Morrissey
FAQ

Morrissey FAQ

All That's Left to Know About This Charming Man

D. McKinney

Backbeat
Books

An Imprint of Hal Leonard Corporation

Published in 2015 by Backbeat Books
An Imprint of Hal Leonard Corporation
7777 West Bluemound Road
Milwaukee, WI 53213

Trade Book Division Editorial Offices
33 Plymouth St., Montclair, NJ 07042

The FAQ series was conceived by Robert Rodriguez and developed with Stuart Shea.

Printed in the United States of America

Book design by Snow Creative Services

Library of Congress Cataloging-in-Publication Data is available upon request.

ISBN 978-1-4803-9448-3

www.backbeatbooks.com

To Dr. Geldwert and Dr. Zhang,
for making sure that my light will never go out

Contents

Foreword

My story of discovering Morrissey is probably like that of many who discovered their favorite band/artist in the pre-Internet era. I was on a lunch break from my job at the Glendale Galleria and went into the Sam Goody to browse the aisles. Record stores and their cardboard displays were a great distraction and time killer in the days when time was something we seemed to have too much of. Music was in three formats at the time; vinyl would soon be the outdated, cumbersome, unportable format that was no match for CDs and cassettes.

Over the intercom, the store was playing a strikingly beautiful track that immediately caught my attention. This man's unique singing voice and lyrics immediately jumped out at me. Then came the next song, and that had its own uniqueness to it as well: acoustic guitar strumming a steady rhythm followed by machine-gun snare and the lyrics "Sweetness, sweetness, I was only joking when I said I'd like to smash every tooth in your head." Each lyric was more provoking as the song continued. I was intrigued, mesmerized. I'd been standing under the speaker, not moving or paying attention to anything else. I loved what I was hearing. Then, the third song I heard was breathtaking. I wanted nothing more at that moment than to keep listening to whatever I was going to hear next. At the end of "The Boy with the Thorn in His Side," I had to know who this was. That day, I purchased *The Queen Is Dead* on cassette, and it began my obsession with this son of a librarian from a place in England called Manchester.

After my Walkman started to melt, it became my life's mission to find every album, every 12″ single, every import, and every magazine article or interview featuring this pale, skinny, awkward-looking lead singer who seemed to defy every macho image of the David Lee Roth lead singer stereotype. He waved flowers on stage, for crying out loud. Morrissey was the perfect lead singer whom every person who forever felt "sixteen, clumsy, and shy" could identify with.

He sang about girlfriends in comas, hairdressers on fire, and twin brothers who were crime bosses. With each passing month, I'd look up at the independent record stores and marvel at the chalkboard that would announce the next single release date. I remember vividly the chills I got when I saw the words "Coming soon: MORRISSEY—'November Spawned a Monster.'" I knew nothing about what the song was going to be about, but wow—reading just the title was like watching the trailer to an exciting summer blockbuster.

For more than thirty years, I've made countless friendships with others and heard about their own first experiences with Morrissey's songs. The stories are different, but the words are the same—words like "unique," "inspiring," "compelling," and "life-changing." Something in his voice and his lyrics captured all of us at a time when we needed someone to sing our lives. People become vegetarians because of him; people read about Oscar Wilde because of him; people become musicians, authors, and artists because of him; people even make the pilgrimage to the Salford Lads Club in Manchester just to be in front of a building where he was photographed.

In his autobiography, Morrissey is clearly obsessed with chart positions. For someone who doesn't seem to care what the "world of crashing bores" finds popular, he is way too hard on himself for not reaching higher on the pop music lists. Why does he care? When all is said and done, history will be more kind to what he wrote than to whatever flavors of the month who will be long forgotten. Time is the true judge of art and its longevity. I would ask Morrissey, how high did Oscar Wilde chart? I feel a great sense of satisfaction knowing I was right about Paula Abdul, MC Hammer, and Vanilla Ice while everyone in my circle of friends was dead wrong about Morrissey. Every one of them eventually conceded my point.

The first chance I ever got to see Morrissey in concert, I was not at all surprised by the fervor, emotion, and hordes of people who tried desperately to reach out to him just to touch him. I expected no less. I knew that everyone who was attending his first US show as a solo artist was there not just to hear his new songs, but also to be in the same room with him. Breathe the same air as him. It was befitting to witness in a championship sports arena the cheers from the audience when someone was lucky enough to battle his or her way past the surprised security guards to hug him.

Having seen Morrissey live frequently over the years, I still have a policy of not researching what the set list will be ahead of time—like waiting until Christmas to open your presents. Admittedly, this practice has gotten more difficult in this time of instant information, but Morrissey is one of only about four artists/bands who could choose to sing any twenty-five songs from any album or any point in his career and I'll know every verse, every chorus, and every note.

Because of my years with my tribute band, I was approached to host a two-hour weekly radio show dedicated to the "songs that made you smile, the songs that made you cry, and the songs that saved your life." Something *this* fun surely couldn't last more than five months, tops. More than five years later, I still feel as though it's too good to be true and that any minute they're going to discover that I still have a key card to get into the building.

Two hours a week, I read Twitter requests and take phone calls from people asking to hear a song that reminds them of a time, a place, a person, or an emotion. I marvel at how many people throughout various parts of the world from different walks of life tune in to this weekly appointment. It continues to be a thrill. And even after spending two hours on the air with those songs, I still listen to the Morrissey catalog on random all the way home.

Jose Maldonado
Lead singer of the Sweet and Tender Hooligans
DJ and host of *Breakfast with the Smiths*
October 2014

Acknowledgments

Not to get all Morrissey-esque on you, but there are some people I would like to personally acknowledge, thank, and give a shout-out to.

I would first like to thank Mike "McBeardo" McPadden for believing in me.

I would also like to thank Steve Markarian for listening to my endless Morrissey stories and for being a good dad and buying tickets so his son Harry could go to a noncanceled Morrissey concert.

To Scott Doyle for being my only friend who can play "Name That Morrissey Lyric," Chris Best for being the best, Missy Gutierrez, Rikki Niehaus, Jackie Smith, K-Lo, the Crills, Maria's son Mark, Anthony the Goat, G. Wolf—and to the Morrissey Haters: Brian Matheny and Mike Cover.

I would like to thank Bernadette Malavarca, Jessica Burr, and everyone else at Backbeat Books.

I would also like to thank Jose Maldonado.

Most importantly, I would like to thank Phillip Holliday for his all of his support and for putting up with me and all my drama. It would not be a Morrissey book if it didn't have any drama.

Introduction
From Metalhead to Suedehead: How I Became a Fan of the Great and Powerful Moz

ou obviously know who my favorite performer is. But guess who is my second favorite?

KISS.

And my third favorite?

Alice Cooper.

Sparks and Devo are my other two favorite bands, so I'm not THAT cheesy.

But still—people always give me a strange look after I am asked about my favorite bands. Morrissey and Gene Simmons have absolutely ZERO in common: Moz likes veg, Gene likes vag. Both of them do have sideburns, so I guess that counts. So what made me go from "Detroit Rock City" to "My Life Is So Shitty"?

I credit my love of music to two things, the first being that I was fortunate enough to have young parents. There was always music in our apartment (and lots of weed). My mom was into Frank Zappa, David Bowie, and Alice Cooper. My dad liked a lot of southern rock, white-boy blues, and Loverboy. Both of them liked oldies and soul music, so being the oldest and only child (at that point), I liked what they liked. I remember someone asking me what my favorite record was, and I had two—*Private Eyes* by Darryl Hall and John Oates, and *Alice Cooper Goes to Hell* (which are still two of my favorite albums). I never got totally into Frank Zappa or Loverboy, but it would have happened eventually if it were not for the second thing that turned me into a musical genius.

MTV.

Oh yes, the glory days of MTV. Dee Snider versus Neidermeyer, Pat Benatar pretending to be a teenage runaway, and Madonna's floppy "Borderline" hat with the bow—it did not get any better than that. The older I got (and the older MTV got), the more I started to lean toward the metal side of things. I still listened to all types of music, but as soon as I was welcomed to the jungle by Guns N' Roses, it was on. Big hair, tight pants, and falsettos became my favorite. It did not help that I was starting to go through puberty, so besides being attracted to thundering drums and hot guitar licks, I was also attracted to thundering bums and hot guitar d . . . well, you know what I mean. I even stayed loyal to the "metal cause" through the grunge years, although I did like Alice in Chains because they were a little harder than the other Seattle bands.

I admit it, I got a little lost in high school. That is because metal kind of died on me. Grunge broke its legs, alternative stomped its head, and hip-hop peed all over it. But that was okay, because like every other teenager, I discovered punk rock. Even my taste in punk rock was tainted by metal—my favorite band was the Misfits, which led me to Samhain, which then led me to Danzig. Man, I loved me some Glenn Danzig. He was going to be my future hairy husband.

After punk, my tastes started to broaden again in the absence of metal. I started listening to goth music and industrial while revisiting my '80s MTV favorites. And it was during this time that I fell in love with my other future hairy husband.

I can tell you exactly when and how it happened.

I was hanging out at my friend Mark's house. It was the usual gang of idiots and the usual Saturday night filled with cigarette smoke, cheap rum, and Jack in the Box tacos. Because I did not smoke and I did not want to listen to the Melvins, I was sitting on the couch in the living room watching *120 Minutes* while everyone else was in the dining room with the turntable.

It was the usual college music crap fest: Hüsker Dü, the Replacements, and lots of PJ Harvey.

And then they showed "Tomorrow" by Morrissey.

At first I rolled my eyes and was all "whatever" about it. But I continued to watch. I watched him slink around France in black and white. I watched him pout at me, asking me about "the one thing that I'll never do." And when he demanded "tell me that you love me" with that sly crooked smile, I was hooked like a fish.

At first I was embarrassed by my Morrissey crush. I was "punk rock" and madly in love with Glenn Danzig at the time—no way could I let anyone know that I preferred sensitive sideburns now. Plus, I still was not all that crazy about his music. I had tried to listen to the Smiths in the past, and I just could not get into it. I liked "How Soon Is Now?," but EVERYONE likes "How Soon Is Now?" And forget about even listening to his solo stuff—my friend Mark poisoned me by playing "Ouija Board, Ouija Board" to show me how dumb Morrissey was: "You're right," I said, "that song is pretty fucking stupid. Let's listen to 'Walk Among Us.'"

But after that, I would feast my twenty eyes on Morrissey's hairless chest and pompadour. I borrowed *Your Arsenal* from a friend and loved it. It was surprisingly harder than I expected it to be, and it encouraged me to check out more of his stuff. Surprise! Most of it was pretty hard, and I loved how the slow jams were over the top. Soon after, I found myself giving up the devil lock and accepting the pompadour poof into my life.

I was now a member of the Church of Morrissey.

Whenever I meet people and Morrissey comes up in the conversation, I find that there are two kinds of people: Morrissey Lovers and Morrissey Haters. I am totally understanding and tolerant of other people's tastes, and I usually don't get mad when people disagree with me—as a record collector, there is nothing I like more than having a conversation with others about music. But when people tell me that they hate Morrissey, and I ask them why, they can never give me a good reason. It is always:

- He is stupid.
- He is whiny.
- He is all gloom and doom.
- He is still stupid.

I never get a good reason because there is not a good reason to not like Morrissey. They realize they can't hate on someone who writes witty and insightful lyrics. They can't hate on someone who was a great front man—Morrissey brought just the right amount of mystery, sexiness, and audience interaction. They can't hate on someone who wants some privacy. And how can you hate someone who wants to save the animals? You can't, so that is why I get barraged with lame arguments, insults, and jokes about my Morrissey love. But the joke is really on them—after all, if you have such passionate feelings (both negative and positive) about someone or something, then it is obviously affecting you more than you would like to admit.

Like him or not, Morrissey has an effect on pretty much everyone.

But don't think for a minute that I am a blind worshipper. I fully believe that the only true fans are real fans, and to be real, you have to remain truthful. I love me some Morrissey, but there are songs that I do not like. He has said stuff that I do not agree with. And there have been times when I just shake my head and roll my eyes. I have met other Morrissey fans who blindly love everything he does and have gotten belligerent if anyone says anything negative. I always point out that underneath all of the hair and satin shirts, he is a normal person like you and me. And then I out-asshole them and remind them that he is human and needs to be loved—just like everybody else does!

So now let's talk about love.

Why do I love Morrissey? I think the one thing I love the most about Morrissey is the "drama." I love the mugging, the curling up in a fetal position on stage, the brooding, and the microphone cord whipping. I love the songs where he is mock crying, mock angry, or mock in love. I love the moaning and groaning and the yelping. I liken him to menopause: sometimes he gets you hot, sometimes he gets you depressed, and he changes your life forever.

I hear a lot of Morrissey fans speak about why they love Morrissey, and usually their #1 reason is "I can relate to him."

Well, I guess that works for some people, but not for me. I am sorry, but I cannot (and could not) relate to Morrissey—I did not grow up in gloomy, dreary, working-class Manchester; I did not feel like an outsider; I am capable of loving someone other than myself; and I prefer cardigans to pullover sweaters. Yeah, we both buried ourselves in music and literature, but other than that, we really have nothing in common. After a long time thinking about what my deep-rooted reason is that I love Morrissey, it suddenly came to me.

I love Morrissey not because I can relate to him, but because he was there for me.

I have loved Morrissey literally for most of my adult life, and he has been the one solid constant thing throughout. Always there with a great album, always there to be judgmental of my meat consumption, and always there when I needed a laugh (or a well-deserved snicker). I knew that if I wanted to feel better or to tune out life, I could just turn on Morrissey.

Morrissey and the Smiths in general proved that you can really just be yourself when it came to music. Sure, they promoted the consumption of flowers during the early years, but other than that—no gimmicks, no bullshit. They brought a new and fresh sound to listeners and paved the way for indie bands to become indie bands. Morrissey also proved with his lyrics that no matter how tragic life was, you had to see the humor in it—because as Morrissey has proven for many people, humor is the only thing that can keep a person going in life.

Morrissey FAQ will look at and explain how a shy and quiet introvert became the hero to millions just like him. Because of the worldwide fan base, fans and information regarding Morrissey are widespread—*Morrissey FAQ* will provide a complete volume of everything a new fan or old vet needs to know about Morrissey.

I want you to think for a minute: Have you ever met people who have admitted that the Beatles saved their life? That Elvis Presley knew how they felt about getting bullied in high school? Not that the Beatles and Elvis aren't just as important as Morrissey, but they're just not as real as Morrissey. Real people have emotions and real people are very much human in nature, and that is why real people can relate to pretty much anyone. And Morrissey is very much real to a lot of people.

Other than the Beatles or Elvis Presley, I cannot think of anyone else but Morrissey who evokes such a crazed and passionate following. From the sweaty dudes who climb up onto the stage to hug him to the legions of fans lined up for his autograph, we are there for Morrissey because he has been there for us. And he represents us: the misunderstood loners, the sexually repressed, and the sardonic chubby people like myself. And although I could not relate to his life, Morrissey represented mine: all of my trials and tribulations, loves current and lost, and late nights lamenting about life.

I have said it once and I will say it again: "There Is a Light That Never Goes Out" is the "Free Bird" of my generation.

I have evened out my musical tastes again, liking a little bit of everything (except Zappa). I am at peace with my eccentric tastes—Black Flag sounds great next to Bell Biv DeVoe on a playlist, and I love to get into conversations with fellow music nerds about Duran Duran stealing everything from Japan (I am talking about you, Nick Rhodes!). Writing *Morrissey FAQ* was quite an adventure for me: I continued to work full time while writing in my spare time, I had two major surgeries, and I dealt with an abnormal number of ups and downs. But the one person who was there for me throughout it all was Morrissey.

My boyfriend was also there for me, but he doesn't have the cool sideburns.

Morrissey
FAQ

Sixteen, Clumsy, and Shy

Morrissey Becomes Morrissey

How do you become a man who's only known by one name? How do you go from a quiet and shy young man to a music legend?

Some are born into stardom; others earn it. I think with Morrissey it is a little of both. When you learn about his upbringing and his childhood, two words come to mind: serial killer.

But luckily for the world, Morrissey chose to slay people with his music. Some may say that the water in Manchester is loaded with talent due to the musical output from that city. Morrissey took that water and made coffee, giving the world the musical wake-up it needed.

Steven

Often mistaken for Stephen, Steven is Morrissey's birth name. In the 2002 documentary *The Importance of Being Morrissey*, Morrissey states that he is named after the American actor Steve Cochran ("whom you've never heard of," according to Morrissey), although some Morrissey theorists think he is named after a dead uncle named Patrick Steven Morrissey. Morrissey has stuck to his story about being named after Steve Cochran throughout the years (even posing for a photo with Steve Cochran's star on the Hollywood Walk of Fame), so I am inclined to believe him. I'm just shocked that Steve Cochran has a star on the Hollywood Walk of Fame, because Morrissey was certainly right about one thing—we've probably never heard of Steve Cochran.

If there is one thing Morrissey hates more than being called Steven, it is being called "Steve." Once hooked up with Johnny Marr, he decided to drop his first name and, in the vein of Cher, only be known by one

Before he crashed down on the crossbar, Steven Morrissey was another Manchester youth with big dreams (and big hair).   *Kerstin Rodgers/ Redferns/ Getty Images*

name. On the rare occasion his first name is used, it is usually wrong and spelled with the *ph*, with such instances being the 2001 compilation *The Very Best of the Smiths.*

And let's be honest—Morrissey really doesn't look like a "Steve."

Oh Manchester, So Much to Answer For

Steven Patrick Morrissey was born on May 22, 1959, at Park Hospital in Davyhulme, Lancashire, Northern England. Before Morrissey's birth, his parents, Peter Morrissey and Elizabeth Ann (Betty) Dwyer, emigrated from Dublin with their daughter, Jacqueline. His father was a hospital porter and his mother was an assistant librarian. Morrissey was raised in the inner city of Manchester, an overcast city with a thriving culture of art, music, history, and architecture. Though it is the ninth-largest city in the United Kingdom by population, Manchester has been ranked as the second city of the United Kingdom in numerous polls. British author, broadcaster, and social commentator Brian Redhead once remarked that "Manchester is the capital of the North of England, where the modern world was born."

In 1965, Morrissey's family moved from Harper Street in Hulme to Queen's Square and finally settled in Stretford on Kings Road in 1969 when their tenement neighborhood was facing demolition. Morrissey has described his first childhood home, saying, "In a way it was like having one's childhood swept away." The new Stretford neighborhood was "bland," according to Morrissey, and he would spend most of his youth sitting in front of the TV for hours on end, staying in his room writing furiously, or reading about Oscar Wilde and James Dean. In a 1984 interview with *Rolling Stone*, he states the following about his two idols: "Wilde and Dean were the only two companions I had as a distraught teenager. Every line that Wilde ever wrote affected me so enormously. And James Dean's lifestyle was always terribly important. It was almost as if I knew these people quite intimately, and they provided quite a refuge from everyday slovenly life."

Morrissey attended St. Mary's Secondary School, which he has always described as "sadistic" and "barbaric," as well as Stretford Technical School. He was surprisingly athletic, which spared him from bullying, but he still found himself feeling lonely and depressed. As a result, he began self-medicating with prescription drugs as a teen. He then began a cycle of taking prescribed antidepressants and barbiturates such as Prozac, Valium, and lithium, which he would eventually wean himself off of, but was still influenced by their effect, as documented in 1988's "Late Night, Maudlin Street" and "Interesting Drug," and most importantly, 2009's "Something Is Squeezing My Skull."

Jacqueline Morrissey Reyner

Morrissey has only one sibling, his older sister, Jacqueline. They were fairly close growing up, with less than a two-year age gap between them. She married in 1983 and had two sons, Sam and Johnny. Sam appeared in Morrissey's "Suedehead" video as the young boy delivering an envelope to Morrissey's front steps, while nephew Johnny turned to music and started a band called Noise Is the Best Revenge, after his uncle's 2005 B-side.

It's Ms. Dwyer

Morrissey's parents divorced when he was seventeen, although according to Morrissey, their marriage wasn't great from the start—it was very straightforward and loveless, with no displays of affection. Although Morrissey has never said anything outrightly negative about his father, Morrissey was and still is very close to his mother, Elizabeth. Since she was an assistant librarian, his first introduction to the literary world (especially to Oscar Wilde) was from her, and she is a fervent music fan—her two favorite artists are Roxy Music and Johnny Mathis. She is also a vegetarian and feels strongly about animal rights.

Elizabeth also handled Morrissey's finances and career once he and the Smiths started to make money. Geoff Travis from Rough Trade endured endless calls from her, making sure they were treating him right, and producer Stephen Street and engineer Danton Supple both had to deal with Elizabeth regarding the money Morrissey still owed them for working on his albums.

Morrissey Senior

Morrissey's relationship with his father, Peter, was neither great nor particularly bad. Peter was supportive of his son's tastes in music (he had no qualms about dropping Morrissey off at a T. Rex concert when he was thirteen). Although not particularly close, Peter and Morrissey have maintained a decent enough adult father-son relationship. Peter has spoken about how proud he is of his son and was even in the audience during Morrissey's 2002 concert at Albert Hall.

The Moors Murders

Morrissey has described his childhood as being morbid with undercurrents of violence. An event that had a profound impact on Morrissey was the Moors murders. Ian Brady and Myra Hindley sexually assaulted and murdered five children between the ages of ten and seventeen between 1963 and 1965 in and around greater Manchester, burying four of the victims on the Saddleworth Moor. This barbaric event left a lasting impression on Morrissey, as it should have, since he (or a friend/relative) could have been a victim of Brady and Hindley. He put his fear down on paper, with it becoming "Suffer Little Children," one of the first songs that he and Johnny Marr worked on together.

Personality Crisis

Morrissey took his first step into the world of popular music by purchasing his first record at age six, 1965's "Come and Stay with Me" by Marianne Faithfull. The older he got, the more his tastes in music turned edgier, and he discovered the New York Dolls at age twelve. His parents encouraged his musical choices—his mother was a big Roxy Music fan herself, and his father drove and dropped him off at his first concert (T. Rex) when he was thirteen.

Morrissey was ecstatic to have had the chance to see the New York Dolls in action after falling in love with them the year before—they were to be the opening act for Roxy Music on November 9, 1972. But unfortunately for Morrissey, it was never meant to be—New York Dolls drummer Billy Murcia passed away two nights before in London from choking on his own vomit after partying too much. Morrissey was standing in the front row awaiting their appearance when a stagehand broke the news. The New York Dolls regrouped with a new drummer and made a return to England in 1973, this time appearing on *The Old Grey Whistle Test*. Morrissey would reminisce about watching their performance: "I was thirteen and it was my first real experience. The next day I was twenty-nine."

Thirty years later (way past the age of twenty-nine), Morrissey was given the actual white Vox Teardrop guitar that New York Dolls guitarist Johnny Thunders played on that episode of *The Old Grey Whistle Test*. To celebrate his new (and probably the best ever) gift, Morrissey posed with it for the cover photo for his 2003 single "Redondo Beach." Morrissey's teenage years were filled with more groundbreaking music, from Bowie and Sparks to Nico and Patti Smith, but he always remained true to the New York Dolls, from wearing homemade New York Dolls T-shirts to school and making decoupaged New York Dolls book covers to playing their self-titled debut album for anyone who would listen.

Athletics

Despite his lanky and dorky appearance (especially while in the Smiths), Morrissey has always claimed that he was exceptionally good at sports, especially track and field. Once he started hanging out with the "different kids," though, he left his potential athletic career behind and focused on anything but school.

Fan Clubs

Although the New York Dolls were broken up by the late '70s, Morrissey continued his support by become the president of the England-based New York Dolls fan club. He met and recruited fellow fans by placing ads in music magazines and writing letters (Mick Jones from the Clash was a member of the club). Through the club, Morrissey met best friend James Maker and future bandmate Billy Duffy.

In May of 1980, Morrissey started the Legion of the Cramped fan club along with a girl named Lindsey Sutton (who was the editor of a Scottish fanzine titled *The Next Big Thing*). He had previously seen the Cramps in 1979, and in 1980 and wanted to share with the world the raw and intense sound of the Cramps.

America Is Not the World

In 1976, Morrissey visited his aunt Mary, who had moved to the United States (specifically New Jersey) in 1969. He found New Jersey pretty miserable (doesn't everyone?), but he was able to make it into New York City and to CBGB, where he procured an autograph from Russell Mael of Sparks. He would continue to visit Aunt Mary, even after she eventually moved to Denver. While grousing around in the snow, Morrissey placed a "musicians wanted" ad in the *Rocky Mountain News* (only John Denver wrote back to him) and applied to work at Target. He was interviewed but was eventually turned down. Too bad—I think Morrissey would look pretty hot in a red polo shirt and comfortable khakis.

Work

It pains me to say this, but Morrissey was pretty much a slacker. He has only worked three jobs—as a launderer in a hospital laundry room, as clerical support for the Inland Revenue, and at a record store. Why on Earth would he quit working at a record store? That is my dream job. When he was not working, he remained on the dole. Specific lines from the Smiths song "Still Ill" reference his hatred for working real jobs, such as "England is mine, it owes me a living" and "If you must go to work tomorrow, well if I were you—I wouldn't bother," as do the entire song "Frankly, Mr. Shankly" and my most often quoted line (especially when I am at my boring nine-to-five job): "I was looking for a job and then I found a job, and Heaven knows I'm miserable now."

At least I have awesome health insurance.

2

Reader Meet Author

Morrissey's Non-Lyrical Writing

Autobiography (2013)

Y ou would think you would know all about Morrissey's life just from listening to his songs, but no—that is why you are reading this book. Oh yeah, you should also pick up his autobiography, titled *Autobiography*. Pretty clever.

Morrissey first clued everyone in back in 2002 about a possible autobiography during a radio interview. Nothing was heard about it again until 2009 when a snippet of it was published as a short story, titled "The Black Moor Lies," that was included in a compendium called *The Dark Monarch: Magic and Modernity in British Art*, published by the Tate St. Ives art gallery. The autobiography was mentioned yet again in 2011 during another interview. Morrissey stated that the book was indeed finished and that he was trying to find an interested publisher.

Cut to 2013—Morrissey inked a deal with Penguin Books to release the obviously titled *Autobiography* as a "Penguin Classic" that September. But shortly before its release, a disagreement occurred between Morrissey and Penguin regarding the contents (Morrissey and Penguin both refused to say what the disagreement was about—only that it was a "content dispute"). Morrissey then decided to take his business elsewhere.

But then, all of a sudden, it was going to be released after all. And it was—*Autobiography* was officially released on October 17, 2013, in the United Kingdom, hitting #1 and setting a new first-week record for a music autobiography. It was released in the United States on December 3, 2013.

Reviews have been mixed about *Autobiography*. Some say it is on par with his musical output—witty, sharp, and utterly brilliant. Others call *Autobiography* whiny, bitchy, and overindulgent. But really, are not all rock biographies overindulgent? The *New York Times* reviewed *Autobiography* and said, "His thoroughgoing distaste for most everything except his musical obsessions might wear on even his fans, but as he writes of a youthful companion, 'anything is forgiven of anyone who makes us laugh.' His well-earned reputation as the saddest of sacks too often obscures his considerable wit. Just saying he's miserable and difficult to handle, as many critics do, is far less clever and crafty than how he puts it, in so many different ways, in songs, interviews and now this memoir."

What turned off readers (and potential readers) was that a big chunk of *Autobiography* is about his feelings regarding the Mike Joyce court case and his complaints about album sales, where his singles charted, and not getting the attention he deserves for being a musical genius. As big of a fan as I am, I have to roll my eyes at this. If he were not a big deal, I would not be writing this book.

We Yanks were waiting with bated breath for our copies of *Autobiography*, but the version we would be "wide to receive" was different from the United Kingdom version. The publisher removed numerous references to Jake Walters, including a childhood photo. No reasons were given, except that it was a licensing issue regarding the photo. Some say that Jake politely asked that certain passages be removed; others say that Morrissey had wanted to downplay his romantic involvement with Jake after the "bombshell" hit with the United Kingdom version. Either way, try to get the United Kingdom version of *Autobiography*.

Exit Smiling (1979)

Exit Smiling is a 1979 booklet by a young Steven Morrissey detailing the lives of his favorite movie stars and their treatment on film. It features future Smiths cover stars and lyrical inspirations, such as Richard Davalos, Shelagh Delaney, Terence Stamp, and Diana Dors. Morrissey submitted it to Manchester-based Babylon Books after they published and distributed his first two booklets, *The New York Dolls* and *James Dean Is Not Dead*, but they declined *Exit Smiling*, despite paying Morrissey an advance of £50. Unfortunately, that £50 advance ended up biting him in the ass come 1998 when Babylon Books decided to print a special limited thousand-copy run of *Exit Smiling*. This upset Morrissey greatly because he was basically powerless to stop its release, plus it looked like crap—Babylon Books used a faxed copy with corrections and notes because that was all they had. Clearly a grab to profit from Morrissey's fame, *Exit Smiling* would have been a great little read that showed insight into Morrissey's film influences if it were not for the bad blood surrounding its publication.

James Dean Is Not Dead (1983)

Morrissey is surprisingly embarrassed by this essay/booklet released in 1983 by Babylon Books. Feeling there was a need to reintroduce James Dean to a new generation, because all previous books written about James Dean were out of print, Morrissey regurgitated what he knew and believed about James Dean and sold it to Babylon Books for £40. *James Dean Is Not Dead* continued to haunt Morrissey throughout his career. After the Smiths became famous, Babylon Books reissued *James Dean Is Not Dead* in 1984 and included Morrissey's name on the cover, whereas the previous edition did not have it. Babylon Books continued to milk Morrissey's fame by again reissuing *James Dean Is Not Dead* in 1997, limited to just one thousand copies, with each copy having a Certificate of Authenticity from Babylon Books. Morrissey's contempt for *James Dean Is Not Dead* and Babylon Books is so strong that he has refused to autograph copies when they're handed to him (and even threw one into the crowd during a *Vauxhall and I* signing event). Morrissey was able to show his love and appreciation for James Dean the right way (or at least, the Morrissey way) with his "Suedehead" video.

The New York Dolls (1981)

After realizing that his countless letters to the *New Musical Express* and *Melody Maker* magazines about the greatness of the New York Dolls were not enough, Morrissey created a fanzine called *The New York Dolls* and included his own writings about the New York Dolls as well as other published interviews and information from other sources. He dedicated the zine to his friend and fellow New York Dolls aficionado James "Jimmy" Maker.

Babylon Books reissued *The New York Dolls* in 1995 during the aftermath of Morrissey's *Vauxhall and I* fame. The reissue included an essay about Morrissey titled "Teenage Fascination: Stephen [*sic*] Patrick Morrissey and the New York Dolls," as well as a discography and time line. It was limited to five hundred copies and came with a Certificate of Authenticity. Unlike with *James Dean Is Not Dead* and *Exit Smiling*, Morrissey does not seem to be as embarrassed about *The New York Dolls* and will speak about it on occasion.

Letters to the Editor

Before Morrissey made a name for himself as Morrissey, he was just Steven Morrissey, amateur music critic. His letters to the *New Musical Express*, *Melody Maker*, and local fanzines have become legendary and are a keen look into the past with his spot-on criticisms, witty zingers, and teenage angst. Here are excerpts from letters about the bands he loved, the bands he hated, and the bands he loved to hate.

On his love of the band Sparks:

> *New Musical Express*, June 1974: "Today I bought the album of the year. I feel I can say this without expecting several letters saying I'm talking rubbish. The album is *Kimono My House* by Sparks. I bought it on the strength of the single. Every track is brilliant, although I must name 'Equator,' 'Complaints,' 'Amateur Hour,' and 'Here in Heaven' as the best tracks and in that order."

On Aerosmith:

> *Melody Maker*, September 1975: "Their music is that of confused struggle, with vocalist Steven Tyler sounding as though he is using the microphone to brush his teeth. They are as original as a bar of soap and have as much to offer seventies rock as Ena Sharples. Aerosmith are just another street-corner rock 'n' roll band, using notorious Zeppelin riffs in an effort to steal our love and devotion. But when one ruminates over the fact that *Toys in the Attic* is the band's third album, thanks, but no thanks, Aerosmith. I'll stick with the New York Dolls for my rock 'n' roll thrills."

On American rock bands in general:

> *Sounds*, December 1975: "The British public are very wary of new bands. Anything that aims to change the day-to-day routine of the rock world is carefully observed before admitted. What a shame the New York Dolls and Jobriath were a little too fond of their satins and silks because I am sure that they both had enough—and more—to please the media. After two albums, several European tours, and a large amount of money spent on publicity, the Dolls are back on the streets of New York with the bands whose path was paved by the Dolls."

On witnessing the Sex Pistols:

> *New Musical Express*, June 1976: "I pen this epistle after witnessing the infamous Sex Pistols in concert at the Manchester Lesser Free Trade

Hall. The bumptious Pistols in jumble sale attire had those few that attended dancing in the aisles despite their discordant music and barely audible lyrics. The Sex Pistols are very New York and it's nice to see that the British have produced a band capable of producing atmosphere created by the New York Dolls and their many imitators, even though it may be too late. I'd love to see the Pistols make it. Maybe they will be able to afford some clothes which don't look as though they've been slept in."

On how much he hated the Ramones (at the time):

Melody Maker, June 1976: "The Ramones are the latest bumptious band of degenerate no-talents whose most notable achievement to date is their ability to advance beyond the boundaries of New York City, and purely on the strength of a spate of convincing literature projecting the Ramones as God's gift to rock music.

The New York Dolls and Patti Smith have proved that there is some life pumping away in the swamps and gutters of New York and they are the only acts which originated from the NY club scene worthy of any praise. The Ramones have absolutely nothing to add that is of relevance or importance and should be rightly filed and forgotten."

Morrissey was still championing the New York Dolls in 1976, so much that the *New Musical Express* agreed with him and published a two-page retrospective about the rise and fall of the New York Dolls:

New Musical Express, November 1976: "Methinks that the Dolls weren't the 'damp squid' that Nick Kent would have us to believe because if you look closely at the increasing number of British 'punk' bands emerging by the shipload, you will see in each one a little bit of the Dolls. I think it's time that *NME* broke the office rules and had an article on the New York Dolls. You know it makes sense."

Complaining about British punk rock and punk bands in general:

Melody Maker, December 1976: "The likes of the Sex Pistols have yet to prove that they are only worthy of a mention in a publication dealing solely with fashion, and if the music they deliver live is anything to go by, I think that their audacious lyrics and discordant music will not hold their heads above water when their followers tire of jumpers and safety pins."

And:

"British punk rock is second to the New York equivalent, in that it does not possess the musical innovation. The New York Dolls, Patti Smith, the Ramones, and Jobriath can withstand accusations of novelty value because, although a great deal of their act was based on image, they also had the musical professionalism and variation to suitably recompense for their image-conscious inclinations. However, although British punk bands are emerging by the truckload, even the most prominent are hardly worthy of serious musical acceptance. So why the space devoted to these acts?"

Morrissey was not too kind about fellow Manchurians Warsaw, a.k.a. Joy Division:

Kids Stuff, July 1977: "Of the new bands, Warsaw, the Worst, the Drones, and the Fall look the most likely to make any headway. Warsaw were formed some time ago by vocalist Ian Curtis and have performed alongside more prominent bands like the Heartbreakers. Although they offer little originality with Ian's offstage antics resembling one Iggy Pop, highlighting their set is 'Another Kill' which is at least memorable, if slightly typical."

But he did like fellow Manchurians Buzzcocks:

New Musical Express, 1977: "Buzzcocks differ only one way from their contemporaries: they possess a spark of originality (that was important once, remember?), and their music gives you the impression they spend longer than the customary ten minutes clutching the quill in preparation to write. Indubitably, Buzzcocks will hardly figure strongly—or even weakly—in the *NME* poll, and in these dark days when Patti Smith, Loudon Wainwright, or even the New York Dolls fail to make an impact on Radio 1 DJs, common sense is therefore not so common. Both this letter and Buzzcocks themselves will probably be filed and forgotten. But for now, they are the best kick-ass rock band in the country. Go and see them first and then you may have the audacity to contradict me, you stupid sluts."

Morrissey started to become less of a passionate music fan and more of a "sarcastic shit-talker" as he continued to pen letters into the late '70s:

New Musical Express, 1977: "After witnessing Johnny Thunders & the Heartbreakers live, my much revered Carly Simon, Loudon Wainwright, Jefferson Airplane, Buffy Sainte-Marie, New York Dolls, Phil Ochs, and Patti Smith albums are presently smoldering on a low light. Don't talk to me about any band but the Heartbreakers because I just won't listen—these boys are newer than the new wave and (surprise!) they can play! What's even more amazing is that the Heartbreakers' music is both memorable and professional, something which is seemingly least expected from a new wave band. The seventies start here.

Steven Morrissey
Kings Rd, Stretford, Manchester

PS: I work for the Inland Revenue—am I still allowed to be a punk?"

And *Kids Stuff*, January 1978: "So you think you're cool 'cos you're on the dole and you think you're hip because you've got a swastika splashed across your torn tee shirt and you think you're tough because the Clash are 'Your Band,' well big deal! If you live in Manchester then I'm running with you, but if you're an out of towner, wipe the mascara out of your eyes 'cos London burned down with boredom and sparks fly in downtown Manchester! And if you're not around to feel the beat, well that's just too bad babbeee!"

This one is my favorite, because it is titled "Ooo, Bitch!":

Sounds, 1978: "The age of romance is upon us again. Jon Savage tips Manchester as the place to be in '78. You remember Manchester—the kids don't think you're tough if you pronounce your T's, and a gig at the Circus was always like guerrilla warfare. Too late, too late, Mr Savage. Save your enthusiasm for the intense drama at the Vortex, but watch you don't smudge your lipstick."

Robert Mackie Letters

In October 1980, Morrissey responded to an ad in *Sounds* magazine from a David Bowie fan in Glasgow, Scotland, looking for pen pals. His name was Robert Mackie, and he and "Steven Morrissey" would write letters back and forth, mostly about David Bowie and other bands, with Morrissey, of course, championing the New York Dolls. Mackie assembled his Morrissey correspondence in 1992 and released a photocopied fanzine titled *Words by Morrissey*. It is actually a really great read, providing insight to Morrissey's pre-Smiths life, and what makes it good are his insults to Mackie, such as "Does being Scottish bother you?," "I was astounded to see the word 'paroxysm' in your epistle—it must have taken you ages to find that one," and "Thank you for the photo. Has anyone ever told you that you look like Grace Jones?" Morrissey's ribbing must not have bothered him too much, because Mackie visited Morrissey in Manchester in 1981, hanging out at bar and going stationery shopping.

Scans of *Words by Morrissey* are available online, and an actual paper copy comes up once in a while on eBay. I have to admit it—I feel that the Mackie letters are the best thing Morrissey has ever written. Every time I read them I find myself laughing out loud. I am sure the "Steven Morrissey" of the letters would have chided me for liking such rubbish.

3

A Vegetarian Slaughters the Dogs

Before He Was a Smith

The Nosebleeds

The Nosebleeds were a local Manchester punk band that had origi-nally started in 1976 after witnessing another local Manchester punk band, Slaughter and the Dogs, open up for the Sex Pistols. They went from having the not-very-punk name of Wild Ram to the very-punk name the Nosebleeds. Singer and front man Ed Garrity became the more punk-sounding Ed Banger, and then they all became Ed Banger and the Nosebleeds.

Ed Banger and the Nosebleeds released a single in 1977 ("Ain't Bin to No Music School") with future Morrissey guitarist Vini Reilly in the band. But after a playing a few gigs, the band broke up, with Ed Banger joining Slaughter and the Dogs, and Vini Reilly creating the Durutti Column.

In 1978, guitarist Billy Duffy joined what was left of the Nosebleeds (drummer Philip Tomanov and bassist Peter Crookes) and, seeing the need for a singer, suggested his friend Steven Morrissey. With Morrissey as the Nosebleeds front man, they played two shows in 1978—one opening for Slaughter and the Dogs and the other opening for Magazine. After those two shows, Morrissey left the Nosebleeds and the band broke up.

Here is where it gets tricky—Morrissey would deny that he was in the Nosebleeds, especially once the Smiths (and himself) gained popularity. When the subject was brought up, Morrissey would answer that he "only wrote songs with Billy Duffy for the Nosebleeds" and that he only spent a couple of weeks hanging out with them (it was more like a couple of months). But unfortunately for Moz, there is actual proof that he was, in fact, singing for the Nosebleeds in 1978. Paul Morley reviewed their May 8,

Harvey Goldsmith Entertainments
with the
New Manchester Review
present

MAGAZINE

PLUS SPECIAL GUEST
JOHN COOPER CLARKE
AND
THE NOSE BLEEDS

THE NEW RITZ
Whitworth Street, Manchester

Monday 8th May 1978

Tickets : Pandemonium, Black Sedan, Virgin,
Hime & Addison, and Paperchase.

Was Morrissey really in the Nosebleeds when they opened up for Magazine? Only Morrissey knows.
Author's collection

1978, show at the Ritz (opening for Magazine) for the *New Musical Express*. Although he fudged on Morrissey's name, referring to him as "Steven Morrisson" (close enough), he was highly complimentary, stating: "Lead singer is now a minor local legend Steven Morrisson, who, in his own way, is at least aware that rock and roll is about magic and inspiration. So the Nosebleeds are now a more obvious rock and roll group than they've ever been. Only their name can prevent them being this year's surprise."

Morrissey and Billy Duffy wrote and played four of their original songs over those two shows in 1978: "Peppermint Heaven," "(I Think) I'm Ready for the Electric Chair," "I Get Nervous," and "The Living Jukebox," as well as a Sylvain Sylvain song that was never released and only available on a bootleg ("Teenage News"). After the Nosebleeds split in 1978, Billy Duffy would end up joining Slaughter and the Dogs, and Morrissey was (supposedly) soon to follow.

Slaughter and the Dogs

Slaughter and the Dogs are a Manchester punk band that took their name from Mick Ronson's 1974 solo album, *Slaughter on Tenth Avenue*, and David Bowie's 1974 album, *Diamond Dogs*. They opened up for the Sex Pistols in 1976 and released one full album and four singles (which was pretty good for a punk band), but in 1978, original singer Wayne Barrett quit.

Billy Duffy, Morrissey's friend and former Nosebleeds bandmate, joined Slaughter and the Dogs, and shortly after that, Morrissey came in to audition for the recently open front man position. He also joined them for a record company audition in London. They must have not been impressed with his awkward teenage moves and angst-filled crooning because Morrissey did not get the job. Slaughter and the Dogs then moved to London and changed their name to the Studio Sweethearts and then back to Slaughter and the Dogs.

Morrissey insists that he was neither a member of Slaughter and the Dogs nor a potential member of Slaughter and the Dogs, despite the decades-old stories of him being in the band. The only proof that he might have been connected to Slaughter and the Dogs is an article he wrote about punk in 1978 for the *Kids Stuff* fanzine, where he mentions the band.

Angels Are Genderless

No one knows (except Morrissey) if his first band really existed or if it was the result of an overactive imagination. In letters written to his pen pal, Robert Mackie, Morrissey states that Angels Are Genderless will start to rehearse once he gets over his jet lag from his trip to visit his aunt Mary in the United States, but nothing else was ever mentioned about it. Angels Are Genderless would be a good metal band name.

Sulky Young and the Tee-Shirts

One day while shopping for albums at a Virgin Records, Morrissey was approached by a friend named Phil Fletcher regarding some mutual friends in the nearby area of Wythenshawe who were also New York Dolls fans. His interest piqued, Morrissey became friends with the local youths, especially with a young guitarist named Billy Duffy. Deciding to start a band, they first referred to themselves as Silky Young and then the Tee-Shirts. The Tee-Shirts rehearsed and landed their first gig fairly soon, but by that time, Billy Duffy had moved on to the Nosebleeds. Morrissey just moved on to his bedroom until Duffy contacted him about following on to the Nosebleeds.

Morrissey the Musician

Despite his musical talent, Morrissey does not actually play any instruments. He is partial to the drums, with Jerry Nolan of the New York Dolls as his inspiration. He has owned various drum kits throughout his life, but nothing has ever come of it. He will pick up a tambourine while on stage to keep the beat.

Morrissey has played on a Smiths album—he was the one banging away on the piano on 1987's "Death of a Disco Dancer."

4

Keats and Yeats Are on My Side

Morrissey's Literary Influences

Alan Bennett

Alan Bennett is a renowned English playwright, known for his dry and witty plays and teleplays. A good deal of Morrissey-penned lyrics are based on lines from Bennett performances, such as "Nature has a language, you see, if only we'd learn to read it" from Bennett's play *Me, I'm Afraid of Virginia Woolf* and Morrissey's line "Nature is a language—can't you read?" from the Smith's 1986 hit "Ask." It makes sense—both are utterly charming and have that natural British sense of humor.

Morrissey befriended Alan Bennett in the early 1990s while both were residing in Camden, where they would drink tea and converse about old film stars. When given the honor of curating the 2004 Meltdown festival, Alan Bennett was the first person Morrissey asked to perform. He agreed and performed his one-man show, *An Evening with Alan Bennett*, with Morrissey beaming from happiness from his seat out in the audience.

John Betjeman

John Betjeman was England's poet laureate from 1972 until his death in 1984. Like Morrissey's writing, Betjeman's poetry is dry and quick-witted, yet filled with a sense of melancholy. In a 1995 interview with *Q* magazine, when asked about the music he would have playing at his funeral, Morrissey answered: "John Betjeman reciting *A Child Ill*." Although it was not quite at his funeral, the poem was played as Morrissey's entrance music during his 2002 tour. During a 2006 appearance on BBC Two's *The Culture Show*, Morrissey announced that Betjeman was one of his all-time heroes.

Beyond Belief

Beyond Belief is a 1967 book by Emlyn Williams that was written about the Moors murders. Morrissey has stated that *Beyond Belief* is one of his favorite books and the inspiration for the Smiths' "Suffer Little Children." Several lines from the book make their way into the song, such as "Wherever he has gone, I have gone" and "Find me, find me."

It is also possible that the book (and the Moors murders in general) inspired more than just "Suffer Little Children." Maureen Smith was Moors murderer Myra Hindley's little sister, and it was she and her husband, Dave, who turned in Ian Brady and Myra Hindley to the police after Dave witnessed them murder one of their young victims. According to legend, Morrissey had already written "Suffer Little Children" before meeting Johnny Marr, so it is safe to assume that the Smiths got their name from Morrissey's obsession with the Moors murders and *Beyond Belief*.

Truman Capote

An American literary genius, Truman Capote became popular after his first novel was published in 1948, the semi-autobiographical *Other Voice, Other Rooms*. He then hit pay dirt in 1958 with his novella *Breakfast at Tiffany's* (fun fact: the 1961 film version of *Breakfast at Tiffany's* features the original version of Henry Mancini's "Moon River," which Morrissey covered in 1994). Capote would then go on to write what is considered to be his masterpiece, 1966's *In Cold Blood*. Morrissey's favorite work by Capote is his collection of interviews with Lawrence Grobel, titled *Conversations with Capote*.

Morrissey has also stated that one of his favorite movies is 2005's *Capote*, starring Phillip Seymour Hoffman as Truman Capote.

Shelagh Delaney

Out of all of his influences, musical or literary, Morrissey has been influenced the most by author and playwright Shelagh Delaney. In a 1986 *New Musical Express* interview, Morrissey stated: "I've never made any secret of the fact that at least 50 percent of my reason for writing can be blamed on Shelagh Delaney, who wrote *A Taste of Honey*."

The song that has the most tastes from *A Taste of Honey* is the Smiths' "This Night Has Opened My Eyes," with almost blatant similarities such as "You can't just wrap it up in a bundle of newspaper. And dump it on a doorstep." Other Smiths songs that received the "taste of Shelagh Delaney

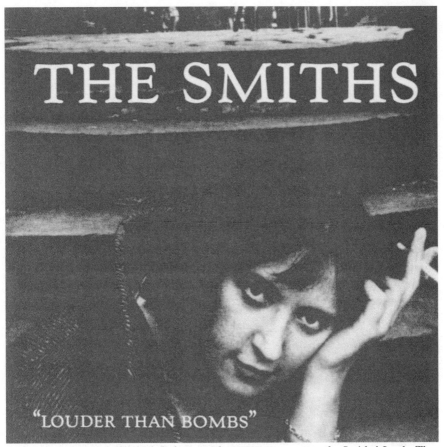

Author and playwright Shelagh Delaney makes an appearance on the Smiths' *Louder Than Bombs* compilation.   *Author's collection*

honey" are "Hand in Glove," "Asleep," "Still Ill," and "These Things Take Time." Photos of Shelagh Delaney were used as cover art for the Smiths' *Louder Than Bombs* compilation and the "Girlfriend in a Coma" single. Morrissey wrote and published a eulogy expressing his love and gratitude for Shelagh Delaney when she passed away in 2011.

Charles Dickens

When asked "What are you reading at the moment?" during a 1992 interview with *Spin* magazine, Morrissey answered: "Well, *Oliver Twist* and a few peculiar magazines, but just because I'm reading them, I'm not necessarily enjoying them. I'm trying to find out what's in them. But *Oliver Twist* is the thing I'm reading on the plane. Charles Dickens is very exciting to me, because he was a terribly gloomy character, terribly embittered, and quite depressed."

Morrissey continued with the Oliver Twist theme by using a sample from the 1948 *Oliver Twist* film adaptation for his 1994 song "Billy Budd."

George Eliot

George Eliot is single-handedly responsible for one of the most memorable opening lines in modern music. The line from her 1871 novel, *Middlemarch*, "To be born the son of a Middlemarch manufacturer, and inevitable heir to nothing in particular" became "I am the son and the heir of a shyness that is criminally vulgar, I am the son and heir of nothing in particular" for the Smiths' classic "How Soon Is Now?"

George Eliot is second only to Charles Dickens when it comes to Victorian writers. Born Mary Ann Evans, she changed her name to George Eliot so she would be taken seriously in a male-dominated field. Morrissey also showed his appreciation for her fresh and frank writing style by including the line "George Eliot knew" in the run-out groove for his 1990 single "Piccadilly Palare."

Herman Melville

Although not mentioned much throughout Morrissey's solo career, Herman Melville may have influenced Morrissey more than he (or anybody) realizes. A copy of *Moby Dick* is featured in the "Interesting Drug" video, and Morrissey's 1994 song "Billy Budd" shares its name with another Melville novel. And we can't forget about poor Johnny Marr, who shares his name with a collection of poems by Melville titled *John Marr and Other Sailors*.

The Murderer's Who's Who

The Murderer's Who's Who was released in 1979 and was THE best guide where one could read and acquire information about serial killers (or killers in general). As one of Morrissey's favorite books, *The Murderer's Who's Who* provided him with information about killers he already knew about (like the Kray twins, Ian Brady and Myra Hindley, Jack the Ripper, and James Hanratty) and enlightened him to other killers he found interesting, like Albert Fish and Thomas Lay. One would say that *The Murderer's Who's Who* was a big influence on Morrissey, considering that three of his best songs ever were written about his favorite killers ("The Last of the Famous International Playboys" about the Kray twins, "Suffer Little Children" about Ian Brady and Myra Hindley, and "Jack the Ripper" about Jack the Ripper, obviously). Morrissey and drummer Spencer Cobrin even wrote and recorded a potential B-side in 1997 titled "Hanratty" about James Hanratty.

So why no songs about Albert Fish or Thomas Lay? Well, he does mention "a good lay" in "Suedehead," so we can pretend that counts for Thomas Lay. If he wanted to pay tribute to Albert Fish, Morrissey could always record a cover of "Fish Heads."

I'm sure Barnes & Barnes could use the money.

Marjorie Rosen

Popcorn Venus is a book by Marjorie Rosen that takes a look at women in film. A feminist at heart, Morrissey was greatly influenced by *Popcorn Venus* with his songwriting for the Smiths and his solo career. *Angel, Angel, Down We Go*; *The Hand That Rocks the Cradle*; and *Little Man, What Now?* are all movies that are referenced in *Popcorn Venus* (and obviously Morrissey song titles). In a chapter about 1960s "beach movies," Rosen asks the all-important question: "How soon is now?"

Elizabeth Smart

Elizabeth Smart is a Canadian writer who wrote the heartbreaking autobiographical book of prose *By Grand Central Station I Sat Down and Wept* (which sounds like a Morrissey-ish title) about her affair with British poet George Barker. Morrissey once again borrowed some of his favorite lines from *By Grand Central Station I Sat Down and Wept* and used them to get his feelings across in lyrics, in such songs as "Shakespeare's Sister," "Late Night, Maudlin Street," "The Headmaster Ritual," and "Reel Around the Fountain." The term "louder than bombs" also came from Smart's book, eventually becoming the title of the Smiths' 1987 compilation.

Oscar Wilde

Oscar Wilde is an Irish author and poet, best known for his 1891 novel *The Picture of Dorian Gray* and for his 1895 play *The Importance of Being Earnest*. He was also known for being imprisoned for "homosexual activity," dressing wildly, bucking the stuffy Victorian system, and being sharp as a tack.

Morrissey began reading Oscar Wilde's children's literature at the tender age of eight, after a suggestion from his librarian mother. "There was a piece called 'The Nightingale and the Rose' that appealed to me immensely then," Morrissey said in a 1984 interview with *Smash Hits*.

Wilde would continue to be a constant inspiration and support system throughout Morrissey's life. Morrissey name-checks Wilde in "Cemetry Gates" ("Keats and Yeats are on your side, but you lose because Wilde is on mine") and uses Wilde's words for cryptic messages in run-out grooves for the "Bigmouth Strikes Again" single ("talent borrows, genius steals") and on the *Hatful of Hollow* vinyl ("The Impotence of Ernest"). There are also other little touches of Wilde throughout Morrissey's solo career—portraits of Wilde have been used as concert backdrops (Tour of the Tormentors); T-shirts and buttons have been worn; snippets of photos have been used in photo shoots, music videos, and live appearances; and even the 2002 documentary about Morrissey takes its name from Wilde's famous play (*The Importance of Being Morrissey*).

In that same 1984 *Smash Hits* interview that was mentioned above, Morrissey summed up his feeling about Oscar Wilde quite nicely: "I'm never without him. It's almost biblical. It's like carrying your rosary around with you."

Wuthering Heights

Wuthering Heights (the book, not the Kate Bush song) is a classic novel written in 1847 by Emily Bronte. Morrissey has mentioned quite frequently that it is among his favorite books, which makes total sense because *Wuthering Heights* is very Morrissey-esque (or is Morrissey very *Wuthering Heights*–esque?) with its story about how love and hate are interchangeable depending on the moment.

Morrissey has been greatly inspired by *Wuthering Heights* and has used key lines in the novel for his own song lyrics—he uses the line "Heaven did not seem to be my home" in his 1997 single "Satan Rejected My Soul," and mostly importantly, the line "You have killed me—and thriven on it, I think. I forgive you" obviously was the basis for Morrissey's 2006 hit single "You Have Killed Me." Morrissey and *Wuthering Heights* have a lot in common—both are a little goth, both are very dramatic, and Morrissey, like the novel's anti-hero, Heathcliff, will die without ever being with the one he truly loves (other than himself).

5

Cosmic Dancers

Morrissey's Musical Influences

T. Rex

On June 16, 1972, Morrissey was barely thirteen and attending his very first concert. I have to admit that T. Rex is a pretty impressive first concert (mine was Huey Lewis and the News).

Surprisingly, Morrissey preferred the pre-glitter and perm version of T. Rex, the folk rock-y Tyrannosaurus Rex, so much that he selected the song "Great Horse" from their 1970 album, *A Beard of Stars*, for his *Under the Influence* compilation. But that is not to say he did not like the glam era T. Rex—he did, and showed his appreciation by covering 1971's "Cosmic Dancer" as the B-side for his "Pregnant for the Last Time" single.

T. Rex has also influenced other musicians whom Morrissey has worked with, like Johnny Marr and Boz Boorer. While T. Rex was Morrissey's first concert, the first album Johnny Marr ever purchased was T. Rex's 1971 "Jeepster" single. Morrissey and Marr both have admitted that the Smiths' 1986 hit "Panic" was their ode to (rip-off of) T. Rex's "Metal Guru" (seriously, put on "Metal Guru" and sing "Panic" over it—it is the same song). Boz Boorer is and was a huge T. Rex fan, starting while a child and continuing into adulthood; he even participated in the rebirth of John's Children, Marc Bolan's 1960s mod band. He also purchased T. Rex's 1971 hit single "Get It On (Bang a Gong)" when he was nine years old.

Morrissey penned the foreword to the 1992 Marc Bolan biography, *Wilderness of the Mind*. Marc Bolan died a very Morrissey-esque death in 1977: while coming home drunk from a party thrown by Rod Stewart, he and his girlfriend, Gloria Jones, skidded off the road and crashed into a tree, instantly killing Bolan and severely injuring Jones.

The New York Dolls' self-titled debut album (1972). *Author's collection*

New York Dolls

No other band has influenced Morrissey more than the New York Dolls. From the flamboyant David Johansen stage moves to the power-charged rock riffs on his later albums, Morrissey has incorporated every aspect of the glammy hammy New York Dolls style into his act (except for the makeup).

Morrissey became enamored with the New York Dolls at age thirteen and continues to sing their praises to the world. He was given the opportunity to witness the New York Dolls in action when they were to open for Roxy Music in 1973, but it was never meant to be—Billy Murcia, the original drummer for the New York Dolls, passed away while partying in London two days before the show, postponing their official United Kingdom debut and leaving teenage Morrissey heartbroken.

Although he never had the chance to see the original New York Dolls lineup (or even the semi-original New York Dolls lineup), he did eventually meet all of the members throughout the 1980s (even Johnny Thunders and Jerry Nolan before they died!).

To get through his teenage angst, Morrissey wrote letters in support of the New York Dolls to various music magazines and zines such as *Sounds* and

Melody Maker while co-creating a New York Dolls fan club and publishing a booklet. While in the Smiths, Morrissey denied his love of the New York Dolls, presenting it as a passing fascination. As his solo career started up, so again did his support of the New York Dolls.

Other than himself, there has been no other artist whom Morrissey has promoted more than the New York Dolls, from constantly speaking about them in interviews, to covering their songs ("Trash," "Human Being," and "Subway Train"), to actually getting them to reunite. When asked by Morrissey to play his 2004 Meltdown festival, David Johansen, Sylvain Sylvain, and Arthur Kane agreed to play and performed on two separate nights. Morrissey immortalized the event by releasing *Morrissey Presents: The Return of the New York Dolls—Live from Royal Festival Hall 2004.*

As with all the other bands that had a major influence on Morrissey, he insists on playing a variety of New York Dolls songs and videos during concert intermissions. He also continues to list the New York Dolls' self-titled debut album as his #1 favorite album of all time.

Angelic Upstarts

Morrissey has preached about the brilliance of the Angelic Upstarts for most of his career, citing them as a major influence on his work. The Angelic Upstarts started in 1977 in South Shields, Tyneside, and immediately took an anti-police and anti-establishment stance with their lyrics. Because of this, they were often associated with the Oi movement, thereby attracting members of the skinhead population.

Morrissey (himself accused of pandering to the skinhead population) would often throw shout-outs to the Angelic Upstarts throughout his solo career—from using a tambourine with the word "MENSI" scribbled on the face (Mensi is the nickname of the Angelic Upstarts lead singer, Thomas Mensforth) to the little girl wearing the Angelic Upstarts T-shirt in the "The More You Ignore Me, the Closer I Get" video (who happens to be the daughter of guitarist Boz Boorer). Although the shout-outs have decreased in his later years, Morrissey continues to show love to one of the most memorable punk bands in English history.

David Bowie

Morrissey has been a fan of David Bowie since his early teenage years, even stating that he has seen Bowie perform in concert fourteen times.

He met David Bowie for the first time in 1990 after Morrissey himself became a superstar. Shortly after that in 1991, Bowie joined Morrissey on stage at the Great Western Forum in Los Angeles to sing T. Rex's "Cosmic Dancer" together, one of the biggest events in Morrissey's solo career. After the success of *Your Arsenal*, Bowie covered Morrissey's "I Know It's Going to Happen Someday" for his Tin Machine *Black Tie White Noise* album. Morrissey and best friend Linder Sterling visited Bowie in New York to hear his version, and Morrissey, of course, cried when he heard it.

With both Morrissey and David Bowie releasing albums on RCA Victor in 1995, they agreed to tour together, with Morrissey being the opener. But playing to half-full arenas and concert halls did not seem to work out for Morrissey—his fans had to fight with Bowie fans to get near the stage, and he could not give a proper encore. Bowie started to make excessive requests of him, wanting Morrissey to cover some of his songs during the set or have David Bowie himself come out and perform with him during Morrissey's set. After ten shows, Morrissey pulled the plug and quit.

Since then, despite having a producer in common (Tony Visconti), Morrissey and David Bowie remain on unfriendly terms. When Morrissey rereleased the single "The Last of the Famous International Playboys" in 2013, he wanted to use a previously unreleased photo of him and David Bowie in New York from 1992 (taken by Linder Sterling) for the cover. David Bowie put a halt to it by threatening EMI Records, who held the rights to most of Bowie's back catalog and released the "Playboys" single. EMI Records sided with Bowie and ordered Morrissey to change the cover.

Buzzcocks

Fellow Manchurians Howard Devoto and Pete Shelley started the seminal punk band in 1976 shortly after witnessing an early Sex Pistols show. Morrissey himself attended one of their first shows as they opened up for the Sex Pistols. Citing their original and campy sound and nonpolitical lyrics, Morrissey (in yet another letter penned to the *New Musical Express* in 1977) championed his affection for the Buzzcocks, stating: "Buzzcocks differ only one way from their contemporaries: they possess a spark of originality (that was important once, remember?), and their music gives you the impression they spend longer than the customary ten minutes clutching the quill in preparation to write."

The Cramps

Morrissey first witnessed the Cramps back in 1979 during their first tour of Great Britain, opening for the Police. Referring to them in 1980 as "the most important US import since the New York Dolls" in a letter published in *Record Mirror* magazine, Morrissey continued to preach his love for the Cramps, even becoming an original member and co-founder of the Legion of the Cramped UK fan club. Morrissey mourned the death of Cramps lead singer Lux Interior by giving him a shout-out during a 2009 performance on *Jimmy Kimmel Live.*

WRITER'S CRAMP

I SENT OFF £1.50 to The Cramps' fan club in May to a Manchester address. My membership cheque was cashed a month ago, but I haven't heard anything from them yet. Can you get in touch with them for me? — **Danny Loker, Bradford.**

NO PROBLEM. The Cramps' fan club, originally based at 384 Kings Road, Stretford, Manchester, and run by ace supporters Steven Morrissey and Lindsay Hutton has now moved to Scotland, c/o Lindsay Hutton, 10 Dochart Path, Grangemouth. Lindsay attributes the breakdown in communication to a lost address during the transition across the border and has been trying to track down the origins of your cheque. Meanwhile, Steven Morrissey has been waiting, fan club kit at the ready, for some sign of human movement from your direction. You lost their address. They lost yours — but your full quota of membership stuff will be with you by the time you read this column.

While Cramps International has built up its audience to well over the hundred mark since kicking off in May this year, Lindsay Hutton feels a membership of nearer 300 would make the membership services he wants to provide, like reasonable T-shirts and posters, and maybe a limited edition record too, more financially viable. The band's management have given him the go ahead to produce a record — now he needs some funds. Anyone interested?

Membership still costs £1.50 a year, or £1.80 with a copy of *The Next Big Thing* fanzine, largely devoted to The Cramps. Cheques, postal orders payable to Lindsay Hutton. People who're interested in launching their own fanzine are also welcome to write to Lindsay for advice and information.

Steven Morrissey leads the Legion of the Cramped fan club.   *Author's collection*

El Vez

Although El Vez was not an inspiration from Morrissey's formative years, Morrissey has admitted that El Vez's style helped spur his interest in Mexican culture. With his Elvis Presley vibe and punk rock heart, El Vez was offered the opening slot for Morrissey's European tour in 1999, but opted to open for him only once in Santa Barbara, California.

Brian Eno

Morrissey was fortunate enough to see the original Roxy Music lineup in 1972 before Brian Eno left the group and has championed Eno's first two solo albums, *Here Come the Warm Jets* and *Taking Tiger Mountain*. Morrissey had also inquired about Brian Eno producing his *Southpaw Grammar* album, but sadly, it never came about.

George Formby

Although known for his lighthearted movies in the 1930s and 1940s, George Formby was a musical hero to Morrissey for his cheeky songs rife with innuendo, such as "Why Don't Women Like Me?," "With My Little Stick of Blackpool Rock," and "When I'm Cleaning Windows," the latter bearing a similarity to Morrissey's "Roy's Keen." In a 1984 interview in the *New Musical Express*, Morrissey said this about his love of George Formby: "For me one of the greatest lyricists of all time is George Formby. His more obscure songs are so hilarious, the language was so flat and Lancastrian and always focused on domestic things. Not academically funny, not witty, just morosely humorous, and that really appeals to me."

Billy Fury

Often referred to as "the English Elvis," Billy Fury had a string of hits in the 1960s and could belt out both rocking tunes and weepy ballads. Morrissey has mentioned his love of Billy Fury quite a bit throughout his career and has praised his contribution to English music in general. He has also promoted Billy in his own way by posing with Billy Fury pics or items in his own promotional photos, such as the cover of the *¡Oye Esteban!* DVD, and in various interviews. During an interview with *The Face* in 1987, when asked if he cried after learning about Billy's death, Morrissey answered, "Persistently. Loudly."

Jobriath

Jobriath was America's answer to David Bowie. Unfortunately, America already liked Bowie, so we did not have room for two. He was pushed by his manager, Jerry Brandt, and his label, Elektra, who promoted him everywhere, culminating with a performance on *The Midnight Special* in 1974. Unfortunately, his records sold poorly, and he was trashed in reviews. When inquiring about Jobriath in the early '90s in hopes of having him support the *Your Arsenal* tour, Morrissey learned that Jobriath had passed away in 1983 from AIDS. To make up for the shabby reception Jobriath received while alive, Morrissey released *Lonely Planet Boy*, a compilation of songs from the two albums Jobriath did release, as well as the unreleased song "I Love a Good Fight," which was released as a single on Morrissey's Attack label.

Joni Mitchell

Amazing singer-songwriter (and cigarette aficionado) Joni Mitchell is the closest thing there is to a "female Morrissey." Already three albums deep by the time Morrissey discovered her 1971 *Blue* album, her next three albums (1975's *The Hissing of Summer Lawns*, 1976's *Hejira*, and 1977's *Don Juan's Reckless Daughter*) were the ones that captivated Morrissey and influenced his lyric style—so much that lyrics in "Shoplifters of the World Unite," "Last Night I Dreamt That Somebody Loves Me," "Sister I'm a Poet," and "Seasick Yet Still Docked" closely mimic Joni Mitchell lyrics from her songs "Amelia," "The Silky Veils of Ardor," and quite a few others (mostly from her *Don Juan's Reckless Daughter* album).

For a promotional piece, Reprise Records coordinated a visit with Morrissey and Joni Mitchell and released it as *Words + Music* in 1996. The interview is great—both of them chat about the songwriting experience and relationships with fans. It is a little hard to find, but grab it if you find it.

Klaus Nomi

The operatic singer from outer space, Klaus Nomi, really was a new wave of new wave. Although not classically trained in opera, Nomi learned his craft from listening to opera records in his youth, while sneaking in rock 'n' roll when he could. After becoming a counterculture hit in 1970s New York City, Nomi was discovered by David Bowie, and he and fellow performer Joey Arias backed Bowie during his 1980 performance on *Saturday Night Live*. With his newfound fame, Nomi fine-tuned his alien-like persona and released two albums, 1981's *Klaus Nomi* and 1982's *Simple Man*. Unfortunately, at the peak of his fame, he passed away in 1983 from complications from AIDS.

Morrissey has continually promoted his affection for Klaus Nomi throughout his own career, speaking about his love of Nomi's music, especially his nonoriginal opera covers. Nomi's version of "The Cold Song" from *King Arthur* was used as the Smiths' entrance music for their first concert in 1982, "Der Nussbaum" by Robert Schumann was used for Morrissey's solo debut in Wolverhampton, and "Wayward Sisters" was used for entrance music for the 1991 *Kill Uncle* tour and the 1992 *Your Arsenal* tour.

Morrissey also included Klaus Nomi's version of Purcell's "Death" on his 2003 *Under the Influence* compilation. It was the final track.

Ramones

Despite his scathing teenage reviews of the Ramones' first albums, Morrissey soon fell in love with the Ramones and their endearing archaic sound. A variety of Ramones songs have been played during various concert intermissions throughout Morrissey's solo career (such as "Cretin Hop," "I Don't Wanna Go Down to the Basement," and "Now I Wanna Sniff Some Glue"). Morrissey included "Judy Is a Punk" on his 2003 *Under the Influence* compilation, citing in the liner notes: "The Ramones do nothing to conceal their disabilities, and once again I am in love."

Morrissey visited the Hollywood Forever cemetery in 2007 and was taken in by its beauty and history. After spending some time at Johnny Ramone's grave, Morrissey decided that he would like to be buried near him. Morrissey revisited Johnny's grave site in 2009 for a photo shoot for *Filter* magazine, using two of the pics from the shoot for his "Something Is Squeezing My Skull" single released later that year.

The Ramones' 1976 self-titled release was Morrissey's #2 pick for his "Morrissey Reveals His Favourite LPs of All Time" list that was featured on thequietus.com in 2010.

Lou Reed and the Velvet Underground

In a letter to pen pal Robert Mackie in 1980, Morrissey stated that he had seen Lou Reed four times in concert. That is four more times than I would see him.

Lou Reed is the unofficial poet laureate of New York City—the dirty and gross (yet cool) New York City—first known for being the non-Nico singer of the Velvet Underground and then for having a strong and successful solo career. The Velvet Underground's 1967 song "The Black Angel's Death Song" was played during concert intermissions during the 1995 Boxers tour and the 2007 *Greatest Hits* tour, and was a selection for Morrissey's 2009 *Desert Island Discs* appearance. Both *The Velvet Underground and Nico* (#8) and *White Light/White Heat* (#7) made appearances on his "Morrissey Reveals His Favourite LPs of All Time" list that was featured on thequietus.com in 2010.

Sparks

Where do I start? I love Sparks and Morrissey does, too!

Sparks consists of brothers from the same mother, Ron and Russell Mael, and an always-tight backing back. Popular in the glam heyday of the early '70s (especially in the United Kingdom), Sparks was like the eccentric cousin of its glam contemporaries—witty, a little strange, and utterly brilliant. Teenage Morrissey was able to grasp the madness of Sparks and shared his insight with the listening public by penning a letter to the *New Musical Express* in 1974 praising the *Kimono My House* album.

Morrissey has taken lyrical cues from Sparks throughout his solo career, such as the classic "London is dead" line from "Glamorous Glue," taken from the Sparks song "Beaver O' Lindy," and "The rain falls hard on a humdrum town—this town has dragged you down" from the Smiths' "William, It Was Really Nothing" gives a wink and nod to the Sparks song "This Town Ain't Big Enough for the Both of Us."

Morrissey finally met the duo in 1991 while on tour in Los Angeles. Becoming fast friends, Morrissey and the Mael brothers frequently correspond and semi-collaborate on projects—Sparks performed at the Morrissey-curated Meltdown festival in 2004, appeared in the 2002 documentary *The Importance of Being Morrissey*, remixed "Suedehead" for the 2005 *Future Retro* compilation, and even wrote and recorded a song about him for the 2008 album *Exotic Creatures of the Deep*, titled "Lighten Up, Morrissey."

Morrissey in turn has included songs by Sparks on various compilations, such as 2003's *Under the Influence* and 2004's *Songs to Save Your Life*. He also plays Sparks songs and videos during concert intermissions.

Buffy Sainte-Marie

Another Canadian songstress (like Joni Mitchell), Buffy Sainte-Marie was a breath of fresh air in the tired old folk scene with her real-life tales of drug abuse and politics. Morrissey purchased her "Soldier Blue" single in 1971 and has commented in various interviews about how much it "changed his life." In 2010, for the rerelease of "Everyday Is Like Sunday," Morrissey created a Spotify playlist and included "Soldier Blue," and he speaks about his love of "Soldier Blue" in his 2013 book, *Autobiography*. He invited Buffy Sainte-Marie to perform at his 2004 Meltdown festival, but she unfortunately had to decline due to prior commitments. Morrissey in turn declined an invitation to appear at a Buffy Sainte-Marie tribute in 2008 because of his boycott of performing in Canada.

Frank Sinatra

Nancy is not the only Sinatra Morrissey is fond of. Frank Sinatra entertained millions of people throughout the world with his crooning and Rat Pack shenanigans. About his musical influences, Morrissey stated in a 2005 interview on the True to You website: "The royal three remain the same: the New York Dolls, Frank Sinatra, Elvis Presley, with Nico standing firm as first reserve."

Morrissey has featured Frank Sinatra's music during concert intermissions and has even crooned a few lines of Sinatra's classic "My Way" while on stage. Both Morrissey and Frank Sinatra share the same taste in Henry Mancini songs—both have covered "Moon River."

Elvis Presley

Billy Fury was repeatedly referred to as "the English Elvis," but only one man comes close to rightfully taking that throne and that is Morrissey.

Besides sharing the same look of sideburns and pompadours, Morrissey and Elvis also share the same vocal style and electrifying stage presence (and obsessive fan base). Elvis's influence on Morrissey was felt even early on during the Smiths, with covers of Elvis's "(Marie's the Name) His Latest

Flame," Elvis's mug on the cover of the "Shoplifters of the World Unite" single, and the witty pun "Are you loathsome tonight?" captured in the run-out groove on the "Ask" single. Johnny Marr also counted Elvis Presley's early music as an influence.

Morrissey continued to show his affection for Elvis well into his solo career by playing a variety of Elvis songs during concert intermissions, such as "I Need Your Love Tonight" and "Tiger Man," as well as using pictures of Elvis as stage backdrops. Morrissey even took the Elvis backdrop idea a step further by featuring huge red letters that lit up to say "Morrissey" as the backdrop for his *You Are the Quarry* tour, similar to the stage setup for Elvis's televised *'68 Comeback Special.* Other than the New York Dolls, there has not been another artist that Morrissey has visually shown his appreciation for, from wearing T-shirts emblazoned with Elvis's face to putting little touches of Elvis into what he is working on, such as the Elvis poster in the bedroom of the young man in the "The Last of the Famous International Playboys" video or putting together an Elvis puzzle on the cover of the *¡Oye Esteban!* DVD. Because I love both Elvis Presley and Morrissey, I often daydream about Morrissey sitting on a rhinestone-studded couch eating an organic (yet fried) peanut butter and banana sandwich and shooting at the TV whenever the Royal Family is shown.

Hey, a girl can dream!

Noel Coward

Morrissey has not been shy about his love and respect for jack-of-all-trades Noel Coward (an English composer, singer, actor, director, and playwright). Morrissey spoke about listening to Noel Coward to his Scottish pen pal, Robert Mackie, in 1981. He paid tribute to Noel Coward by quoting him on stage in 2006, stating: "I believe that since my life began, the most I've had is just talent to amuse."

Sacha Distel

The non–Serge Gainsbourg singer from France whom all the cool kids know, Sacha Distel has been a favorite of Morrissey's for some time now. He has had the honor of being a Morrissey concert backdrop (2006's Tour of the Tormentors), and an old Scopitone of Distel singing "Où ça, où ça" was played during the intermission on the same tour. With Distel's dark hair and good looks, it is easy to see why Morrissey was so fond of him.

While curating the 2004 Meltdown festival, Morrissey had inquired about having Sacha Distel perform on one of the nights. Unfortunately, he was too sick to perform and had to decline, and then passed away from cancer a month later at age seventy-one. On stage later that year in Paris for the *You Are the Quarry* tour, Morrissey introduced himself as "Sacha Distel" as a tribute.

Sex Pistols

One thing Morrissey and I both agree on is that the Sex Pistols were a New York Dolls rip-off. Go ahead and get all "How dare you!" But it is true. They were supposed to be the new New York Dolls—after the New York Dolls broke up in 1975, then-manager Malcolm McLaren promised original Doll Sylvain Sylvain that he would recruit musicians and come up with a new band for him to play with. And what he came up with was the Sex Pistols, a group of ragtag youth who were anti-establishment and pretty much anti-everything. Obviously a dirtier and more anarchic version of the Monkees, the Sex Pistols did bring change to popular music (and music in general), but they only did what the New York Dolls had done previously (and better).

Morrissey witnessed the Sex Pistols a total of three times in Manchester at the Manchester Free Trade Hall (with the Buzzcocks and Slaughter and the Dogs opening). Although he first lavished praise on the Sex Pistols with a letter to the *New Musical Express* (see the chapter "Reader Meet Author") about their first Manchester concert, Morrissey eventually called them out for what they were—New York Dolls rip-offs.

He eventually gave them some props in a 2006 interview with the *New Musical Express*, stating: "I think they changed the world, and I'm very grateful for that. I saw them three times at the very beginning and they were breathtaking and very necessary and I simply felt gratitude. Everybody on the planet has shortcomings, and most people can't see it through, but it doesn't matter because most people give nothing and they gave so much and they've sustained."

6

These Charming Women

Morrissey's Feminine Side

Sandie Shaw

B oth Morrissey and Johnny Marr have referred to themselves as "incurable Sandie Shaw fans" and for good reason—this chick was everywhere in 1960s England. According to Morrissey, her performance of her first #1 hit, "(There's) Always Something There to Remind Me," in 1964 was little Steven Morrissey's first exposure to real music. With two more #1 hits and a slew of other chartbusters, Sandie Shaw was the UK's "Barefoot Pop Princess" because instead of wearing her eyeglasses, she would perform barefoot so she could "feel the stage." Sandie Shaw also was the first English winner of the Eurovision contest, performing a poppy, perfect performance of "Puppet on a String."

After she cooled her heels in the 1970s, Sandie teamed with B.E.F. (British Electric Foundation) to record a version of "Anyone Who Had a Heart" in 1982, bringing her back into the spotlight.

And then the Morrissey Magic happened!

Being the "incurable" fans they were, Morrissey and Johnny Marr had Rough Trade's Geoff Travis give a letter written and signed by both Morrissey and Marr and cassette of music to Nik Powell, the head of Virgin Records and Sandie Shaw's husband. After a little reluctance, Sandie decided to work with the Smiths and in 1984 released a cover of their debut song, "Hand in Glove," with Morrissey and Marr's "I Don't Owe You Anything" and "Jeane" as the B-sides. It reached #27 on the UK chart, her first hit in fifteen years.

Morrissey would continue to work with Sandie Shaw throughout the '80s. She recorded and released a song about him titled "Steven (You Don't

Eat Meat)" and the discarded *Viva Hate* track "Please Help the Cause Against Loneliness." Unfortunately, Morrissey and Sandie fell out around 1990, although a reason has never been made public. She continues to speak highly of him, while he just does not speak about her at all.

Nancy Sinatra

Despite being called a "pizza waitress" by Rex Reed, Nancy Sinatra proved him (and everybody else) wrong when she unleashed her talent upon the world. She signed to her father's Reprise label in the early 1960s and released a couple of mediocre torch songs. Nancy hit pay dirt when she met Billy Strange and Lee Hazlewood and they wrote "These Boots Are Made for Walkin'," her first #1 hit ("Somethin' Stupid," a duet with her father, was her only other #1). Nancy continued to have several hits throughout the rest of the '60s, even scoring the primo gig of singing a James Bond theme song (1967's "You Only Live Twice"). She continued her successful partnership with Lee Hazlewood, and they released popular duets like "Jackson," "Some Velvet Morning," and "Summer Wine." Nancy also had a so-so film career, starring along Elvis Presley in the movie *Speedway*.

Morrissey says that Nancy sought him out to become friends; Nancy said it was he who sought her out to become friends. Either way, they're friends and former neighbors (as chronicled in the 2002 BBC documentary *The Importance of Being Morrissey*). Nancy released her 2004 album, *Nancy Sinatra*, on Morrissey's Attack label, which featured her cover of Morrissey's "Let Me Kiss You" from his 2004 album, *You Are the Quarry*. Both singles were released on the same day.

Kirsty MacColl

Kirsty MacColl was an English singer-songwriter who is best known for "Fairytale of New York," her duet with the Pogues' Shane McGowan. Sadly, she is also known for her untimely and controversial death.

Kirsty was signed to Stiff Records in 1979 and released her first single, "They Don't Know About Us." At the time, it failed to chart but gained popularity in 1983 after English comedienne Tracy Ullman covered it and sent it to #2 on the charts. She had a few marginal hits afterward (including her own cover of Billy Bragg's "A New England"), and she started contributing on albums mainly produced by her then-husband Steve Lillywhite for bands such as the Talking Heads, Simple Minds, and of course, the Smiths.

Kirsty MacColl was a dear friend of and collaborator with both
Morrissey and Johnny Marr.   *Author's collection*

Kirsty first worked with the Smiths in 1985 on an early version of "Bigmouth
Strikes Again" and then again on "Ask" and "Golden Lights." Because of this
collaboration, Kirsty became dear friends with both Morrissey and Johnny
Marr, working with both of them individually—she sang on Morrissey's
"Interesting Drug" and on several of her own albums with Johnny. As a
matter of fact, both "Interesting Drug" and her Johnny Marr–involved
album *Kite* were released in April 1989.

In December 2000, Kirsty was on vacation with her family in Cozumel,
Mexico. While scuba diving in a restricted area, a speedboat owned by
supermarket millionaire Guillermo González Nova wrongfully entered the
restricted area and struck Kirsty as she pushed her son Jamie out of the way
of the speeding vessel. Kirsty was killed instantly.

Because of the suspicious circumstances around her death (a boat hand
being blamed for driving the boat instead of the owner, Mexican authorities
doing little to investigate and take action, and a million other ridiculous
excuses), her friends and the music community have rallied together to
bring justice to Kirsty and her family. Her mother, Jean MacColl, penned
Sun on the Water, a book about the despicable injustice regarding Kirsty's

death, and the BBC documentary *Who Killed Kirsty MacColl?* has brought worldwide attention to the matter.

Kirsty's "fairy tale" unfortunately ended early, but her musical legacy continues to live on year after year in "a new England."

Chrissie Hynde

Chrissie Hynde is a singer, guitarist, and animal rights activist, best known for being the tough and sultry front woman for the Pretenders. After moving to London from Ohio in 1973, Chrissie worked at an architectural firm, wrote for the *New Musical Express*, and became a sales associate at Malcolm McLaren and Vivienne Westwood's clothing store, SEX. After hanging around London and France and playing with assorted bands (like Masters of the Backside, an early version of the Damned), Chrissie started the Pretenders with Pete Farndon, James Honeyman-Scott, and Martin Chambers. They released their first album in 1979, with their third single, "Brass in Pocket," hitting #1 on the Billboard charts in early 1980.

After the deaths of two of the original members in 1982, Chrissie kept the Pretenders going with a rotation of musicians. In 1987, Chrissie hooked up with Johnny Marr, and he joined the Pretenders. And three years after that, she kept the Smiths train a-rolling by hooking up with Morrissey in 1991. They hit it off famously, with Hynde supplying backing vocals for Morrissey's "My Love Life" and appearing as a dancing 1950s bobbysoxer in the video for his "Sing Your Life." The Pretenders recorded a cover of Morrissey's "Everyday Is Like Sunday" for the soundtrack to the 1995 film *Boys on the Side*. Both Morrissey and Chrissie Hynde are active members of PETA and big animal rights supporters.

Marianne Faithfull

Marianne Faithfull is a singer-songwriter who was born into royalty, became a homeless addict, and then bounced back to become rock royalty. With her mother being a Hungarian aristocrat, her image in the early '60s was that of a delicate yet slightly rough-around-the-edges princess. But with sharing the same manager with the Rolling Stones came the opportunity to party with the Rolling Stones (and dating Mick Jagger). She soon became addicted to drugs, and even though she had a few hits and co-wrote "Sister Morphine" for the Rolling Stones, she ended up addicted and homeless on the streets. Despite recording two albums (1971's *Rich Kid Blues* and 1975's *Dreamin'*

My Dreams) and appearing in a 1973 David Bowie TV special, she wouldn't get her triumphant comeback until 1979 when her seminal album *Broken English* was released. She continued to release albums into the next three decades and has worked with music superstars like Metallica, Nick Cave, Blur, Emmylou Harris, Roger Waters, and Joe Jackson.

Morrissey fell in love with Marianne Faithfull when he was six years old—he purchased her 1965 single "Come and Stay with Me" and said it had a lasting effect on him throughout his life. In a 1997 interview with Len Brown, Morrissey said that he loved "the sound and the feel" but "didn't know what the words meant" in "Come and Stay with Me." He was also a fan of "The Sha La La Song," the B-side to her 1965 hit "Summer Nights," so much that he introduced Johnny Marr to the song and he fell for it, too. After a few failed attempts in the '90s, Morrissey and Marianne Faithfull finally met and became fast friends. Marianne has even covered a Morrissey song—her version of his 2006 single "Dear God Please Help Me" appeared on her 2008 album, *Easy Come, Easy Go.*

Patti Smith

If it wasn't for Patti Smith, there would be no Smiths.

Morrissey was introduced to Johnny Marr by mutual friend Billy Duffy at a Patti Smith concert on August 31, 1978. He also met her earlier in the afternoon in a music store, where he received a guitar pick inscribed with the name of the most controversial title in her catalog—"Rock n' Roll Nigger."

Patti Smith is a rock 'n' roll icon. When I think of New York, I instantly think of two people: Lou Reed and Patti Smith. Although not born or raised there (she moved to New York City in 1967), Patti Smith embodies the feeling and attitude of New York City—tough and dirty, yet intellectually fun.

Morrissey has spoken at great lengths about his admiration for Patti Smith, calling her first album, *Horses,* "life changing," and he considers her three following albums (*Radio Ethiopia, Easter,* and *Wave*) also to be equally important. After establishing an e-mail friendship in the 2000s, Morrissey and Patti Smith became in-person friends, and Patti even was the opening act for the Los Angeles stop on his 2013 tour.

To show his gratitude for her pioneering attitude and sound, Morrissey recorded and released a cover of her 1975 song "Redondo Beach" as a single in 2004.

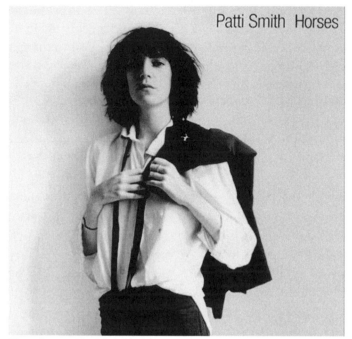

Horses by Patti Smith (1975).   *Author's collection*

Nico

Nico, the Yoko Ono of the Factory.

She was originally born in Germany, made her way to Paris to model, and then became an actress by accident—while visiting the set of Federico Fellini's *Il Dolce Vita*, he cast her in a small part. She also played the lead role in Jacques Poitrenaud's *Strip-Tease* and sang the theme song, originally written by Serge Gainsbourg. Nico then made her way to New York, where she hooked up with Andy Warhol and his Factory gang. At the suggestion of Warhol, Nico joined the Velvet Underground on vocals, much to the displeasure of Lou Reed and John Cale. She also recorded four solo albums throughout the late '60s and early '70s, and those albums happen to be some of Morrissey's favorite albums, especially 1970's *Desertshore*.

In 1981, while down and out and addicted to heroin, Nico took up residence in Manchester, England, living downstairs from Morrissey's best friend, Linder Sterling. Although never meeting her face to face, Morrissey would see her walking around town and would receive updates on her activities from Linder. Sadly, Nico continued on a downward spiral with heroin and eventually died while living with her son in Ibiza, Spain.

She fell off her bike while trying to score some hash.

Linder Sterling

Linder Sterling is a graphic/performance artist, singer, feminist, and Morrissey's best friend. A fellow Manchester youth, Linder hooked up with the Buzzcocks' Howard Devoto while at a Sex Pistols show, and they moved in together. She started making collages with a variety of cut-out pictures from housewares ads and porno mags. One of her better known masterpieces is the cover art of the Buzzcocks' "Orgasm Addict" single—a naked woman's body with a steam iron for a head and smiling mouths for nipples. She also created the cover for Magazine's 1978 album, *Real Life*.

Linder started her own band, Ludus, shortly after. Causing controversy with her pro-feminist lyrics, Linder continued to inspire young Morrissey, whom she had met in 1976 while at a different Sex Pistols show. They became fast friends—reading feminist literature, strolling through the cemetery, and peeking into homes. Their friendship continued to build on each other's support for their separate musical projects—Morrissey supporting and writing press releases for Ludus and Linder photographing Morrissey and being the muse for some of his best songs, like "Cemetry Gates." Linder has also made vocal guest appearances on different Morrissey songs—she sings the harmony vocals on "Driving Your Girlfriend Home," and Morrissey name-checks her in "I Won't Share You." Linder released a photo book in 1993 titled *Morrissey Shot* that included various photos she had taken of Morrissey on his first solo tour in the United States. She took the photos for the covers of *Your Arsenal, Beethoven Was Deaf*, and the remastered *Southpaw Grammar*.

Joan Armatrading

Joan Armatrading is a British singer-songwriter known for her tough yet soulful voice, with three of her singles having made it to the Top 40 (1976's "Love and Affection," 1980's "Me Myself I," and 1983's "Drop the Pilot"). In her 1982 song "The Weakness in Me," there is a line that sounds very "Suedehead"-ish ("Why do you come here? And pretend to be passing by? When you know I've got troubles enough."). Joan Armatrading, like Morrissey, has also taken great strides to keep her personal life personal and has refused to talk about any significant other in her life, although it was reported back in 2011 that she had entered a civil partnership.

Cilla Black

Cilla Black, an English singer known for her obnoxious and over-the-top singing, is also known for her association with the Beatles. John Lennon and Paul McCartney discovered her at Liverpool's Cavern Club and introduced her to manager Brian Epstein, who signed her to EMI Records. Her first single ("Love of the Loved") was written by Lennon and McCartney, yet did not go over so great on the UK chart (only reaching #35). Her second single, "Anyone Who Had a Heart," was written by Burt Bacharach and Hal David, reaching #1 on the UK chart.

Despite her success throughout the 1960s and 1970s, Cilla Black fell out of favor by becoming a television host on cheesy programs like *Surprise, Surprise* and *Blind Date*. Morrissey still cared for Cilla Black and pretty much forced the Smiths into recording a cover of Black's 1968 B-side "Work Is a Four-Letter Word" in 1987. This decision (and song) was not liked by Johnny Marr and contributed to the breakup of the Smiths.

Cilla Black is and was a big supporter of the British Conservative Party and supported Margaret Thatcher throughout the 1980s. I think it's safe to say that Morrissey is no longer a fan.

Cagney and Lacey

Morrissey is man after my own heart with his love of this police drama (although I have to say that my favorite is *Columbo*). Morrissey would admit to watching *Cagney and Lacey* throughout its run in the 1980s and liking it because of its strong female characters and realism regarding modern police work. Smiths album cover star Richard Bradford would also guest star on later episodes of *Cagney and Lacey* as Detective Lacey's father.

Timi Yuro

Timi Yuro was introduced to a young Morrissey by his mother, Elizabeth, who was also a big fan. Timi grew up in Los Angeles and started singing at her parents' restaurant. She caught the eye of a rep from Liberty Records who signed her right away. Her debut release, "Hurt," reached an impressive #4 on the US chart—listeners who loved her deep and soulful voice were shocked to find out that Timi was not black, but Italian (some listeners also assumed she was Japanese because of her name).

Like Morrissey, Timi Yuro preferred to sing sad songs from the heart, and unfortunately her life ended in the same vein. After making somewhat of a comeback in 1976 due to "Hurt" becoming a hit for Elvis Presley, she was diagnosed with throat cancer and finally passed away from it in 2004.

Morrissey showed his love and appreciation for Timi Yuro by recording her 1968 song "Interlude" with Siouxsie Sioux.

Viv Nicholson

After winning huge after betting on the football pools in England, white-trash warrior Viv Nicholson and her husband, Keith, became something of tabloid fodder, starting with Viv parading her newfound fortune in front of the press, stating that she was going to "spend, spend, spend" her money. Those three little words would continue to haunt Viv for the rest of her life, because that is what she did—she spent all of her money until she was broke and bankrupt. As an attempt to earn money, she released a single titled "Spend, Spend, Spend" and then wrote and published an autobiography titled *Spend, Spend, Spend* in 1976. A teleplay based on the book was pro-duced in 1977 (titled *Spend, Spend, Spend*), and in 1998, a successful musical was written and brought to life in London's West End.

Guess what it was called?

Morrissey always admired Viv Nicholson, because despite all of the setbacks she had to deal with (which were mostly her own fault), she never let it stop her from doing what she wanted and always kept her head high. To celebrate that, Morrissey and the Smiths decided to use a photo of Viv not once but twice on the cover of a single—she appeared on the cover for the 1984 single "Heaven Knows I'm Miserable Now" and 1985's "Barbarism Begins at Home." She almost made it onto a third Smiths single—Rough Trade reissued "The Headmaster Ritual" in 1988 on a compact disc single and used a photo of Viv sitting at an easel. At this time, she was a Jehovah's Witness and objected to some of the lyrics in "The Headmaster Ritual" (the "spineless bastards" line).

Morrissey had become friends with Viv Nicholson during the 1980s and even joked around about getting married, but for whatever reason, they stopped being friendly to each other in the mid-'90s. Probably because she became a Jehovah's Witness.

7

There Is a Light That Never Goes Out

Cinema-Inspired Album Art

Billie Whitelaw in *Charlie Bubbles*

Cover: "William, It Was Really Nothing"/"How Soon Is Now?"

Billie Whitelaw owned this movie, so it was only appropriate that she graced the cover of the "William, It Was Really Nothing"/"How Soon Is Now?" split (both of those songs being big hits for the Smiths). Albert Finney directs and stars in this film about a writer who revisits his roots in Manchester after making it big in London. Written by Morrissey's favorite author, Shelagh Delaney, it proves the old adage of "you can't go home again."

The original cover for the "William, It Was Really Nothing"/"How Soon Is Now?" split was a picture of man sitting in bed with a speaker, originally from an ad for A/D/S speakers. For legal reasons, the 1987 reissue has the Billie Whitelaw cover, although the "speaker man" cover is the most available.

Richard Davalos in *East of Eden*

Cover: *Strangeways, Here We Come; The Smiths: Best . . . I; The Smiths: . . . Best II*

Richard Davalos is one of the non–James Dean actors in the 1955 film *East of Eden* and instantly became one of Morrissey's favorite actors. He featured Davalos in two of his books (*James Dean Is Not Dead* and the semi-unpublished *Exit Smiling*) and a screen shot of Davalos from *East of Eden* for the cover of *Strangeways, Here We Come*. Alas, he wasn't the first choice

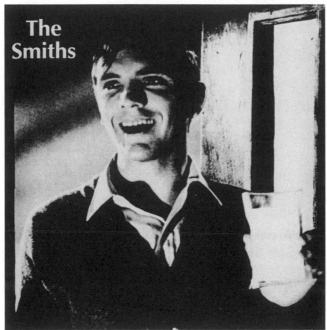

The Smiths' "What Difference Does It Make?" single (1984).
Author's collection

Original "What Difference Does It Make?" cover star Terence
Stamp at first didn't approve of the use of his image for the single.
Morrissey's milky goodness was substituted on certain 12" singles
until Stamp finally changed his mind and granted the Smiths
permission to use his image. *Author's collection*

for the album cover—Morrissey wanted a screen shot of Harvey Keitel from Martin Scorsese's *Who's Knocking at My Door?*, but Harvey Keitel wouldn't grant permission.

Richard Davalos would make two more appearances on the Smiths releases: his mug graced the covers of 1992's *Best . . . I* and *. . . Best II* compilations. It's kind of sad, but most people today only know him (and his face) from the Smiths' covers and not from any of his acting work.

Joe Dallesandro in *Flesh*

Cover: *The Smiths*

Joe Dallesandro was discovered by Andy Warhol and Paul Morrissey in 1967 and then was discovered by the better Morrissey in 1984 and used on the cover of the Smiths' self-titled debut album. Fun fact: Joe Dallesandro (and his crotch) is also the cover star of the Rolling Stones' 1971 hit album, *Sticky Fingers*.

Alain Delon in *L'Insoumus*

Cover: *The Queen Is Dead*

Alain Delon starred in the 1964 movie *L'Insoumus*, and two images from the film were used for the Smiths' *The Queen Is Dead* album—one for the front cover and one on the dust sleeve. His Morrissey connection doesn't end there—he also starred in the 1968 film *Girl on a Motorcycle* with a prehomeless Marianne Faithfull, and he's the father of Nico's son, Ari.

Terence Stamp in *The Collector*

Cover: "What Difference Does It Make?"

Despite the number of lyrical references to *The Collector* (such as "Take me and mount me like a butterfly" from the Smiths' "Reel Around the Fountain"), Morrissey was not so much a fan of the movie as was Johnny Marr. Still, the image of Terence Stamp as the psycho stalker from *The Collector* is one of the most recognizable Smiths covers.

But it almost did not happen. After the single was released in 1984, Terence Stamp was not happy with the usage of his image and objected to it. The Smiths then re-staged the scene with Morrissey in place of Stamp (although holding a glass of milk instead of a chloroform rag) and were set on using that version when Stamp changed his mind and let them go ahead with his image. I wonder if it was a glass of soy milk Morrissey was holding?

Sean Barrett in *Dunkirk*

Cover: "How Soon Is Now?"

Although neither Morrissey nor Johnny Marr has really mentioned anything about *Dunkirk* being one of their favorite movies, a still of actor Sean Barrett from *Dunkirk* was used for one of the covers of the Smiths' 1985 "How Soon Is Now?" single.

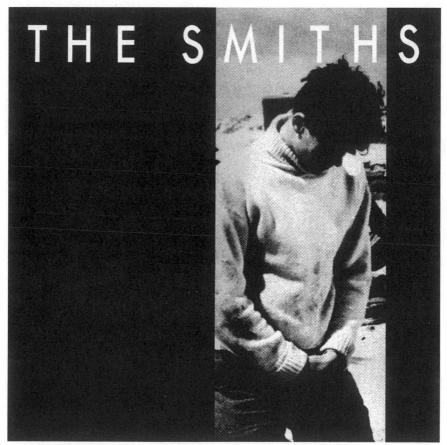

Actor Sean Barrett from the 1958 film *Dunkirk* was used for one of the many "How Soon Is Now?" single covers.   *Author's collection*

Mystery Child in *Zacharovannaya Desna*

Cover: "The Joke Isn't Funny Anymore"

Not much is known about this mystery child, and not much is known about why Morrissey and/or Marr chose this image for the Smiths' "The Joke Isn't Funny Anymore" single. Morrissey used this image again as the backdrop for his 1988 solo/Smiths goodbye show at Wolverhampton.

Avril Angers in *The Family Way*

Cover: "I Started Something I Couldn't Finish"

This unnamed and unknown baby from the 1964 film *Zacharovannaya Desna* was used for the cover of the "The Joke Isn't Funny Anymore" single.   *Author's collection*

Murray Head in *The Family Way*

Cover: "Stop Me If You Think You've Heard This One Before"

Theater and film star Avril Angers was indeed one of Morrissey's favorite actresses, especially for her role in 1967's *The Family Way*. Because of this, Avril and her ridiculous hat graced the cover of the Smiths' 1987 single "I Started Something I Couldn't Finish."

Murray Head (in his pre-Bangkok days) also appeared in *The Family Way* and graced the cover of the Smiths' 1987 "Stop Me If You Think You've Heard This One Before" single.

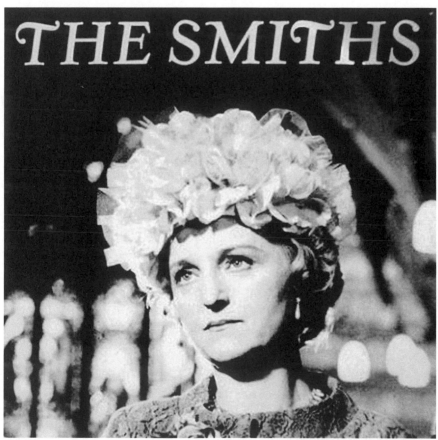

Avril (and her hat) on the cover of the Smiths' 1987 single "I Started Something I Couldn't Finish."   *Author's collection*

John Garfield in *Humoresque*

Cover: *Ringleader of the Tormentors*

John Garfield himself did not appear on the cover of 2006's *Ringleader of the Tormentors*, but Morrissey did in an homage to Garfield's violinist who falls in love with Joan Crawford and is "tormented" about their affair.

Fun fact: In 1981, Canadian-based comedy show *SCTV* (*Second City Television*) parodied *Humoresque*, with cast member Catherine O'Hara in the Joan Crawford role and violinist Eugene Fodor in the John Garfield role. Catherine O'Hara is the sister of singer Mary Margaret O'Hara, who supplied the female moans and groans in Morrissey's 1990 hit "November Spawned a Monster." Morrissey is fan of Mary Margaret O'Hara and her albums.

Unknown Soldier in *In the Year of the Pig*

Cover: *Meat Is Murder*

A still of a solider from the Vietnam War documentary *In the Year of the Pig* was used on the cover of 1985's controversial *Meat Is Murder* album. In the documentary, the writing on his helmet is "Make War Not Love," whereas it says "Meat Is Murder" on the album cover.

Jean Marais in *Orpheus*

Cover: "This Charming Man"

A still of actor Jean Marais looking lovingly into his reflection from the 1950 film *Orpheus* was used as the cover of the Smiths' 1983 single "This Charming Man." It was almost used for the unreleased "Reel Around the Fountain" single (even appearing in advertisements for the single), but plans for that single were scrapped, making Jean Marais truly a "charming man."

Candy Darling in *Women in Revolt*

Cover: "Sheila Take a Bow"

While both Candy Darling and Joe Dallesandro appeared in Andy Warhol's 1968 *Flesh*, it was from his 1971 film *Women in Revolt* that the Smiths used a still of actress Candy Darling for their 1987 single "Sheila Take a Bow."

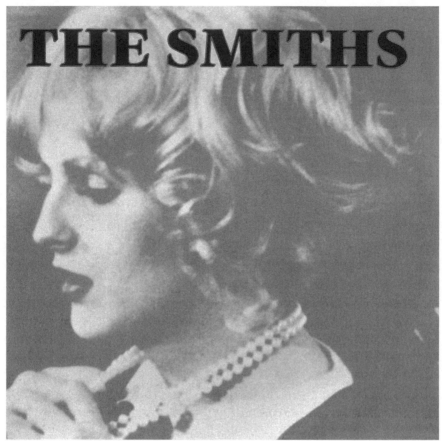

A still of actress Candy Darling from the 1971 film *Women in Revolt* was used for the Smiths' 1987 single "Sheila Take a Bow."

Diana Dors in *Blonde Sinner*

Cover: The Smiths' *Singles*

Morrissey favorite Diana Dors made her official appearance on the Smiths' 1995 *Singles* compilation. The still of her forlorn face is taken from the 1956 film *Yield to the Night*, or as it is known in American, *Blonde Sinner*.

Yootha Joyce in *Having a Wild Weekend*

Cover: "Ask," "Some Girls Are Bigger Than Others"

A still of English actress Yootha Joyce from the 1965 film *Having a Wild Weekend* was used for the Smiths' 1986 single "Ask." The same still was used for the 1986 "Some Girls Are Bigger Than Others" single, but with a red tint. Yootha was known for her role as Mildred Roper on the UK television show *Man of the House*, the original version of the popular US television show *Three's Company*. Yootha was also friends with Smiths friend/accomplice Kirsty MacColl's parents.

Robert Duncan in *The Uncle*

Cover: "The Headmaster Ritual"

The still of child actor Robert Duncan in the 1965 film *The Uncle* was only used on the 12″version of the Smiths' 1985 single "The Headmaster Ritual."

Richard Bradford in *Man with a Suitcase*

Cover: "Panic"

Richard Bradford is a handsome American actor who starred in the 1960s television show *Man with a Suitcase*, playing a loner gun-for-hire in England. Surprisingly (and unlike with other Smiths album art), Richard Bradford was totally down for the Smiths using his face on the cover of their 1986 single "Panic." He had heard they were a good band, but according to Bradford, they forgot to put the vinyl in the jacket that they sent to him, so he never actually listened to "Panic."

Fun fact: "Panic" is one of only two Smiths album covers that simply say "Smiths" and not "The Smiths" (the other being the single for "Bigmouth Strikes Again").

8

Good Looking Men About Town

The Men That Made Morrissey

B eing a lyrical genius can only take you so far—support staff is needed to shape your ideas, and mentors are needed to encourage and inspire you (no matter how depressed you are). Besides, listening to the same New York Dolls album can only take you so far, too.

The following men (sadly, no women) have been the driving force behind Morrissey's career and Morrissey himself.

Kevin Armstrong, Guitarist and Co-writer: 1989–1990

Kevin Armstrong was a session musician who had previously played with David Bowic and Thomas Dolby. He first met Morrissey in 1987 when he was considered to replace Johnny Marr as the Smiths' guitarist. He declined any thought of it and continued with his session work. After working with Sandie Shaw on her 1988 *Hello Angel* album, Armstrong once again had the chance to work with Morrissey and took him up on his offer to play guitar on the upcoming *Bona Drag* tracks.

Kevin Armstrong also co-wrote "He Knows I'd Love to See Him" and "Piccadilly Palare," which both ended up on *Bona Drag*. After the album was done, Armstrong and Morrissey amicably parted ways.

Boz Boorer, Guitarist and Co-writer: 1990–present

Guitarist Boz Boorer has been Morrissey's right-hand man since joining his backing band in 1990. He has played guitar (obviously) and co-written a number of Morrissey's favorite and much-loved hits, such as "Jack the Ripper," "Speedway," "Now My Heart Is Full," and "The More You Ignore Me, the Closer I Get" (fun fact: Boz's daughter Billie-Rose is the little girl featured in the video for "The More You Ignore Me, the Closer I Get"). Boz has also provided the clarinet and banjo on a number of Morrissey's songs.

Despite being younger than Morrissey, Boorer has had a longer professional career in music. He was only fifteen when he started with the Polecats, who had hits with their rockabilly covers of David Bowie's "John, I'm Only Dancing" and T. Rex's "Jeepster," and a big hit in the United States with their 1983 single "Make a Circuit with Me" ("Jeepster" was even produced by future Morrissey producer Tony Visconti.) What's funny is that in Morrissey's 1981 letters to pen pal Robert Mackie, the singer talks shit about the Polecats' cover of "John, I'm Only Dancing." I'm sure Boz has never let Morrissey live that one down.

Morrissey first met Boorer in 1990 while looking for a "rockabilly-ish" band for a "rockabilly-ish" EP that never materialized. Good friend Chas Smash recommended Boorer to Morrissey, and he was impressed enough to bring him along on the *Kill Uncle* tour. Since then, Boorer has proven to be irreplaceable to Morrissey, even taking on double duties as a producer and jack-of-all-musical-trades (Boz produced the 1994 Morrissey and Siouxsie Sioux duet, "Interlude"). In his spare time, he has also played with Kirsty MacColl and Adam Ant, as well as fronted his own band, Boz and the Bozmen.

Longtime guitarist and collaborator Boz Boorer was rocking with the Polecats long before Morrissey had met Marr.
Author's collection

Jonny Bridgwood, Bassist: 1990, 1993–1997

Jonny Bridgwood was first brought in to play for Morrissey in 1990 for the "Pregnant for the Last Time" single, but then was let go in favor of Gary Day (who was in guitarist Alain Whyte's three-piece rockabilly band). Two years later, Gary Day was let go and Bridgwood was brought back to record 1994's *Vauxhall and I*. Once again, he found himself dropped for the recording of the "Hold On to Your Friends" single, but then—surprise! He was brought back for 1995's "Boxers" single, and then he finally got to unpack his things and stay for a while, playing on both 1995's *Southpaw Grammar* and 1997's *Maladjusted* and their tours. Bridgwood left Morrissey's band in 1997 due to financial issues with Morrissey and his feelings about the music becoming repetitive.

Dean Butterworth, Drummer: 2002–2004

Although not a member of the famous pancake syrup family, Dean Butterworth was equally smooth and silky with his drumming. But that was the problem—it was too smooth for Morrissey (who has always recruited hard drummers for his backing band). He liked Butterworth enough to keep him on for the recording of 2004's *You Are the Quarry* album and the subsequent tour, but Butterworth could sense Moz's unhappiness and left on his own to join the lame rock band Good Charlotte.

Matt Chamberlain, Drummer: 2005

One of the two Matts that have drummed for Morrissey, Matt Chamberlain was only featured on 2005's *Ringleader of the Tormentors*. The recording session went well, due to Chamberlain having previously worked with producer Tony Visconti on two David Bowie albums (2002's *Heathen* and 2003's *Reality*). He was replaced immediately after recording *Ringleader of the Tormentors* with Matt Walker.

Spencer Cobrin, Drummer and Co-writer: 1991–1997

Spencer Cobrin has been referred to as "the best drummer Morrissey's ever had," and I pretty much agree. Cobrin was young, talented, and just happy to be playing the drums. Sadly, his relationship with Morrissey ended on bad terms, and they have not spoken or played together since 1999.

Spencer Cobrin was brought onboard for the 1991 *Kill Uncle* tour and "rockabilly" EP that never materialized. Already being friends with and working with bassist Gary Day and guitarist Alain Whyte made the transition comfortable, and Cobrin impressed Morrissey enough to ensure a spot for the recording of 1992's *Your Arsenal*. For unknown reasons, both Cobrin and Day were kicked out of the band shortly before the recording of 1994's *Vauxhall and I*. He was brought back again for the recording of the "Boxers" single and 1995's *Southpaw Grammar*. He was retained for 1997's *Maladjusted*, but for this album, Cobrin gave Morrissey some songs he had been working on, and three were chosen: "Now I Am a Was," "Wide to Receive," and one of my personal favorites, "Lost." After the *Maladjusted* tour wrapped up, Cobrin and bassist Jonny Bridgwood left the band, due to financial issues with Morrissey.

In typical Morrissey fashion (regarding money), he got pretty shitty with Spencer Cobrin, faxing him horrible letters filled with tripe and accusations. Spencer has moved on, and he has drummed for other bands and has composed movie soundtracks.

Gary Day, Bassist and Co-writer: 1991–1993, 1999–2006

Gary Day is the most recognizable and most beloved of Morrissey's bass players. Coming from the same rockabilly scene as Boz Boorer, Spencer Cobrin, and Alain Whyte, Gary Day was a skilled bass player and had great stage presence, especially when he would trade his electric bass for the classic stand-up bass and slap away during Morrissey's more rockabilly-ish songs, like "The Loop" and "Pregnant for the Last Time."

Both Day and Cobrin were excused from Morrissey's band and tour after the *Your Arsenal* tour concluded. Day went back to playing in his previous rockabilly band, the Nitros, and even started his own record label until Morrissey brought him back for the "Boxers" single in 1995 and then again for Morrissey's 1999 tour. Day continued to work for Morrissey in the recording studio and on tour, co-writing the B-sides "Mexico," "Noise Is the Best Revenge," and "You Know I Couldn't Last." Sadly, he was replaced in 2007 by Morrissey's current bass player, Solomon Walker.

Michael Farrell, Keyboardist: 2004–2007

Michael Farrell was Morrissey's first "real" keyboard player, joining the *You Are the Quarry* tour in 2004. His keyboarding was a welcome sound—it brought a fullness to Morrissey's songs and made the piano-based songs easier to perform live (such as "Trouble Loves Me" and "Last Night I Dreamt That Somebody Loved Me"). He was also a multi-instrumentalist who played the trumpet and trombone (as a former trombone player myself, I love his trombone solo in "I Just Want to See the Boy Happy" from 2006's *Ringleader of the Tormentors*). He also co-wrote "At Last I Am Born" and the terrible B-side "Sweetie-Pie" (although the terribleness wasn't Farrell's fault). Michael Farrell left Morrissey's band in 2007 to spend more time with his family.

Joe Moss, Smiths Manager: 1982–1983

Joe Moss is a local Manchester businessman who befriended a young Johnny Marr and became the first manager of the Smiths. Moss first saw success with the manufacturing and selling of Indian-styled sandals and clothing in the 1970s and officially created his own clothing company called Crazy Face after he started manufacturing and selling "loon pants" (bell bottoms). He soon opened up a couple of Crazy Face boutiques, with one of them being in Manchester.

Johnny Marr worked next door to the Crazy Face boutique at X-Clothes and would hang out with Moss on his lunch break, talking about records, music, and life. Although Moss was sixteen years older than Johnny, they both found each other to be kindred spirits and got along famously. Soon their talk of records and music would lead to discussion about starting a band. Marr knew of a bassist and drummer whom he could work with, but did not know of anyone who would be his ideal front man. To encourage Marr in his front man odyssey, Moss showed him a documentary about songwriting partners Leiber and Stoller, and how they first met (Stoller just showed up on Leiber's doorstep and asked him if he wanted to work together). This stuck with Johnny, and a short time later, Johnny told Moss he had heard of a guy in Stretford who might be a good front man. Moss promised Marr that if this new partnership worked out, they could rehearse at the Crazy Face manufacturing plant and he would help with band management.

Once the Smiths were created, Joe Moss funded the recording of their first single, "Hand in Glove," in early 1983 (he and his wife Janet were properly thanked on the back of the album cover). He continued to manage the Smiths until the end of 1983 and then quit—after the birth of his daughter, he wanted to become a "family man," and he also realized that they needed a "real" manager, someone who knew the music business better than he did. To this day, both Morrissey and Marr recognize that if it were not for Joe Moss believing in them and supporting their music, there would be no Smiths.

Moss remained friendly with the Smiths as they became indie rock superstars. He even got back into the music scene by managing the group Marion (who opened for Morrissey in 1995) and Johnny Marr in his solo career.

I guess they really were "kindred spirits."

Mark Nevin, Guitarist and Co-writer: 1990–1992

After the breakup with producer and co-writer Stephen Street after the release of 1988's *Viva Hate*, Morrissey was in need of a new co-writer for his second album, 1990's *Kill Uncle*. New guitarist Kevin Armstrong, producer Clive Langer, and ex-Smiths bassist Andy Rourke had all submitted new songs, but they were all pretty meh. Drummer Andrew Paresi knew Mark Nevin and asked him to submit some of his songs to Morrissey for consideration. He did, but he sent a cassette to Morrissey under the pseudonym "Burt Reynolds," as instructed by Paresi.

Morrissey liked what Nevin had sent him and wanted to hear more. As Nevin was mailing yet another package addressed to "Burt Reynolds," he saw Morrissey taking a stroll nearby. He walked over and gave him the package; Morrissey became embarrassed about the whole "Burt Reynolds" thing and silently took the package and left. He must not have been that embarrassed, though, because he asked Nevin to be his guitarist and co-writer for the upcoming *Kill Uncle* album.

Eight of the ten tracks on *Kill Uncle* were written by Nevin, and because of that, he gets a lot of the blame for how poorly the album was received. Nevin blamed it on Morrissey's writing style—he was a fan of writing and recording the lyrics separately from the music and took the songs for what they were, never adding or suggesting any changes to the music. Despite the poor reception of *Kill Uncle*, Morrissey asked Nevin to write songs for the soon-to-be-discarded rockabilly EP, and he did—submitting "The Loop," "You're Gonna Need Someone on Your Side," "Pregnant for the Last Time," and "Born to Hang." Three of those songs made it on to other projects ("You're Gonna Need Someone on Your Side" went to 1992's *Your Arsenal*, "Pregnant for the Last Time" was released as a single in 1991, and "The Loop" ended up as a B-side for the 1991 "Sing Your Life" single), and

Nevin was under the impression that he was going to be Morrissey's guitarist for his next album, 1992's *Your Arsenal* (nicknamed "Kill Auntie").

Until it was time for the *Kill Uncle* tour to begin. Mark Nevin was still under contract with RCA after his previous band, Fairground Attraction, broke up. RCA demanded the one last album they were owed, and Nevin fulfilled their demand by recording and touring that last album with a new band under the name Sweetmouth. Morrissey hired Boz Boorer to take Nevin's place, along with the rest of his new backing band (Spencer Cobrin, Gary Day, and Alain Whyte). Both Boorer and Whyte also took over writing duties from Nevin, although two Nevin tracks did find their way onto *Your Arsenal*—the aforementioned "You're Gonna Need Someone on Your Side" and "I Know It's Gonna Happen Someday."

Andrew Paresi, Drummer: 1987–1991

Andrew Paresi was essentially a session drummer, and coincidentally, that is how he met Stephen Street. Stephen Street was working on a single for a new band called A Pair of Blue Eyes, in which Andrew Paresi was the drummer. After impressing Street, he was offered the chance to try out for Morrissey's new backing band. He also impressed Morrissey and got along with guitarist Vini Reilly, so he was in.

He was a good fit for a band that really had no idea what they were doing—Paresi was a quick learner and easy going, but really skilled at his drumming. From the pounding and thundering beat of "I Don't Mind If You Forget Me" to the gentle backing drums on "Late Night, Maudlin Street," Andrew Paresi could do it all—and he did it all for 1988's *Viva Hate*.

And it was unknown to everyone (except Morrissey) why he was replaced with ex-Smith Mike Joyce on drums for the recording of "Interesting Drug" and "The Last of the Famous International Playboys." But Paresi was not out of the band for long—while working with guitarist Kevin Armstrong and producer Clive Langer on Sandie Shaw's 1989 *Hello Angel* album, Langer recruited both of them to record Morrissey's "Ouija Board, Ouija Board" single and 1990's almost album *Bona Drag* and for-sure album *Kill Uncle*.

Unfortunately, after *Kill Uncle*, Andrew Paresi was replaced by Spencer Cobrin for the *Kill Uncle* tour and the recording of Morrissey's new album. Paresi continued to play the drums after that and then went into radio comedy. His 2005 Radio 1 show was titled *I Was Morrissey's Drummer*.

John Peel, DJ, BBC Radio 1: 1967–2004

One of the best-known radio DJs throughout the world, John Peel started his broadcasting career in the United States in Dallas, Texas. After several other radio gigs throughout the southwestern United States, he made his way back to his home country of England in 1967 and took the midnight to two in the morning shift on Radio London, in which he played all the up-and-coming rock music (like the Rolling Stones) while also playing more underground music, like folk and psychedelic rock. After Radio London ceased operation, he moved on to the BBC's new pop music station, Radio 1. His new show was pretty much the same as his Radio London show—showcasing new bands, playing records from old bands, playing spoken word poetry, and fielding call-in questions from listeners. Peel was always on the lookout for new bands that he liked, and that is where the Smiths come in.

In the late 1970s and early 1980s, John Peel played a lot of what was new—punk rock, new wave, and indie rock. Longtime producer John Walters had seen the Smiths' second show in London in 1983 and recommended them to Peel. He brought them into the studio in 1983 to record four songs for his famous *Peel Sessions* segment. It was a great success, with songs from that session being included on the *Hatful of Hollow* compilation. The Smiths would perform on the *Peel Sessions* a total of four times throughout their short career.

In a 1987 article about the Smiths in the *Observer* magazine, John Peel had this to say about Morrissey's writing: "More than one Morrissey lyric has caused my laughter to tinkle among the teacups. His ability to indicate a whole way of life by briefly highlighting a darkened corner of that life is matched only by his skill at delivering his lyrics in a manner that leaves the listener with no choice but to consider seriously what is being sung. These are rare gifts in popular music."

After the Smiths broke up, John Peel and Morrissey and Marr drifted apart, although Morrissey and his *Viva Hate* band were booked to perform some new solo tracks on the *Peel Sessions*. Although it was attempted, it did not work—Morrissey did not like how the producers and staff treated himself and the band, as if they were amateurs. That was the last time Morrissey had any communication with John Peel.

Sadly, John Peel passed away in 2004 from a heart attack at age 65. But his legacy lives on in the hearts of music fans young and old, and certainly in the hearts of the Smiths and Morrissey fans for giving them their "big break."

John Porter, Smiths Producer: 1983–1987

John Porter was originally a guitarist, but then became a bass player when asked by friend and former bandmate Bryan Ferry to join Roxy Music for the recording of their second album, *For Your Pleasure*. This led to a successful partnership with Ferry and the rest of the members of Roxy Music—Porter continued to play bass for Roxy Music and on four of Ferry's solo albums, as well as saxophonist Andy Mackay's 1975 solo album, *In Search of Eddie Riff*.

By 1983, John Porter was a well-known and respected producer, having produced albums for Killing Joke. He was brought into the studio by Rough Trade's Geoff Travis to see if he could remix (and would be interested in remixing) the Smiths' debut album, which was originally recorded by Troy Tate. Porter insisted that it would be easier to start fresh, so that they did—rerecording their album with Porter at the controls.

John Porter and Johnny Marr hit it off and became friends, and Porter a mentor to the young guitarist. Despite *The Smiths* sounding better than the previous Troy Tate recordings, it still wasn't great, due to the pressure from Rough Trade and time constraints. Porter continued to work on a number of singles for the Smiths, such as "This Charming Man," "What Difference Does It Make?," "Heaven Knows I'm Miserable Now," "William, It Was Really Nothing," "How Soon Is Now?," and "Panic." He was under the impression that he would be producing the next Smiths album, but when it came time to record, he was replaced by Stephen Street, whom Morrissey had met during the recording of "Heaven Knows I'm Miserable Now" (Street was the engineer). It was rumored that Morrissey was jealous of the close relationship that had formed between Porter and Marr, so he decided to "team up" with Street to form their own special recording studio friendship. The Smiths continued to use Street for the rest of their albums and eventually started to do some of the producing themselves.

John Porter became the leading producer for blues musicians such as Buddy Guy, Taj Mahal, B. B. King, and John Mayall. He now resides in New Orleans.

Vini Reilly, Guitarist: 1987–1988

Vini Reilly is a guitarist from Manchester whom Morrissey had never met prior to working on 1988's *Viva Hate*, despite having some past connections. Vini Reilly was the guitarist in the original lineup of Ed Banger and the Nosebleeds. Once Vini and Ed Banger left, Morrissey joined the Ed Banger-less Nosebleeds as the lead vocalist, only to perform two shows as their front man in 1978. Vini Reilly was also the first act signed to Manchester's Factory Records—his solo work was given the name the Durutti Column.

Morrissey met Vini Reilly through *Viva Hate* producer and bassist Stephen Street, who previously produced the Durutti Column's *The Guitar and Other Machines* album. He introduced Morrissey to Reilly, and they hit it off. Despite doing a great job on *Viva Hate* and getting along with Morrissey (they would often make trips back to Manchester to hang out), Reilly would soon claim that he wrote a majority of the music for *Viva Hate*, despite Stephen Street's claims that he wrote the music for *Viva Hate*. Morrissey and drummer Andrew Paresi both back up Street's claims. The fighting did not last too long, since Stephen Street produced the next Durutti Column album in 1989.

Stephen Street, Producer and Engineer: 1984–1987; Co-writer, Producer, and Bassist: 1987–1989

Stephen Street has a long history with Morrissey, going back to the Smiths. He began as an engineer for the 1984 single "Heaven Knows I'm Miserable Now," and that led to job of engineering their 1985 album *Meat Is Murder* and 1986's *The Queen Is Dead*. The Smiths then chose him to produce their last album, 1987's *Strangeways, Here We Come*.

A musician and writer himself, Street submitted a tape of songs he had written for potential B-sides for the *Strangeways, Here We Come* singles, but since the Smiths were no more by the time it came to releasing singles, Morrissey adopted Street's songs for his 1988 debut album *Viva Hate*. He also adopted Street to produce it and play bass.

Now as the producer of *Viva Hate*, Street assembled a backing band for Morrissey (guitarist Vini Reilly and drummer Andrew Paresi), and together, they recorded and released *Viva Hate* to critical acclaim and two Top 10 singles. Although Street continued to submit songs to Morrissey, things were turning sour over owed royalties for his writing and producing work on *Viva Hate*. He continued to work with Morrissey on the Street-penned B-side "Will Never Marry" and playing keyboards on the upcoming singles "The Last of the Famous International Playboys" (which he also wrote) and "Interesting Drug." Unfortunately, he and Morrissey stopped working together in 1989, but Morrissey had the balls to still record and release some of Street's songs, like "Ouija Board, Ouija Board," "At Amber," and "Journalists Who Lie."

Stephen Street went on to produce huge and award-winning albums by Blur and the Cranberries.

Troy Tate, Smiths Producer: 1983

Troy Tate (formerly of the Teardrop Explodes) was the first producer of the Smiths' 1983 debut self-titled album. Picked by Rough Trade boss Geoff Travis as a "perfect match" for the young and inexperienced Smiths, Tate spent a good month with the Smiths recording fourteen of their originals, capturing the real and raw sound they were known for in their live concerts. At first Morrissey was extremely pleased with the new album recordings, but then he started to grouse about them to the higher-ups at Rough Trade. Geoff Travis then brought in John Porter to rerecord the album.

Rumors abound as to why Troy Tate was given the boot—some say that Morrissey was not happy with the songs' lack of fullness; yet other people close to the production have mentioned that they believe that Morrissey was jealous of Troy Tate and Johnny Marr's new friendship. But no one can argue that the John Porter version of *The Smiths* did sound more polished and hit-friendly.

Some of the original Troy Tate recordings did make it out of the studio— his recording of the Smiths "Jeane" ended up as the B-side on the "This Charming Man" single, and his version of "Pretty Girls Make Graves" was the B-side to "Last Night I Dreamt That Somebody Loves Me." *The Troy Tate Sessions* is a bootleg that can be found online that has his original version of *The Smiths*.

Woodie Taylor, Drummer: 1993–1994

Woodie Taylor was also a member of the rockabilly scene and friend of guitarist Boz Boorer. He joined Morrissey's band after the dismissal of Spencer Cobrin to record 1994's *Vauxhall and I*. Although Morrissey was pleased with his drumming on *Vauxhall and I*, he asked Cobrin back to work on the B-sides "Moon River" and "A Swallow on My Neck," but then turned around and asked Taylor back to work on the 1995 "Boxers" and "Sunny" singles. He was kept on for the first round of recording in France for the 1995 album *Southpaw Grammar*, but he was dismissed after that. And then—you guessed it—Spencer Cobrin was brought back for the second attempt at recording *Southpaw Grammar* and then stayed until 1997.

Woodie Taylor now goes by M. J. Taylor and currently plays drums in the British indie pop band Comet Gain.

Jesse Tobias, Guitarist and Co-writer: 2004–present

After guitarist and co-writer Alain Whyte unexpectedly left the 2004 *You Are the Quarry* tour, Morrissey was in search of a new guitar player. Keyboardist Michael Farrell had previously worked with Jesse Tobias and his ex-wife (Tobias's ex, not Farrell's) in a band called Splendid, and recommended him to Morrissey. Morrissey liked his look and his guitar playing and brought him on board.

Although Alain Whyte was still penning songs for Morrissey, Jesse Tobias also started to submit songs to Morrissey, with five of his songs making it to 2006's *Ringleader of the Tormentors* (four of the songs ended up being the four singles). Jesse Tobias is currently one of Morrissey's guitarists and co-writers, having worked on 2009's *Years of Refusal* and 2014's *World Peace Is None of Your Business*.

He is also not too bad on the eyes, if you know what I mean.

Tony Visconti, Producer: 2005

Tony Visconti is a legendary producer who produced Morrissey's 2006 album *Ringleader of the Tormentors*, making it one of the best albums in his catalog. And no, he is not the "Visconti" Morrissey croons about in the album's first single, "You Have Killed Me"—that honor belongs to Italian film director Luchino Visconti.

Tony Visconti was born and raised in Brooklyn and, after studying music and playing in regional groups, made his way to England. He became room-mates with David Bowie and produced his seminal albums, 1969's *Space Oddity* and 1970's *The Man Who Sold the World*. He was known as a founding father in the glam rock world and would also work on legendary albums like *Electric Warrior* by T. Rex, *Indiscreet* by Sparks, *The Idiot* by Iggy Pop, and *Black Rose* by Thin Lizzy.

Visconti had almost worked with Morrissey two previous times (before *Ringleader of the Tormentors*): he almost produced either the Smiths' 1986 *The Queen Is Dead* album or their 1986 single "Panic" (Morrissey remembers it as *The Queen Is Dead*; Johnny says it was "Panic"). He was also in the running to produce Morrissey's 1992 album, *Your Arsenal*, but the producing job went to ex–David Bowie guitar player Mick Ronson (Visconti had previously worked with Ronson on David Bowie's *The Man Who Sold the World*). It would be Bowie again who would connect Morrissey to Tony Visconti . . . and opening act/background singer Kristeen Young . . . and drummer Matt Chamberlain. Visconti produced David Bowie's 2002 album, *Heathen*, and 2003's *Reality*. He recommended Young and Chamberlain to Bowie for those albums and to Morrissey for *Ringleader of the Tormentors*.

Ringleader of the Tormentors went to #1 on the UK chart and had four great singles. When it came time to record what would be 2009's *Years of Refusal*, Tony Visconti assumed the job was his. Morrissey, on the other hand, said that it was not and chose *You Are the Quarry* producer Jerry Finn. In a 2008 interview with *Hot Press* magazine, Morrissey had this to say about the issue: "Tony wasn't ever in line for the job. He had started working with a band, Kentucky, and tied himself up with that. I wanted to try Jerry Finn again—he had produced *You Are the Quarry*, and we were in the enviable situation of having worked both with Tony and Jerry and had really enjoyed both. I'd love to do another album with Tony, and I feel blessed to have eventually found two ideal producers. They are both fantastic in equal measure. I wish I had met them earlier."

As I write this, Tony Visconti has not produced another Morrissey album.

Matt Walker, Drummer: 2006–present

Solomon Walker, Bassist: 2007–present

Matt and Solomon Walker, a.k.a. the Walker Brothers, both joined Morrissey's band around the same time (2006–2007). Matt joined first, starting with the 2006 Tour of the Tormentors. Solomon played with Morrissey and the band in Chicago in 2006 when bassist Gary Day was unable to attend. Once Morrissey let Day go, he invited Solomon to join his brother as his full-time bassist.

Alain Whyte, Guitarist and Co-writer: 1991–2009

Other than Johnny Marr, no other writer has been able to connect with the "Morrissey Magic" like guitarist Alain Whyte. Actually, Whyte has surpassed Marr by sheer volume—Whyte has written eighty-one songs with Morrissey, with sixteen of those being singles, and then six of those being Top 10 hits on the UK chart. Not too shabby for a guy hired for his "rockabilly skills."

In 1991, Morrissey had completed work on the *Kill Uncle* album and had an itching to make a rockabilly album. After recruiting guitarist Boz Boorer, he then met and adopted the Memphis Sinners, a rockabilly band whose members were Spencer Cobrin, Gary Day, and Alain Whyte. After pretending to be a rockabilly band for the "Sing Your Life" video, they became his band in real life. Although Alain irritated Morrissey enough with his constant talking, Morrissey liked him enough to accept and perform some of his songs, such as the B-side "Pashernate Love" and "We Hate It When Our Friends Become Successful." After that it was on—Alain became Morrissey's writing machine, pumping out such Morrissey favorites as "You're the One for Me, Fatty," "Alma Matters," "Irish Blood, English Heart," and "I'm Throwing My Arms Around Paris."

Whyte continued to play guitar and write for Morrissey until 2004, when it was rumored that he had health problems. He dropped out of the *You Are the Quarry* tour and has not performed live on stage with Morrissey since then, although he continued to record and write on 2006's *Ringleader of the Tormentors* and 2009's *Years of Refusal.* He now lives in Los Angeles.

9

How Marr-Velous

The Beginning of the Smiths

Johnny Marr and Andy Rourke

ohnny Marr met Andy Rourke while attending high school in Wythenshawe, and they started playing music together, with Rourke actually teaching Johnny chords and riffs. They started a band in 1980 with some other Wythenshawe friends and named themselves White Dice. White Dice had an American rock 'n' roll sound, and although they recorded a demo with Elvis Costello's manager, Jake Riviera, they never did anything more and broke up shortly after. Marr and Rourke then started their punk-funk project, Freak Party.

In 1981, Freak Party was no more and Johnny Marr had moved to Manchester proper, leaving Andy Rourke behind. While working at X-Clothes, a cool clothing boutique, Johnny became friends with Joe Moss, who ran a different cool clothing boutique called Crazy Face. Joe introduced Johnny to early rock 'n' roll and rhythm and blues and stirred his creative juices, so much that Johnny ached to find someone compatible and someone just as into old music as he was.

After meeting and not instantly connecting with other musicians (including Matt Johnson of The The, whom Marr would eventually team up with after the Smiths), Johnny Marr remembered a strange and lanky individual whom he had met four years earlier through his friend Billy Duffy.

Billy Duffy and Steven Pomfret

Billy Duffy was a schoolmate of Johnny Marr and Andy Rourke in Wythenshawe, and they became friends despite playing in separate bands (Marr and Rourke in White Dice and Duffy in the Nosebleeds with Morrissey). In the summer of 1978, Duffy, Marr, and other friends went to the Manchester Apollo to check out the Patti Smith concert. Morrissey was also there and bumped into Duffy and Marr. Being all New York Dolls and Patti Smith fans (obviously), Duffy introduced the two, and they exchanged pleasantries. Although they did not speak much at the show, Morrissey himself (and Morrissey's legend) left an impression on Johnny Marr that he was never able to shake.

Steven Pomfret was another bandmate of Morrissey and Billy Duffy who was also a mutual friend of Johnny Marr. After Duffy had moved to London, Pomfret was the only link Marr had to Morrissey, and Marr recruited Pomfret to escort him to Morrissey's house. Once Morrissey came to the door, Pomfret stepped back and left the two to talk. Although Pomfret initially worked with the both of them on some pre-Smiths rehearsals, he decided it was not working out, and he left with no ill feelings.

Morrissey and Johnny Marr

At that fateful post–Patti Smith meeting, Morrissey invited Marr upstairs to his bedroom, and they proceeded to hang out, mostly talking about the New York Dolls, Patti Smith, and similar writing/composing partners Leiber and Stoller. After spending the afternoon together, Morrissey agreed to create music with Marr.

Leiber and Stoller, Lennon and McCartney, and Morrissey and Marr.
Clare Muller/Redferns/Getty Images

Together in Marr's apartment, Morrissey and Marr worked on three songs: "Suffer Little Children," "The Hand That Rocks the Cradle," and "Don't Blow Your Own Horn" (which was never recorded). After seeing how well their first time creating music had gone, they were inseparable. Morrissey and Marr continued to write songs and work with various musicians until December 1982 when the final lineup of the Smiths was complete.

Mike Joyce and Andy Rourke

Mike Joyce first met Johnny Marr through Pete Hope, a mutual friend. Joyce was a punk drummer at first, playing with the bands the Hoax and Victim. Getting sick of the punk routine, Joyce decided to try out for the Smiths. Despite Joyce being high on 'shrooms during his audition, Morrissey and Marr liked what they heard, and Joyce became the third Smith.

Andy Rourke was the last official Smith to join, although he and Johnny Marr had the oldest relationship. Replacing original Smiths bassist Dale Hibbert, Rourke rejoined Marr in a musical setting and took over bass duties, himself becoming the fourth Smith.

10

I Really Don't Know and I Really Don't Care

"I'm really ready to be burned at the stake in total defence of that record. It means so much to me that I could never explain, however long you gave me. It becomes almost difficult and one is just simply swamped in emotion about the whole thing. It's getting to the point where I almost can't even talk about it, which many people will see as an absolute blessing. It just seems absolutely perfect to me. From my own personal standpoint, it seems to convey exactly what I wanted it to."

—Morrissey, *Melody Maker*, March 3, 1984

The self-titled debut album by the Smiths was eagerly awaited by the music fans of England after their four successful appearances on BBC Radio 1 and their breakthrough single, "Hand in Glove." After signing with the Rough Trade label in mid-1983, they immediately started recording their album with Troy Tate, who was picked by Rough Trade head Geoff Travis to oversee the project.

Although Morrissey and Marr had issues with the how the album was sounding, they relied on Travis to make the final decision about the album's future. Travis thought it was crap, but because he was low on funds, he asked friend and known producer John Porter if he could "fix it up." Porter listened to it and came to the conclusion that it would be easier (and cheaper) just to start from scratch. Despite being crunched for time, Travis and the Smiths agreed to give it another try.

Besides there being pressure to get the album done by the end of the year, drama was brewing within the Smiths themselves. Morrissey was unhappy about the contract they had signed with Rough Trade and felt that he was not getting adequate compensation. During one of the recording sessions, Morrissey up and disappeared. After being gone from the studio for five hours, he finally called and filled everyone in on his whereabouts—he had impulsively left the studio and took the train to London to visit Geoff Travis because he was unhappy about how the money owed to the Smiths was split. Morrissey threatened to quit the band unless his and Johnny Marr's share was raised to 40 percent each, leaving Andy Rourke and Mike Joyce with 10 percent each. Rourke and Joyce agreed to the split because with the band being so close to "making it," they did not want it to end. Of course, none of this agreement was actually put to paper and signed off on, and it came back to bite Morrissey and Marr in the ass during the 1996 court case.

Despite the album getting done in time (and for as cheaply as possible), Morrissey and Marr were not happy with how it had turned out (yet again). They felt that Porter had butchered everything and buried everything that was special about their sound. Even though the Troy Tate records weren't great, they at least kept a little bit of the Smiths' raw and honest sound. The Porter version was too subdued and too slick, but it was what they had, and they were stuck with it.

The Smiths was released in February 1984, and it reached #2 on the UK chart (Simple Minds' *Sparkle in the Rain* kept it from reaching #1). Despite all of the productions problems, Morrissey and the Smiths were happy with the aftermath. Morrissey considers *The Smiths* to be his most personal album, mainly because all of the songs were written in his formative years, from a teenager to a young man. Johnny considered it a "learning experience." And the fans considered *The Smiths* to be one of the best debut albums of all time—it certainly was not one of their best, but every great band has to start somewhere.

"Reel Around the Fountain"

I feel that I can be honest with you at this point in the book.

I hate this song.

It is so boring, and Morrissey just drones on. And it is a shame that they picked "Reel Around the Fountain" to lead the album with, because a lot of people are not as patient as me and would probably turn it off halfway into this song and then never listen to it again.

But I am sure there is something good to say about "Reel Around the Fountain."

Like how Paul Carrack played the piano on the track. I really like his former band, Ace.

"Reel Around the Fountain" was Morrissey's take on losing his virginity. And when it came to his interests, Morrissey blew his load with this song—he used lines from Shelagh Delaney's *A Taste of Honey* and *The Lion in Love* and took the title from one of his favorite books, *Popcorn Venus* (the author refers to a scene in Federico Fellini's *La Dolce Vita* where Anita Ekberg is dancing around the Trevi Fountain as "reeling around the fountain"). Johnny's inspiration for his guitar part in "Reel Around the Fountain" was the old R&B song "Handy Man" by Jimmy Jones.

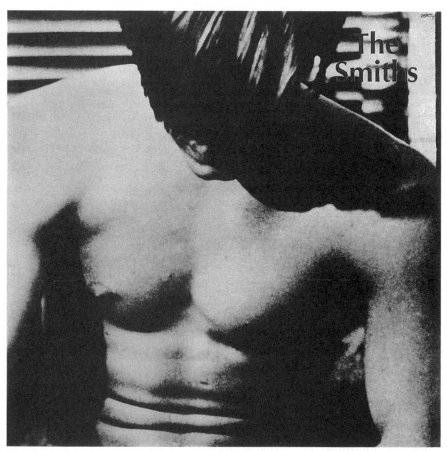

The Smiths' 1984 self-titled debut. Two Morrisseys are associated with this album: Morrissey himself and the singer and director Paul Morrissey (the cover photo is of actor Joe Dallesandro in Paul Morrissey's 1968 film *Flesh*).   *Author's collection*

"Reel Around the Fountain" did have a little drama surrounding it. Originally slated to be released as a single, it was hastily pulled due to a story in the *Sun* about how one of their earlier songs, "Handsome Devil," was about child sexual abuse. It wasn't—but now everyone was careful not to offend. When it was found out that "Reel Around the Fountain" mentioned a child, people got nervous, and the single was canned.

"You've Got Everything Now"

One of the better songs on side A of *The Smiths*, "You've Got Everything Now" once again features lines inspired by *A Taste of Honey* and *The Lion in Love* by Shelagh Delaney. Morrissey sings about being smarter than most of his classmates, yet they have gone on to have successful lives while Morrissey still lives at home and is on the dole. "You've Got Everything Now" does feature one of Morrissey's great falsetto moments.

"Miserable Lie"

"Miserable Lie" has always had the miserable reputation of being a song about Morrissey's relationship with best friend Linder Sterling, due to a reference about living with a girl in Whalley Range in Manchester. When asked about the connection, Morrissey admitted that he did live with Linder in Whalley Range, but he didn't stay there for long. This is also the first song where Morrissey sings about his negative feelings regarding his body image ("I look at yours, you laugh at mine").

Whereas "You've Got Everything Now" had a couple of great little falsetto moments, "Miserable Lie" is nothing but Morrissey falsetto for 75 percent of the song. It gets tiresome and annoying, making it falsetto overkill on song that has some of the best lyrics on the album.

"Pretty Girls Make Graves"

"Pretty Girls Make Graves" gets its title from Jack Kerouac's 1958 novel, *The Dharma Bums*—the main character (who is celibate) states that when he sees a pretty girl, he reminds himself that "pretty girls make graves." Morrissey is in the same boat in "Pretty Girls Make Graves"—he meets a girl and she is ready to get down, but he feels inadequate, so she leaves him to go bone another ready-and-willing guy. It's fine if you choose not to have sex, but Morrissey is such a whiny little bitch in this song, I would dump him, too.

Fun fact: A woman's voice makes an appearance on "Pretty Girls Make Graves" and says "Oh, really?" That voice belongs to Morrissey's girlfriend at the time, Annalisa Jablonska. Some say that they were not really boyfriend/girlfriend, but in the 1981 letters to pen pal Robert Mackie, Morrissey states that he is dating Annalisa and that they are both bisexual.

Oh, really?

"The Hand That Rocks the Cradle"

"The Hand That Rocks the Cradle" is a song of firsts. It was the first song Morrissey properly wrote, even pre-Smiths. Richard Boon, a friend of Morrissey and the manager of the Buzzcocks, has mentioned hearing Morrissey sing "The Hand That Rocks the Cradle" without any music in his bedroom in 1980. After Morrissey connected with Johnny Marr in 1982, it was one of the first songs they worked on together. Morrissey's lyrics and melody reminded Marr of Patti Smith's song "Kimberly" and suggested they base "The Hand That Rocks the Cradle" on that. It was the first demo they ever recorded and the first song they played live at their first show in October 1982 at the Manchester Ritz. Morrissey and Marr were going to name the Smiths debut album *The Hand That Rocks the Cradle* but decided on the humble title of *The Smiths*.

"Still Ill"

One of the best and most loved Smiths songs, "Still Ill" was a late addition to the debut album, with Morrissey and Marr writing it between the aborted Troy Tate session and the John Porter rerecord (Marr wrote the guitar part the same night he wrote the guitar part for "This Charming Man"). "Still Ill" is Morrissey's tale about being . . . well, still ill (and still being Morrissey). Still ill from being in love ("Under the iron bridge we kissed and although I ended up with sore lips") to not working ("England is mine and it owes me a living") to life in general ("And if you must go to work tomorrow, well if I were you I wouldn't bother. For there are brighter sides to life and I should know because I've seen them, but not very often"). A staple in the Smiths' live shows, Morrissey still performs "Still Ill" in concert.

I guess he's been ill for a very long time.

"Hand in Glove"

"Hand in Glove" was written by Morrissey and Johnny Marr in early 1983. Marr came up with the guitar riff one night while visiting his parents. Afraid he would forget his fantastic new riff, Marr had his girlfriend, Angie, drive him over to Morrissey's house, and he continued to play the riff while riding in the passenger seat. Once they arrived at Morrissey's house, they recorded the riff onto a cassette and Morrissey got busy writing the lyrics, completing them that same night.

Morrissey once again took inspiration from favorite author Shelagh Delaney, as well as singer-songwriter Buffy Sainte-Marie, with his line "And everything depends upon how near you stand to me" based on her line "Everything depends upon how near you sleep to me" from her 1971 song "Bells." The Smiths loved "Hand in Glove" and all agreed that it would be their first single.

The Smiths' manager, Joe Moss, agreed to pay for the recording of "Hand in Glove" in February 1983, and all were pleased with how it turned out—Marr's guitar was rough and raw, and Morrissey's lyrics were brutally honest and went along perfectly. Even the touch of Marr's harmonica added just

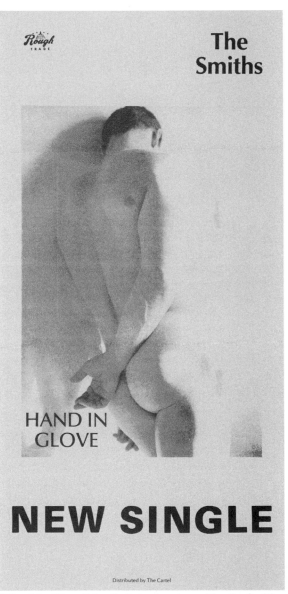

"Hand in Glove," the first single released by the Smiths.
Author's collection

the right sound. All members of the Smiths and Joe Moss were proud of their new single, and it is what sold Geoff Travis at Rough Trade on them. He tentatively signed the Smiths and agreed to release the single and then work on a real contract with the band.

It was released in May 1983, but did not even break the Top 100 on the UK chart, although it did hit #3 on the UK Indie chart. The Smiths were disappointed, but the "Hand in Glove" single did lead the band to other positive things—they started to receive more coverage in the press, and that led them to their first "Peel Session" with BBC Radio 1 DJ John Peel. It also led to their collaboration with singer Sandie Shaw, who liked "Hand in Glove" enough to cover it. Her version (backed by a Morrissey-less Smiths) reached #27 on the UK chart.

Not happy with the Troy Tate recording of "Hand in Glove" for their debut album, the Smiths insisted on using their previous single version for the album. Second producer John Porter agreed, but "cleaned" it up and changed the fade-in and fade-out on the original version. Although not as heavy-sounding as the original single, the version of "Hand in Glove" on *The Smiths* is certainly one of the better tracks on the album.

The B-side to the 1983 single release of "Hand in Glove" is a live recording of "Handsome Devil" at the Hacienda Club from April 1983. It was released on 7" vinyl.

"What Difference Does It Make?"

Even before its official release on 1984's *The Smiths*, Morrissey hated "What Difference Does It Make?" Don't believe me?

He also told *Q* magazine, in September 1992: "There's a couple of songs I don't like. In fact, I didn't really like them at the time. Like 'What Difference Does It Make?,' I thought was absolutely awful the day after the record was pressed . . ." Morrissey spoke to *Jamming!* in December 1984, and said: "For me, almost all the records have been absolutely perfect, but I can't deny that there are some that haven't aged so gracefully—'What Difference Does It Make?' . . . I regret the production on that now. But that's the only regret, although I might seem like the kind of person that has many regrets."

Morrissey felt that his lyrics were simple and not his usual sharp and witty outlook on life. It was one of the songs the Smiths performed on their first "Peel Session" in 1983 and, in Morrissey's eyes, the best and most definitive version of the song. Unfortunately for him, producers Troy Tate and John Porter disagreed, and both recorded their separate versions. Morrissey was able to trump both of them—he still hated those versions (and the song in general) so much that in 2008 when Warner Brothers was releasing *The Sounds of the Smiths* compilation, Morrissey instructed them to use the original Peel Session version, because it was the lesser of two evils. At least for him—the rest of the world loved "What Difference Does It Make?" It reached #12 on the UK chart in January 1984.

The B-sides for "What Difference Does It Make?" are "Back to the Old House" and "These Things Take Time." It was released on 7″ vinyl, 12″ vinyl, and compact disc single.

"I Don't Owe You Anything"

"I Don't Owe You Anything" was originally written to lure Sandie Shaw into using songs written by Morrissey and Johnny Marr. She liked it, but not as much as "Hand in Glove," and ended up using it as a B-side for her own "Hand in Glove" single. "I Don't Owe You Anything" is the snoozer on *The Smiths*, with its sleepy guitar and lounge-esque keyboards in the background. It is the closest thing to yacht rock that Morrissey and the Smiths have ever recorded.

"Suffer Little Children"

Like "The Hand That Rocks the Cradle," "Suffer Little Children" was written before Morrissey hooked up with Johnny Marr and was rife with Morrissey's feelings about the Moors murders and child killers Ian Brady and Myra Hindley.

Eerily spooky and the only track on *The Smiths* to have the adequate atmosphere (and adequate production), "Suffer Little Children" was a fitting tribute to the deceased Manchester youth from the very much alive Manchester youth. Morrissey expected it to draw attention, but its release was pretty uneventful until September 1984, when the grandfather of Moors murder victim John Kilbride heard it playing on a jukebox in a pub (it was the B-side to the "Heaven Knows I'm Miserable Now" single). Understandably upset, he went to the press and a big deal was made. Because of past issues regarding "child abuse" on earlier Smiths songs "Handsome Devil" and "Reel Around the Fountain," stores such as Boots and Woolworths pulled *The Smiths* and refused to sell it. A press release in the September 15, 1984, issue of *Melody Maker* magazine states

Morrissey's feelings and intentions when writing and recording "Suffer Little Children."

Because of the outcry regarding the content of "Suffer Little Children," Morrissey met with Ann West, who was the mother of Moors murders victim Lesley Ann Downey. Morrissey and Ann West became friends over the grief they both shared over the death of her daughter.

I'd Like to Drop My Trousers to the World

Meat Is Murder

"Of all the political topics to be scrutinised, people are still disturbingly vague about the treatment of animals. People still seem to believe that meat is a particular substance not at all connected to animals playing in the field over there. People don't realise how gruesomely and frighteningly the animal gets to the plate . . . "
—Morrissey, *New Musical Express*, December 22, 1984

After dealing with the bullshit of two producers and two completely different (and both inferior) albums, the Smiths decided to record their follow-up album *Meat Is Murder* themselves. Johnny had learned enough about working the board from John Porter, but still needed a little help with the finer details. After working with engineer Stephen Street on one of their previous singles (1984's "Heaven Knows I'm Miserable Now"), they invited him to help with the production of *Meat Is Murder*. The band liked Street because he was around the same age as they were, plus he was not "too experienced," meaning that he was still game for trying new things and learning along the way.

Although the Smiths were living in London when the bulk of *Meat Is Murder* was written, they decided to record it back north in Liverpool. The quality of sound, lyrics, and overall feel on *Meat Is Murder* is way better than on *The Smiths*. Only a couple of the songs were performed previously, so the album sounded fresh. And other than the title track, "Meat Is Murder," and "The Joke Isn't Funny Anymore," all of Morrissey's songs are sharp, witty, and do not sound like they came from a teenager's diary.

Meat Is Murder was released in February 1985 and immediately went to #1 on the UK charts, dethroning Bruce Springsteen's *Born in the U.S.A.* (THANK GOD!). The Smiths also found themselves getting bigger here in the United States due to their B-side-turned-single, "How Soon Is Now?" (we Americans love "How Soon Is Now?"), and they would find themselves touring the United States for the first time. Although not their best album, *Meat Is Murder* was *their* album—it finally showcased what the Smiths truly could do and did much more for the Smiths than *The Smiths* ever could.

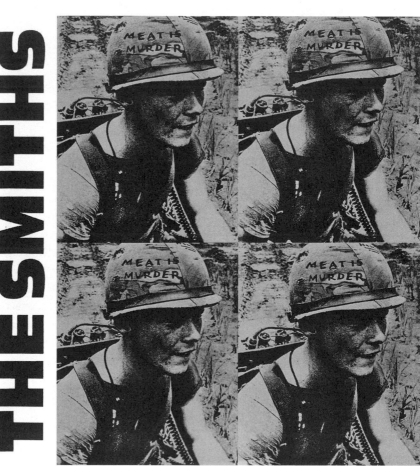

The Smiths' second album, 1985's *Meat Is Murder*. It knocked Bruce Springsteen's *Born in the U.S.A.* album out of the #1 spot on the UK chart. Good.   *Author's collection*

"The Headmaster Ritual"

Taking over where Pink Floyd's *The Wall* left off, "The Headmaster Ritual" goes back to Morrissey's teen years when he attended St. Mary's Secondary Modern School in Stretford, Manchester. Morrissey has never kept it a secret how much he hated attending school there due to their participation in corporal punishment and humiliation. The Manchester Education Committee tried to do damage control by attempting to have the song banned from the radio (it wasn't) and even had Mr. Morgan, the headmaster himself, on the radio to defend himself. Of course, he had nothing but pleasant things to say about young Steven Morrissey.

The music for "The Headmaster Ritual" was created early on in the Smiths, during the botched Troy Tate sessions in 1983. After resurrecting it a year later, Johnny fine-tuned it, and Morrissey easily added his lyrics, making it a great, yet critical, opening track.

"The Headmaster Ritual" was released as a limited single in 1985 and then again in 1988 after the Smiths had broken up. The B-sides for "The Headmaster Ritual" are "Oscillate Wildly" and live versions of "Nowhere Fast," "Stretch Out and Wait," "Shakespeare's Sister," and "Meat Is Murder."

"Rusholme Ruffians"

"Rusholme Ruffians" is Morrissey's take on hanging out at the Rusholme Fairgrounds in Manchester. As he explains it: "As a child I was literally educated at fairgrounds. It was a place of tremendous violence and hate and stress and high romance and all the true vital things in life. It was really the patch of ground where you learned about everything simultaneously whether you wanted to or not."

"Rusholme Ruffians" is full of hot, exciting fairground action, such as getting stabbed, killing yourself, and falling in love. Besides the actual Rusholme Fairgrounds themselves, Morrissey drew on two other sources of inspiration—actress and comedienne Victoria Wood and her own fairground story *Fourteen Again*, and Elvis Presley's 1961 hit "(Marie's the Name) His Latest Flame." The two songs are so similar that "(Marie's the Name) His Latest Flame" was played as an intro to "Rusholme Ruffians" in concert for the Smiths' 1987 live album, *Rank*. With its added "fair-like" sound effects, "Rusholme Ruffians" does indeed take the listener back to the days when it was actually fun to visit the fair.

I wonder if funnel cake is vegetarian-friendly?

"I Want the One I Can't Have"

"I Want the One I Can't Have" is, in my opinion, the best track on *Meat Is Murder*. Johnny Marr's bright-sounding guitar brings the song to life, and Morrissey is at his sassiest best, feeling sexually frustrated and bitching about "couples" and their selection of bedding.

So why is he complaining about sleeping on a double bed? Everybody sleeps, right? In an interview with the *New Musical Express* in 1984, Morrissey explains why he is so sickened by couples making a sensible bed purchase: "That came from a sense I had that, trite as it may sound, when people get married and are getting their flat—not even their house, note—the most important thing was getting the double bed. It was like the prized exhibit; the cooker, the fire, everything else came later. In the lives of many working-class people the only time they feel they're the centre of attention is on their wedding day. Getting married, regrettably, is still the one big event in their lives. It's the one day when they're quite special."

You would think Morrissey owned stock in twin beds. And for someone who is always championing and romanticizing the English "working class," he spends just as must time knocking them down in "I Want the One I Can't Have." Morrissey has stated time and time again that he did not like his singing on the album version of "I Want the One I Can't Have," so much so that he made Warner Brothers remove "I Want the One I Can't Have" from the 2008 compilation *The Sound of the Smiths*, but he has made up for his shortcomings by performing it fairly often in his solo career.

"What She Said"

You know that punchline that is super popular right now?

The "That's what she said" punchline?

You can thank Morrissey and Marr for it.

"What She Said" is the Smiths' (well, at least Morrissey and Marr's) tribute to author Elizabeth Smart and her 1945 prose poem, *By Grand Central Station I Sat Down and Wept*. Morrissey used lines almost verbatim from Smart's work to transform his tale about a depressed young man (probably Morrissey), making it more poignant.

Despite its sad theme, "What She Said" is actually a rocking song and some of Johnny Marr's best guitar work, along with a great thumping bass line from Andy Rourke. Because of this, "What She Said" was always a concert favorite due to its even more intense live sound.

"That Joke Isn't Funny Anymore"

This album isn't fun anymore.

After four upbeat and rocking songs, we get the first slow jam on the album. "That Joke Isn't Funny Anymore" is actually a really good song,

An advertisement for *Meat Is Murder*.   *Author's collection*

despite its downer title. It is a dark and moody song about Morrissey being miserable while on a date (or at least hanging with someone in a parked car). After complaining about how a joke "hit too close to home" and how it is not cool to "kick them when they fall down," they eventually have sex in the car, with Morrissey stating "I just might die with a smile on my face after all."

The "That Joke Isn't Funny Anymore" single was released in July 1985, five months after *Meat Is Murder* was released. It was not a bad selection for a single, but it did not chart well (#49 on the UK chart) because everyone had already heard it and listened to it for last five months. Plus with its dark and heavy demeanor, it was not exactly "radio friendly." "That Joke Isn't Funny Anymore" and "Hand in Glove" are the only two singles in the Smiths' catalog that failed to chart inside of the Top 40 on the UK chart.

"Nowhere Fast"

It was smart thinking to put "Nowhere Fast" after "That Joke Isn't Funny Anymore," because you need to wake up and "Nowhere Fast" is such a great upbeat song. Morrissey sings about how boring and nondescript his town is—all of the townspeople are idiots because "each household appliance is like a new science" to them (but in the 1950s, most household appliances were like a new science, but I digress). He claims that if he felt "a natural emotion" he'd be so shocked he would probably "jump in the ocean." Last time I checked, depression was a natural emotion, so jump already.

Morrissey's lyrics are not really the show-stopper here (even though they are great), but it is the rest of the Smiths who really shine. Other than "Shakespeare's Sister" and "Vicar in a Tutu," "Nowhere Fast" is the closest song they have to a shit-kicking tune, and it really does rock— Johnny Marr's guitar sizzles and squeals while Andy Rourke and Mike Joyce provided the tight yet bouncy back end. The song itself sounds like a train to complement Morrissey's line "And when a train goes by it's such a sad sound." "Nowhere Fast" truly is the underrated gem in the Smiths catalog.

"Nowhere Fast" is also the first time Morrissey takes a dig at the Royal Family with this classic line: "I'd like to drop my trousers to the Queen, every sensible child will know what this means." It would be the first of many digs that Morrissey would write about the Royal Family.

"Shakespeare's Sister" from 1985's *Meat Is Murder*.   *Author's collection*

"Well I Wonder"

Yet another song on *Meat Is Murder* that uses Elizabeth Smart's 1945 prose poem, *By Grand Central Station I Sat Down and Wept.* "Well I Wonder" uses such *Grand Central* lines as "The fierce last stand of all I have" and "Do you hear me where you sleep?," and it is indeed a very beautiful song, with Johnny Marr's guitar gracefully surrounding Morrissey's echoing lyrics about not being noticed. The Smiths also thought it would enhance the loneliness by adding the sound of rain to the song. It did—I feel very lonely right now while writing this.

"Well I Wonder" was never released as a single, although it did show up as a B-side to the "How Soon Is Now?" single.

"Barbarism Begins at Home"

As a bass player myself, this is probably my favorite Smiths song for the bass alone, and Andy Rourke should get a lot more props for this funkified Smiths song. I know, you didn't think it was possible to have a longer Smiths song than "How Soon Is Now?" (at 6:46), but surprise!—"Barbarism Begins at Home" is longer, coming in at 6:57. When played live, the Smiths have even dragged it out to the fifteen-minute mark. I would already be in the beer line at minute seven.

Another song about Morrissey not getting any pudding because he didn't eat his meat, "Barbarism Begins at Home" tells us once again about the horrors of corporal punishment in English schools. Originally written by Morrissey and Marr before the ill-fated Troy Tate session, it became part of the Smiths' live set before it was recorded and released on *Meat Is Murder*. Interestingly enough, Johnny Marr is the one who speaks about hating this song. It is probably because his fingers are tired from playing it for fifteen minutes straight.

"Meat Is Murder"

"Meat Is Murder," like its namesake album, is Morrissey's attempt to educate the public about disgusting meat consumption and to go into further detail about his animal rights beliefs. Up until this point, critics and reporters had mocked him about his herbivore lifestyle, chalking it up to him being "eccentric" and "quirky." Morrissey wanted to prove that he was hardcore and not fucking around about animal rights and living a vegetarian lifestyle, so he wrote "Meat Is Murder" as a response.

The song is a scary tune, with the sounds of animals screaming and crying (yes, animals cry). Morrissey's lyrics chide the listener for eating fried chicken and sizzling steaks, and show that animal slaughter isn't cute or funny. It is "murder."

Johnny Marr had been working on a creepy waltz-type of song beforehand, and when approached by Morrissey to record his mantra, Johnny was in agreement with Morrissey's beliefs and gave him the song. Producer Stephen Street added the animal and slaughterhouse sound effects, giving it the uncomfortable sound Morrissey wanted.

Morrissey has claimed that the song "Meat Is Murder" has turned thousands of people to a meat-free lifestyle.

"How Soon Is Now?"

I know, I know—"How Soon Is Now?" was not on the original release of *Meat Is Murder*, but it was on the US release, plus it is a fan favorite and a big hit, so I am just going to include it. It was first released as a B-side for the 1984 "William, It Was Really Nothing" single and then as a single on its own in 1985, reaching #24 on the UK chart.

Seymour Stein, the head of Sire Records, referred to "How Soon Is Now?" as "the 'Stairway to Heaven' of the 80s." He should have added, "Only not a shit pile." Released in 1985, "How Soon Is Now?" sounds like no other song from that period or any other song in the Smiths' catalog. Set to Johnny Marr's pulsating, Bo Diddley guitar and another slide guitar, Morrissey croons, "I am the son and the heir of a shyness that is criminally vulgar. I am the son and the heir of nothing in particular," which is adapted from a line in George Eliot's novel *Middlemarch* ("To be born the son of a Middlemarch manufacturer, and inevitable heir to nothing in particular."). It is a haunting piece of music that still defines the band . . . and that is the problem with it.

Most hardcore Smiths/Morrissey fans argue that despite "How Soon Is Now?" being the Smiths' best-known song, it really is not a fair representation of their sound. And they are right—it really does not sound like anything else in their catalog. But that doesn't mean it can't still be a good song—the reason it is so successful with fans and non-fans is because it is a cool-sounding song that is radio friendly. "How Soon Is Now?" is usually most music fans' first listen to the Smiths, and once they realize they like it, they check out some more songs. That is what's called "building a fan base."

"How Soon Is Now?" is the Smiths song that has probably been covered the most, with Richard Butler's band Love Spit Love doing the most popular of covers—it was used in both the 1996 movie *The Craft* and the 1998 television show *Charmed* (witches be loving them some Smiths). As a matter of fact, I used to sing "How Soon Is Now?" at karaoke night until my friend started to drunkenly shout, "Sing that song from Charmed!" And then I would tell her, "That joke isn't funny anymore." She still didn't get it.

Morrissey Fan: 1. Blonde Friend: 0.

12

Take Me Out to Dear Old Blighty

The Queen Is Dead

"Some things we did are not as good as they're remembered. The Queen Is Dead is not our masterpiece. I should know. I was there. I supplied the sandwiches."

—Morrissey in *Q* magazine, April 1994

But were they veggie sandwiches?

The Smiths' *The Queen Is Dead* album is often referred to as their "Best Album Ever," so much so that it has become a sore topic (obviously) with the band. I don't know why it has to be that way—why can't the audience like one album and the band like another? It has been my experience that with most creative people that is usually the case—they are always critical of the popular work and usually consider the not-so-popular work their best (even I am guilty of that). Either way, there is no denying that *The Queen Is Dead* is probably their best work. Song-wise, I don't think it is any better than *Meat Is Murder*, but it does have better production values, more depth, and the "Free Bird" of all Smiths songs—"There Is a Light That Never Goes Out."

Plans for *The Queen Is Dead* started before *Meat Is Murder* was finished a year before, with Johnny Marr creating an early version of "Never Had No One Ever." Realizing that their popularity was getting to be too much, the Smiths decided to retreat and hole up once again in Manchester. Marr bought a house in the village of Bowdon, and that is where the Smiths would come together to write, work out ideas, and go over business. But it was the business side of the Smiths that would start to cause drama in the creative side.

Morrissey was unhappy with the way Rough Trade was handling their business. Despite *Meat Is Murder* reaching #1 on the UK charts, their singles were doing pretty much nothing, due to the lack of planning and support from Rough Trade ("How Soon Is Now?" and "Shakespeare's Sister" did not even crack the Top 20, and "That Joke Isn't Funny Anymore" did not even reach the Top 40, despite it being released from a #1 album). Morrissey brought this all to Marr's attention—since the Smiths did not have a manager, Marr handled the majority of their business. Between trying to write music for the Smiths' new album and dealing with all of the business aspects of the band, it was starting to take its toll on Marr, so much so that they were rethinking staying with Rough Trade. A shady lawyer had begun to hound the Smiths, trying to take over the business side of their work.

The Queen Is Dead was finished in December 1985 and was originally scheduled for a February 1986 release. Rough Trade was not happy that their premier group was thinking about leaving the label, refusing to release the album until an agreement could be made and settled upon. On top of all of their business problems, the Smiths were dealt another setback with having to deal with bassist Andy Rourke's drug addiction. After it became obvious that the drugs were affecting his playing, and after being caught buying drugs in a police sting, Rourke left the band to get the help he needed, and Marr recruited ex–Aztec Camera guitarist Craig "The Fifth Smith" Gannon to take his place. It did not take Rourke long to get clean, so they had Gannon play rhythm guitar to help flesh out their sound (and to give Marr a little bit of a break). Unfortunately, Craig Gannon's time in the Smiths was short, and he was out of the band six months later.

Rough Trade and the Smiths came to a tentative agreement, and *The Queen Is Dead* was finally released in June 1986 to rave reviews. It reached #2 on the UK charts, with Peter Gabriel's *So* sledgehammering it away from the #1 spot. At that time, *The Queen Is Dead* was the Smiths' most creative work, with its sampling, realistic writing, and fuller sound. The stress of dealing with their business bullshit took its toll on the Smiths, but the stress of it all only made the band work harder and smarter, creating what is still referred to as their "Best Album Ever."

"The Queen Is Dead"

An appropriate beginning to an appropriate song on an appropriate album, the above sample (a song from World War I taken from the 1962 movie *The L-Shaped Room*) speaks volumes about England at the time—with Thatcherism at an all-time high and the Royal Family still disgusting in his eyes, Morrissey longed for the days when England was truly "dear old Blighty."

The majority of "The Queen Is Dead" lyrics are about Buckingham Palace trespasser Michael Fagan and what Morrissey would do if he were in his shoes. Michael Fagan managed to break into Buckingham Palace in 1982 and actually got into the Queen's bedroom. He didn't kill her—they just spoke a little while until the palace guards came to remove him. In "The Queen Is Dead," Morrissey states that he would have done more than talk—he would have killed her with simple tools like "a sponge" and "a rusty spanner." He also finds the time to make fun of Prince Charles and the monarchy in general.

"The Queen Is Dead" was also the Smiths' attempt to show critics that they really could rock, and that there was more to them than just deep lyrics and jangly guitar. It was a blistering opening track that gave the fans a look into a different side of the Smiths and a different kind of album.

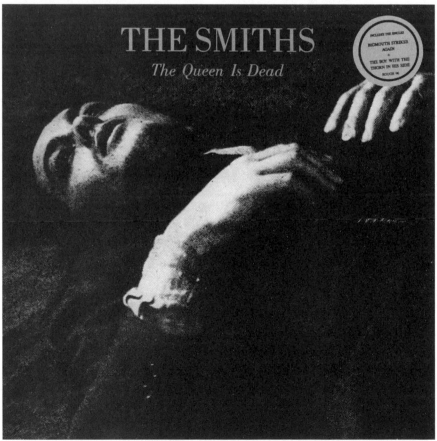

The Smiths' third album, 1986's *The Queen Is Dead*. It was stopped from reaching #1 on the UK chart by Peter Gabriel's *So* album.   *Author's collection*

"Frankly, Mr. Shankly"

If "There Is a Light That Never Goes Out" is my generation's "Free Bird," then "Frankly, Mr. Shankly" is my generation's "Take This Job and Shove It."

Due to the behind-the-scenes drama regarding the Smiths' business affairs with Rough Trade, Morrissey wrote "Frankly, Mr. Shankly" as his "fuck off" letter to Rough Trade boss Geoff Travis (and making fun of Travis's attempt to impress Morrissey with his "bloody awful poetry"). With "Frankly, Mr. Shankly," Morrissey stresses that it is okay to want to be famous. In an interview with the *New Musical Express* in June 1986, Morrissey has this to say about being too famous to work for Mr. Shankly:

> Yes . . . fame, fame, fatal fame can play hideous tricks on the brain. It really is so odd, and I think I've said this before—God, I suddenly sounded like Roy Hattersly—when one reaches so painfully for something and suddenly it's flooding over one's body, there is pain in the pleasure. Don't get me wrong, I still want it, and I still need it, but even though you can receive five hundred letters from people who will say that the record made me feel completely alive—suddenly doing something remarkably simple like making a candle can seem more intriguing in a perverted sense than writing another song. But what is anything without pain?

With its vaudevillian sound and upbeat rhythm, "Frankly, Mr. Shankly" is the song that makes quitting your job fun. Lord, have I daydreamed of the day I could sing this while throwing a cup of coffee in my boss's face and then leaving the office world for good!

Fun fact: The Smiths approached Linda McCartney and asked if she would play piano on "Frankly, Mr. Shankly." She frankly said no.

"I Know It's Over"

"I Know It's Over" is hands-down the best "weeper" the Smiths ever recorded and Morrissey has ever written (I don't consider "There Is a Light That Never Goes Out" to be a "weeper"). Fans will argue that "Last Night I Dreamt That Somebody Loved Me" is the ultimate Smiths "weeper," and while it is a great song, "Last Night I Dreamt That Somebody Loved Me" is not as deep and not as emotionally layered as "I Know It's Over."

Even Johnny Marr was super-impressed with how Morrissey knocked it out of the depression ballpark with "I Know It's Over": "Morrissey's vocal on 'I Know It's Over'—I'll never forget when he did that. It's one of the highlights of my life. It was that good, that strong. Every line he was hinting at where he was going to go. I was thinking, 'Is he going to go there? Yes, he is!' It was just brilliant," Marr told *Record Collector* magazine in November 1992.

As in his 1995 song "Southpaw," Morrissey once again refers to his mother, even when he is dead and is about to be buried (but before he returns as a zombie). He introspectively looks back on his life—the love he felt and lost and the realization that he wasn't worthy of receiving love after all. "I Know It's Over" is Morrissey's tale of how, despite trying to maintain and hold on to life, he realizes that life will never hold on to him and decides to end it all.

Written by Morrissey and Marr in just one night, "I Know It's Over" still remains a favorite of fans and Morrissey himself, as he still performs it live as a solo artist.

"Never Had No One Ever"

One of the oldest songs on *The Queen Is Dead*, "Never Had No One Ever" was originally written back in 1984 as the Smiths were finishing their work on the *Meat Is Murder* album. Inspired by Iggy and the Stooges' 1973 song "I Need Somebody," Johnny Marr wrote the music for "Never Had No One Ever" as a powerfully sad song that would fit perfectly along with Morrissey's lyrics about being an outsider. Predating his 2004 "Irish Blood, English Heart," "Never Had No One Ever" has Morrissey touching upon his feelings about being born Irish, but raised English: "On *The Queen Is Dead*, 'Never Had No One Ever,' there's a line that goes 'When you walk without ease, on these, the very streets where you were raised, I had a really bad dream, it lasted twenty years, seven months and twenty-seven days. Never had no one ever.' It was the frustration that I felt at the age of twenty when I still didn't feel easy walking around the streets on which I'd been born, where all my family had lived—they're originally from Ireland but had been here since the fifties. It was a constant confusion to me why I never really felt 'This is my patch. This is my home. I know these people. I can do what I like, because this is mine.' It never was. I could never walk easily," Morrissey told *Melody Maker* magazine in September 1986.

"Cemetry Gates"

No, it is not a typo. It really is spelled that way. No one knows why—whether it was intentional or a mistake. My guess is that the Smiths spelled it that way due to Morrissey's pronunciation of "cemetery" in the recording of the song.

"Cemetry Gates" falls along the same lines as "Frankly, Mr. Shankly" with its vaudevillian sound and witty verse. Morrissey did indeed visit cemeteries for fun—he and best friend Linder Sterling would spend many a pleasant afternoon traipsing through the tombstones. As for his sentiments regarding plagiarizing the works of worldly authors, Morrissey penned the lyrics as a rebuttal to all of the critics who would accuse him of ripping off his favorite authors (Shelagh Delaney, Elizabeth Smart, etc.) for his own lyrics. Morrissey would claim that his lyrics paid tribute to the authors who comforted him during rough times and encouraged his own writing.

"Bigmouth Strikes Again"

"I would call it a parody if that sounded less like self-celebration, which it definitely wasn't. It was just a really funny song," Morrissey told *Melody Maker* magazine in September 1987.

Morrissey wrote "Bigmouth Strikes Again" as an act of martyrdom, upset that the music press still was highly critical of the Smiths and their

"Bigmouth Strikes Again" single from 1986's *The Queen Is Dead.*
Author's collection

success. As a satirical gesture, Morrissey compares himself to Joan of Arc being burned at the stake. Morrissey does deserve a little street cred—when played live, Morrissey has upgraded his melting electronic listening device from a Walkman to an iPod.

I don't think Apple Care will cover a melting iPod.

"Bigmouth Strikes Again" was the second single to be released from *The Queen Is Dead*, and although it was a big hit for the Smiths, it was not technically a hit—it only reached #26 on the UK charts. Although good friend Kirsty MacColl was asked to come in to provide the backing female vocals on "Bigmouth Strikes Again," her vocals were scrapped, and Morrissey's voice was filtered through a harmonizer, making it sound like a woman's voice (albeit a really weird-sounding woman).

"Money Changes Everything" and "Unloveable" are the B-sides to "Bigmouth Strikes Again." It was released on 7″ vinyl and 12″ vinyl.

"The Boy with the Thorn in His Side"

Although "The Boy with the Thorn in His Side" appears on 1986's *The Queen Is Dead*, it was released as a single prior to the album's release. Yet another song about how the music press is always wrong about him and misconstrues everything he says ("How can they hear me say those words and still they don't believe me? And if they don't believe me now, will they ever believe me?"), "The Boy with the Thorn in His Side" is reminiscent of the Smiths' early work—jangly and light, but with dark, angsty lyrics. Morrissey stated in 2003 that "The Boy with the Thorn in His Side" is one of his favorite songs that he has written—the other song being 1994's "Now My Heart Is Full."

"The Boy with the Thorn in His Side" was originally released as a single in September 1985, reaching #23 on the UK chart. Its B-sides are "Asleep" and "Rubber Ring." It was released on 7″ vinyl, 12″ vinyl, and compact disc single.

"Vicar in a Tutu"

Easily the weakest song on *The Queen Is Dead*, "Vicar in a Tutu" is a farcical tale about a cross-dressing man of the cloth, and is another attempt by the Smiths to infuse a little bit of rockabilly into their sound (like with "Nowhere Fast" and "Shakespeare's Sister"). It almost didn't make the album—the Smiths were set to put B-side "Unloveable" on the album, but scrapped it in favor of the jaunty "Vicar in a Tutu."

"There Is a Light That Never Goes Out"

If you really listen to the lyrics and think about them, they're pretty cheesy. But it still didn't stop "There Is a Light That Never Goes Out" from being the best song the Smiths have ever recorded. Of course, they don't believe that, but 7,586,104 fans can't be wrong.

"There Is a Light That Never Goes Out" is a true love song—Morrissey's lyrics clearly suggest that anything is made better as long as you are with the one you love, even death ("To die by your side, well the pleasure, the privilege is mine"). Some say that the song is autobiographical—Johnny Marr did drive Morrissey around a lot because Morrissey did not have a driver's license, but Marr is quick to point out that other people drove Morrissey around, too. Whatever the case may be, "There Is a Light That Never Goes Out" continues to be an anthem for true love (and double-decker buses).

Despite the obvious, the Smiths never played "There Is a Light That Never Goes Out" as an encore during live shows (even though the song screams encore and lighters). In his solo career, Morrissey will play "There Is a Light That Never Goes Out" as an encore, as witnessed in the 2004 DVD, *Who Put the M in Manchester?* He also released it as a split single in 2005 with his cover of Patti Smith's "Redondo Beach" (both songs appear on 2005's *Live at Earls Court*), reaching #11 on the UK chart. It had been previously released in 1992 to promote the Smiths' . . . *Best II* compilation, but it only reached #25 on the UK chart.

Other than "How Soon Is Now?," "There Is a Light That Never Goes Out" is a favorite Smiths song for bands to cover. Dum Dum Girls, Braid, Neil Finn, Noel Gallagher, and Miley Cyrus have all covered "There Is a Light That Never Goes Out."

"Some Girls Are Bigger Than Others"

"The whole idea of womanhood is something that to me is largely unexplored. I'm realising things about women that I never realised before and 'Some Girls' is just taking it down to the basic absurdity of recognizing the contours to one's body. The fact that I've scuttled through twenty-six years of life without ever noticing that the contours of the body are different is an outrageous farce!" Morrissey told the *New Musical Express* in June 1986.

As a former busty girl myself, I think it's about time we back pain sufferers got our own anthem, and it took Morrissey to give it to us. "Some Girls Are Bigger Than Others" is Morrissey's ode to women's breasts and how men (and the public in general) ridiculously think of them. Johnny Marr first wrote the music to "Some Girls Are Bigger Than Others" in 1985 during sound checks and fine-tuned it later that year, loving the silky guitar riffs and flowing rhythm throughout. He dropped it off at Morrissey's house, and then a couple days later, Morrissey presented him with the lyrics he wrote for his beautiful song.

Lyrics about tits.

Johnny went with it, and it did turn out to be a beautiful, yet sarcastic, song. So what is the deal with the music fade-out in the beginning? According to engineer Steven Street, the Smiths wanted to mimic the ending fade-out in 1985's "That Joke Isn't Funny Anymore," so they created one in the beginning of "Some Girls Are Bigger Than Others," wanting it to sound like opening and closing the door to a music hall blasting music.

"Some Girls Are Bigger Than Others" was not the best ending track for an awesome album, but it is still a good song (and one of their most memorable). I would like to take this time to thank Morrissey for thinking about how my breasts are viewed by society (and for sticking up for "the girls").

Thanks, Morrissey!

13

Let Me Whisper My Last Goodbyes

Strangeways, Here We Come

"It's a very uplifting record, even if the titles lead one to consider it a rather dour record. I don't know how far my judgement is valid—being an obviously immensely depressed person—but it's not really morbid."

—Morrissey, *Q* magazine, 1987

D o you want to know the best thing about the making of the Smiths' 1987 album, *Strangeways, Here We Come*?

After a long day of writing and recording, the band would stay up all night drinking wine and listening to the *Spinal Tap* soundtrack, and then make little Stonehenges with their empty cigarette packs.

You're welcome.

Because *Strangeways, Here We Come* was released after the break-up of the Smiths, people think it was recorded with bad vibes. But according to the Smiths, that was not the case at all. In a 1994 interview for *Q* magazine, Morrissey defends his and Johnny Marr's opinion about the album: "*Strangeways, Here We Come* is the Smiths' best album. Well, it is. We're in absolute accordance on that. We say it quite often. At the same time. In our sleep. But in different beds."

Unlike for the three previous Smiths albums, Morrissey and Marr really didn't have anything ready to go, sans "Girlfriend in a Coma," nor did they preview any new songs in concert like they had done in the past. They would be creating *Strangeways, Here We Come* from scratch together, making it their strongest album to date.

Although the actual recording of the album was great, things behind the scenes were not so great. Johnny Marr was getting burned out with handling the business side of the Smiths (they were still without a decent manager). He was also getting burned out with the sound of the Smiths in general, wanting to move in a different direction. Morrissey was still content with his usual style of writing songs, based on his own personal experiences and his love of old movies. Johnny was just burned out on everything, period.

That is why he suggested the band take a couple weeks off to go on vacation—to get some sunshine, rest, and recharge. Morrissey ignored Marr's request and insisted on going back into the studio to record the B-sides for the *Strangeways, Here We Come* singles. Johnny Marr had had enough—he announced to the band that he was done. It was announced to the public in August that the Smiths were no more.

Strangeways, Here We Come was finally released in September 1987. It certainly was a great album, and the critics and the fans loved it, but it always had a sad feeling about it. When listening to it, you were reminded that the

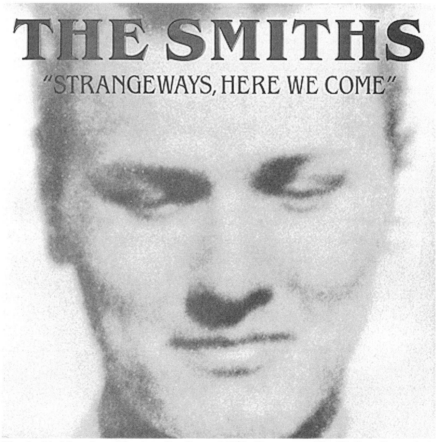

The Smiths' fourth and final studio album, 1987's *Strangeways, Here We Come*. It was their highest-charting album in the United States, reaching #55 on the US chart. Sadly, it was also their last album.   *Author's collection*

Smiths were gone, and they could not even enjoy the best album they ever recorded. Although none of the songs were ever played live (obviously), Morrissey took it upon himself to do a little postmortem *Strangeways, Here We Come* concert in Wolverhapmton with Andy Rourke, Mike Joyce, and Craig "The Fifth Smith" Gannon. Among Morrissey's first solo songs, they performed "Stop Me If You Think You've Heard This One Before" and "Death at One's Elbow." It wasn't much, but it was a sweetly sad send-off to what was the Smiths.

"A Rush and a Push and the Land Is Ours"

Wanting to get away from his typical "jangly" guitar song, Johnny Marr insisted that *Strangeways, Here We Come* open with a song with no guitar on it, as if to tell the world, "This is a different Smiths album."

And different it is—"A Rush and a Push and the Land Is Ours" has that vaudevillian sound going for it, but it totally works for the theme of the song. Morrissey starts as the ghost of "Troubled Joe" and then sings about how he does not want to fall in love again. No one is certain why Troubled Joe killed himself, but because it is a Morrissey song, he probably hung himself because he wasn't loved.

"I Started Something I Couldn't Finish"

No one liked this song except Johnny Marr. With a guitar riff reminiscent of David Bowie's 1973 "The Jean Genie," "I Started Something I Couldn't Finish" is a glam-ish take on Morrissey hitting on a chick and then getting rebuffed. You know what else he couldn't finish? Bitching about this song.

"I Started Something I Couldn't Finish" was the second single released from *Strangeways, Here We Come*, and it reached #27 on the UK chart. Its B-sides are live versions of "Some Girls Are Bigger Than Others" and a cover of James's "What's the World," and the 1983 Troy Tate version of "Pretty Girls Make Graves." It was released on 7″ vinyl, 12″ vinyl, and cassette single.

"Death of a Disco Dancer"

One of two songs on *Strangeways, Here We Come* with "death" in the title, "Death of a Disco Dancer" is (according to the Smiths and fans), one of the better songs on *Strangeways, Here We Come*. Eerily similar to the Beatles' "Dear Prudence," with its swirling guitar riff and Morrissey's seductive vocals, it almost feels like you are falling down the rabbit hole. Or at least smoking some good-quality hash.

"Death of a Disco Dancer" does indeed sound a bit hippie-ish, and its lyrics do nothing but feed into that ("love, peace, and harmony"). Although Morrissey has never officially confirmed what the lyrics of "Death of a Disco Dancer" are truly about, it is safe to say that the lyrics are supposed to encourage people to do something about senseless violence in their town and not turn away.

"Death of a Disco Dancer" also has the honor of being the only Smiths song that Morrissey has played any instrument on (sans harmonizer). He created and plays the piano part.

"Girlfriend in a Coma"

Everyone's favorite *Strangeways, Here We Come* track, "Girlfriend in a Coma" is the Smiths song that is the closest thing they have had to a "novelty song" (quick—someone call Dr. Demento!). Also the shortest song in their catalog, "Girlfriend in a Coma" is a quick two minutes of Morrissey heartbroken that his girlfriend is indeed in a coma, and he runs through a gamut of emotions (and they are surprisingly pretty normal): he goes from sad to angry to introspective about their past relationship and guilty about fighting with her and then angry again. He finally accepts that it is indeed "serious" and gives her his last goodbyes.

Johnny Marr wanted to give "Girlfriend in a Coma" a more upbeat reggae sound and used the 1970 reggae single "Young, Gifted, and Black" by Bob & Marcia as an influence. He also created the strings part on "Girlfriend in a Coma" synthetically instead of using a real orchestra, giving the song its dramatic soap opera-ish thunder (he is credited on the album as "Orchestrazia Ardwick" for his strings creations). One of the funniest songs in the Smiths' catalog, Morrissey himself has stated that "Girlfriend in a Coma" is one of his favorite Smiths tracks.

"Girlfriend in a Coma" was released in August 1987 and reached #13 on the UK chart. Its B-sides are "Work Is a Four-Letter Word" and "I Keep Mine Hidden." It was released on 7″ vinyl, 12″ vinyl, and cassette single.

"Stop Me If You Think You've Heard This One Before"

Because Morrissey is guilty (even then) of getting redundant with his lyrics, he and the Smiths wrote and recorded "Stop Me If You Think You've

Heard This One Before" as satirical take on the critics who would lambaste Morrissey for not getting original. So he did—"Stop Me If You Think You've Heard This One Before" is about everything from love to riding bikes and crashing to mass murder.

It was the "mass murder" line that would eventually land them in a little bit of a conundrum—"Stop Me If You Think You've Heard This One Before" was set to be released as a single in August 1987 and promo copies were sent to radio stations. Unfortunately for the Smiths, a young loner named Michael Ryan killed sixteen people in the village of Hungerford before turning the gun on himself, and the radio stations felt that the "And plan a mass murder" line would be insensitive to the victims' families (if it were released today, all it would get would be a "Too soon?" comment on Facebook). It was, however, released as a single in the United States, because let's face it, we're used to mass murders.

"Stop Me If You Think You've Heard This One Before" is one of the better songs on *Strangeways, Here We Come* and has even had the honor of becoming a track on the popular video game *Rock Band* (even I've sang along to it on *Rock Band*). It was covered successfully by Mark Ronson (son of future *Your Arsenal* producer Mick Ronson) and Daniel Merriweather, reaching #2 on the UK chart.

The B-sides for "Stop Me If You Think You've Heard This One Before" are "Work Is a Four-Letter Word," "Girlfriend in a Coma," "I Keep Mine Hidden," "Pretty Girls Make Graves," and a live version of "Some Girls Are Bigger Than Others." It was released on 7″ vinyl, 12″ vinyl, and compact disc single.

"Last Night I Dreamt That Somebody Loved Me"

"Last Night I Dreamt That Somebody Loved Me" is the masterpiece of *Strangeways, Here We Come*. It is heady, torchy, overly dramatic, and goth-y all at the same time, and with it being the final single released from *Strangeways, Here We Come* (and technically the last single released by the Smiths in general), it made the music and lyrics of "Last Night I Dreamt That Somebody Loved Me" even sadder.

Not that it was a sad event writing and recording it—Johnny Marr came up with the guitar one night coming back from a concert on a whim, and Morrissey was able to whip up some lyrics. Morrissey also nailed his vocal part on the first take, providing just the right amount of heartbreak and sorrow to make "Last Night I Dreamt That Somebody Loved Me" a truly memorable track for the Smiths. And once again, Johnny "Orchestrazia Ardwick" Marr provided the orchestral moments synthetically. An equally dramatic cover of "Last Night I Dreamt That Somebody Loved Me" was released by the Eurythmics in 2004, but my favorite version is Morrissey's on the 2005 live album, *Live at Earls Court*—I love how he rolls his *r*'s for the "right one."

"Last Night I Dreamt That Somebody Loved Me" was the final single released by the Smiths, and it was released in December 1987, reaching #30 on the UK chart. Its B-sides are "Rusholme Ruffians," "Nowhere Fast," and "William, It Was Really Nothing." It was released on 7″ vinyl, 12″ vinyl, and compact disc single.

"Unhappy Birthday"

Every party has a pooper and that's why we invited Morrissey.

"Unhappy Birthday" is Morrissey's tale of wishing an enemy an "unhappy birthday." Despite its sour-puss topic, "Unhappy Birthday" is a fun song and one of the better tracks on *Strangeways, Here We Come*. It is surprisingly simple, with Johnny Marr's beautiful guitar strumming along to Morrissey's bitter lyrics ("Because you're evil and you lie and if you should die, I may feel slightly sad (but I won't cry)"). I can't tell you how many times I get a picture of Morrissey and the line "I've come to wish you an unhappy birthday" posted on my Facebook by friends on my actual birthday.

It's too bad—I would love to see what Morrissey would pick out and buy someone for a birthday present.

"Paint a Vulgar Picture"

"No, it wasn't about Rough Trade at all. So I was a bit confused when Geoff Travis, the Rough Trade big boy, despised it and stamped on it. It was about the music industry in general, about practically anybody who's died and left behind that frenetic fanatical legacy which sends people scrambling," Morrissey told the *New Musical Express* in February 1988.

As the longest track on *Strangeways, Here We Come*, "Paint a Vulgar Picture" is the Smiths' obligatory song about the record industry and how it treats people (every band has one of these songs). Because of the Smiths' drama with Rough Trade (and soon-to-be-new label EMI Records), Rough Trade head Geoff Travis assumed the song was about him. Although Morrissey denies this (as stated in the quote above), it is safe to assume that Travis was correct in his assumptions. Morrissey's morose tale is about a musician who is dead—dead from the bullshit of dealing with the record industry (and pressure from the music industry in general)—and no one cares. Morrissey would again touch on this topic with 2004's "You Know I Couldn't Last."

"Death at One's Elbow"

The second song on *Strangeways, Here We Come* with "death" in the title and the obligatory Smiths "rockabilly-styled" song, "Death at One's Elbow" is a surprisingly fun song loaded with sound effects and corpses.

Morrissey was influenced by the diary of Joe Orton, a 1960s English playwright who was bludgeoned to death with a hammer by his lover, Kenneth Halliwell. Morrissey came up with the song's title after reading this quote regarding the death: "As the corpse is downstairs in the main living room, it means going out or watching television with death at one's elbow."

Morrissey changed the relationship in "Death at One's Elbow" to reflect a male/female relationship, but he kept the sentiment quite the same.

"I Won't Share You"

"I Won't Share You" is the swan song of *Strangeways, Here We Come* and, sadly, to the Smiths in general. It was well known that Morrissey would become highly jealous of anyone who dared to have any kind of relationship with Johnny Marr (save Johnny's wife, Angie), like manager Joe Moss, producer John Porter, and producer Troy Tate. "I Won't Share You" is and has always been rumored to be Morrissey's jealous love song to Johnny Marr, making it a pretty sad and ominous ending track.

With its beautiful guitar, unique autoharp parts, and sad harmonica at the end, "I Won't Share You" is a fitting end to a beautiful, unique, and sad band.

14

It Was a Good Lay

A fter Johnny Marr left the Smiths, Morrissey, Andy Rourke, and Mike Joyce decided to try out a new guitarist. Friend and fellow Manchurian Ivor Perry (of the band Easterhouse) tried to fill Marr's big shoes, but couldn't. Marr also held partial rights to the Smiths name, so any chance of Morrissey and the band proceeding to record and perform as the Smiths was nil.

Unable to admit that the Smiths were truly through, Morrissey was completely lost. A solo career had never crossed his mind, yet he was practically forced to go solo—it was the Smiths that had signed to EMI Records in 1986, but their contract stated that an album was due, no matter what the status of the band was. Morrissey realized this and decided to fearfully push forth. He contacted former Smiths producer and engineer Stephen Street to help create his new solo album.

Morrissey threw himself into the new album despite feeling depressed and uncertain. Stephen Street would also be playing bass; Vini Reilly of the Durutti Column and Andrew Paresi, a session musician, were used as Morrissey's backing band. Sandie Shaw was also enlisted to help with backing vocals, yet nothing with her voice was used. Morrissey originally asked if Mike Joyce and Andy Rourke would be willing to work on his new album, but they politely declined, themselves still depressed and in shock about the dissolution of the Smiths.

As a perfectionist, Morrissey would scrap songs if he felt they were just not working. "Safe, Warm Lancashire Home," "Lifeguard on Duty," "Treat Me Like a Human Being," "I Don't Want Us to Finish," and "Please Help the Cause Against Loneliness" were attempted, but never "worked." Sandie Shaw provided backing vocals on "Please Help the Cause Against Loneliness" that never saw the light of day, but she ended up rerecording her own version for her 1988 album, *Hello Angel.*

A session outtake of "Treat Me Like a Human Being" was released on the 2012 remastered special edition release of *Viva Hate*. Both "Lifeguard on Duty" and "Please Help the Cause Against Loneliness" appeared in outtake form on the 2010 rerelease of *Bona Drag*.

The first two songs somewhat completed were "Bengali in Platforms" and "Suedehead." With the Smiths no more and the uncertainty of Morrissey's efforts, EMI sent out a representative to check on his progress. "Suedehead" was played for them, and they loved it. This affirmation was a great relief for Morrissey and gave him strength and reassurance to continue recording. For the first time since the breakup of the Smiths, Morrissey felt that he was capable of creating amazing music without Johnny Marr's collaboration.

The album was completed in December 1987, and Morrissey and the band decided to record Morrissey's solo debut for John Peel at the BBC studios in London. Nothing went right—Morrissey was in a bad mood, the BBC employees were being jerks, and band members had a hard time cooperating. It was never broadcast nor released to the public.

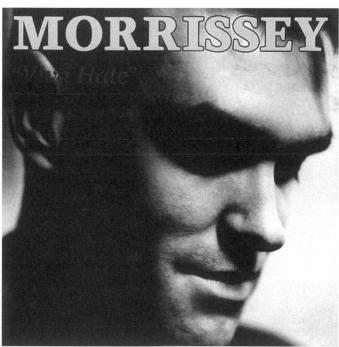

Morrissey's solo debut, 1988's *Viva Hate*. The original album title was *Education in Reverse*, but Morrissey changed his mind at the last minute.   *Author's collection*

Viva Hate was finally released in March 1988, although up until January 1988, the title of the album was *Education in Reverse* (some early album releases in Australia and New Zealand do in fact have this title). The title change was due to Morrissey's still-lingering bitter feelings about the demise of the Smiths. The first single from *Viva Hate*, "Suedehead," was released in February 1988 and reached #5 on the UK Singles chart (higher than any previous Smiths release).

"Alsatian Cousin"

Don't laugh—I had to look up what "Alsatian" was. It means "people from Alsace, France."

The more you know . . .

This hard rocking-ish opener tells the story of an affair between a teacher and student, with such clues as "Leather elbows on a tweed coat" and "But on the desk is where I want you!" Morrissey sings so passionately and seems so intrigued, yet also sounds so disgusted by the afterschool activities, it makes you wonder of any of it was based on a true story from his past. Stephen Street has stated that his bass line in "Alsatian Cousin" was an homage to the thundering bass of Grandmaster Melle Mel's "White Lines (Don't Do It)," which is actually a sample/rip-off of Liquid Liquid's post-punk song "Cavern." Rip-off or not, the bass line, along with Morrissey's seething contempt for hot teacher-on-student humping, makes this the first in a long line of outstanding album opening tracks.

"Little Man, What Now?"

Some say this song is about Jack Wild, a child star who played the Artful Dodger in 1968's *Oliver!*, and on Sid and Marty Krofft's *H. R. Pufnstuf*, some say this song is about Roger Tonge, a child actor on the long-running soap opera *Crossroads*, but most say it's about Malcolm McFee, who starred in the popular '60s sitcom *Please Sir!* Too bad—I was really hoping it was about Danny Bonaduce.

A song about a washed-up child star who ends up on a "Where Are They Now?"–type show, its lyrics suggest that Morrissey was the only person on Earth who remembered the actor. A sad, but poignant, take on fame being a cruel mistress—but fortunately, Morrissey will never get to experience the feeling of being forgotten.

"Everyday Is Like Sunday"

The second single from *Viva Hate*, "Everyday Is Like Sunday" is one of Morrissey's biggest hits, reaching #9 on the UK chart. In this song set in a sad little seaside town that time forgot (or ignored on purpose), Morrissey begs for a nuclear bomb to drop and destroy it. One of the lyrics that has always mystified fans is the "Share some greased tea with me" that appears toward the end of the song. Research has shown that no one knows quite what it means—supposedly Morrissey has stated that greased tea means "tea in a cup that hasn't quite been washed so therefore has a slight film across the top." I always understood it as a reference to the typical "boardwalk atmosphere"—performers with no shirts on, rigged games, cheap souvenir stands, and greasy disgusting food. Obviously I'm only familiar with the Venice boardwalk and not the sleepy yet charming boardwalks of England that Morrissey is preaching about, but his lyrics bring home the memories of a disappearing time, when fun was simple and tea wasn't greasy.

"Everyday Is Like Sunday" is the only Morrissey solo song to bc used in a television commercial. In 2008, the NFL (of all things) used it in commercials promoting its upcoming professional football season, using some generic Nickelback-ish singer. "Everyday Is Like Sunday" has been covered

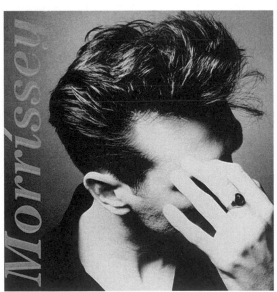

"Everyday Is Like Sunday," the second single released from 1988's *Viva Hate*.   *Author's collection*

by the Pretenders, Natalie Merchant–less 10,000 Maniacs, Armageddon Dildos, Mr. Lawrence, Colin Meloy, and my international favorite, Mikel Erentxun.

The B-sides for "Everyday Is Like Sunday" are "Disappointed," "Sister I'm a Poet," and "Will Never Marry." It was originally issued on 7″vinyl and 12″vinyl. It was reissued in 2010 on two different 7″vinyl singles and on compact disc single.

"Bengali in Platforms"

One of the three "racist" Morrissey songs, "Bengali in Platforms" tells the tale of a Bengali who tries to fit in with Western culture and fails miserably. As England's #1 loner, Morrissey warns the Bengali that "Life is hard enough when you belong here" and advises him to "Shelve your Western plans." You better listen to him, Bengali—Morrissey knows about not fitting in!

"Bengali in Platforms" originated before *Viva Hate* was even conceived. After Johnny Marr left the Smiths, Morrissey, Andy Rourke, and Mike Joyce attempted to keep the band going and hired Ivor Perry, formally of the band Easterhouse to become their new guitarist. Ivor joined them in the studio in July 1987 to work on some B-sides, and although the entire session was a disaster, an early version of "Bengali in Platforms" was a result of it.

"Angel, Angel, Down We Go Together"

Named after the 1969 movie *Angel, Angel, Down We Go*, "Angel, Angel, Down We Go Together" is the delightfully oddball song on *Viva Hate*. Totally orchestral, the song features Morrissey crooning about supporting a depressed individual while trying to talk him out of killing himself. It turns out that the tortured individual whom Morrissey wanted to save was none other than Johnny Marr. In a 2002 article in *Mojo* magazine, Morrissey stated: "'Angel, Angel, Down We Go Together' was written with Johnny Marr in mind and it is the only song I have written with him in mind, post-Smiths. I saw him in the music industry being used and being manipulated and I felt I was in a similar situation."

For the record, although I find the *Viva Hate* version of "Angel, Angel, Down We Go Together" beautiful, my favorite version is the fast-paced, hard-rocking version featured on the 1992 concert video, *Live in Dallas*.

"Late Night, Maudlin Street"

In my opinion, "Late Night, Maudlin Street" is the best track on *Viva Hate*. Moody and pleasantly rambling, Morrissey sings about life on Maudlin Street in 1972. Many say that "Maudlin Street" is a metaphor for Manchester, England, and Morrissey's mundane teenage years. One of his longest songs (clocking in at seven minutes and forty seconds), it's filled with amazing lines that only Morrissey could come up with, such as "Love at first sight, it may sound trite, but it's true you know" and "No, I cannot steal a pair of jeans off a clothesline for you." Tales of taking drugs, hitchhiking, getting arrested, grandmothers dying, hitting puberty, and getting stitches make "Late Night, Maudlin Street" the most insightful glimpse into Morrissey's life and into Morrissey himself.

The title "Late Night, Maudlin Street" was believed to be taken from Bill Naughton's book of short stories *Late Night on Watling Street*. Maudlin Street School is also the name of the school in *Carry On Teacher*, one of Morrissey's favorite films.

"Suedehead"

This song is easily Morrissey's best-known song and biggest hit. It was the first single released from *Viva Hate* and rose to #5 on the UK chart in February 1988 (reaching higher than any song by the Smiths). "Suedehead" is such a dreamy song, I'm surprised Freddy Krueger doesn't make an appearance. Supposedly this is yet another song written about Johnny Marr, but most likely it's about a stalker. Think about it: "Why do you come here?," "You had to sneak into my room just to read my diary?," and "Why send me silly notes?" are all questions asked throughout the song. I think Johnny has better things to do than break into Morrissey's house.

Recorded early on in the *Viva Hate* sessions, "Suedehead" brought in a new independent sound for Morrissey. Interestingly enough, the line "It was a good lay" was censored when published in the liner notes so as to not cause a bunch of pearl-clutching. Morrissey has never gone on record about who the "good lay" was, but given his reverence for animals, we can assume he wasn't singing about chickens.

The B-sides to "Suedehead" are "I Know Very Well How I Got My Name," "Hairdresser on Fire," and "Oh Well, I'll Never Learn." It was released on 7″ vinyl, 12″ vinyl, compact disc single, and cassette single.

"Break Up the Family"

Because *Viva Hate* was released so soon after the breakup of the Smiths, assumptions were that "the family" in "Break Up the Family" was the Smiths. But it really is yet another song about Morrissey's youth and living in Manchester in 1972. According to Morrissey, it's about a group of friends he hung out with in Manchester. As with most groups of friends, it's better to "break up" the group in order to grow than to stay together and wilt. Morrissey realized this and chose to leave his group of friends to focus on himself and his future.

This song strays a little bit from the typical Morrissey sound, albeit with that mellower *Viva Hate* sound. It kind of has—dare I say—a funky adult contemporary sound? Either way, it's still a harmonious recollection of Morrissey's youth, which seems to be the overall theme of *Viva Hate.*

Viva Hate advertisement.   *Author's collection*

"The Ordinary Boys"

Despite the title "The Ordinary Boys," this song is actually about the extraordinary boys—the loners and free-thinkers who choose not to follow the herd like sheep, a situation Morrissey knew all too well. "The Ordinary Boys" was accidentally leaked on early mispressings of the "Suedehead" 12″ single, giving fans a sneak listen before the album was released ("The Ordinary Boys" was never released as a single on its own). Fun fact: An English indie band christened themselves the Ordinary Boys and actually played Morrissey's 2004 Meltdown festival. Their lead singer, Samuel Preston, sadly started to use only his last name to copy Morrissey. I guess he truly was an "ordinary boy."

"I Don't Mind If You Forget Me"

I don't know why fans don't like this song. Some have even gone so far as to refer to it as the weakest song on *Viva Hate*. I think it's great—it's an uptempo jam that wakes you up after the mellow fest that is "Break Up the Family" and "The Ordinary Boys." Yet another song supposedly about Johnny Marr, "I Don't Mind If You Forget Me" is supposed to be about how Johnny felt the need to leave and move on and how Morrissey didn't care.

"Dial-A-Cliché"

The cliché Morrissey sings about in "Dial-A-Cliché" is that of all boys having to grow up to be a "man" and not themselves, a role that was more enforced during Morrissey's childhood than it is today, although I'm sure there are still some out there who feel that all men should be strong and tough. A richly acoustic song that blends perfectly with Morrissey's voice, "Dial-a-Cliché" has early demos with Morrissey singing in a higher pitch that didn't have the same listening effect and didn't feel right to him. Fans are glad that he decided to go deeper.

"Margaret on the Guillotine"

In the same spirit as "The Queen Is Dead," "Margaret on the Guillotine" is Morrissey's answer to the call of the dissatisfied people of England about the Margaret Thatcher regime. Morrissey is pretty blunt with this song—calling for her immediate death, asking when is she finally going to die, and telling the people of England to just kill her already. Despite its assertive lyrics, "Margaret on the Guillotine" is a very simple, almost folksy song with the sweetest guitar flowing into your ear while its seething lyrics enter your brain and make you want to assassinate a world leader. The Special Branch (the equivalent of the FBI in the United States) actually visited Morrissey to make sure he wasn't a threat and to make sure he didn't have a guillotine.

15

Because It's Not Your Style

Kill Uncle

If you ask any Morrissey fans their opinion about *Kill Uncle*, it usually goes something like this: "*Kill Uncle* is okay, but *Bona Drag* is better!"

And they're pretty right on. *Kill Uncle* is the redheaded stepchild of the Morrissey catalog, always playing second fiddle to the "not technically a studio album" *Bona Drag*. In fact, 1990's *Bona Drag* was supposed to be Morrissey's second solo album. After working on and completing a few songs, Morrissey was feeling confident enough to release "Ouija Board, Ouija Board" as a single.

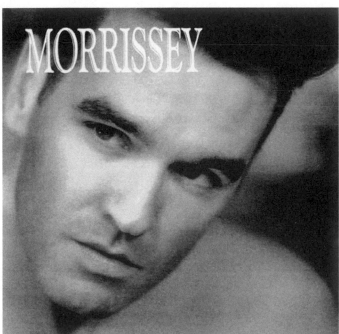

The poor reception of the "Ouija Board, Ouija Board" single prolonged the creation and release of Morrissey's second solo album.

Author's collection

The critics hated it, and it failed to reach the Top 10.

Morrissey became depressed and scrapped *Bona Drag*. Later that year, *Bona Drag* was resurrected from the dead and made into a compilation album containing the new songs, B-sides, and previous hits "Everyday Is Like Sunday" and "Suedehead."

After witnessing the positive praise for *Bona Drag*, Morrissey decided to give an official second album another try. With his new co-writer, Mark Nevin, producing duo Clive Langer and Alan Winstanley, and help from members of Madness and Elvis Costello's Attractions, *Kill Uncle* went into production at Morrissey's favorite studio, Hookend.

Despite not being a hit, *Kill Uncle* has its moments. Although most of the songs are "good," most of them aren't very deep, despite the heaviness of the song topics. They all have a certain gentleness to them due to the

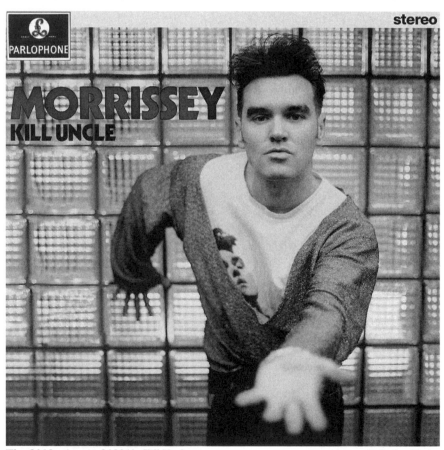

The 2013 reissue of 1991's *Kill Uncle*.   *Author's collection*

amazing guitar work of Mark Nevin, yet none are strong enough to earn any street cred. There are some positive aspects of *Kill Uncle*. It was the first time Morrissey toured as a solo artist, with sold-out crowds and a legendary appearance on *The Tonight Show with Johnny Carson*. He also formed his backing back for this tour—Boz Boorer, Gary Day, Alain Whyte, and Spencer Cobrin, who have continued to be Morrissey's co-writers and support for the majority of his solo career. Finally, it established Morrissey as a true solo recording artist, ensuring that the successes of *Viva Hate* and *Bona Drag* weren't a fluke.

"Our Frank"

"Our Frank" is the opening track of *Kill Uncle* as well as its first single, reaching #26 on the UK chart. Not about a specific person, but about open conversations, "Our Frank" is one of the better songs on *Kill Uncle*, although it was the first single of Morrissey's solo career that did not make the Top 20.

If you listen closely to "Our Frank," you can hear a little touch of "Our House" by Madness. Producers Clive Langer and Alan Winstanley also produced "Our House," and the piano on "Our Frank" was played by Seamus Beaghen, Madness's keyboard player. And, you know, they both contain the word "our."

The B-sides for "Our Frank" are "Journalists Who Lie" and "Tony the Pony." It was released on 7″ vinyl, 12″ vinyl, compact disc single, and cassette single.

"Asian Rut"

"Asian Rut" is the second Morrissey song to be accused of having racist undertones. It's actually anything but racist—Morrissey tells a tale about a boy (who happens to be of Asian descent) getting revenge on the white hoodlums who killed his friend.

"Sing Your Life"

When people reference "Rockabilly Morrissey," usually it's in regards to this song.

"Sing Your Life" was the second single from *Kill Uncle*, reaching #33 on the UK chart. With its classic rockabilly thump and vintage sound, "Sing Your Life" took Morrissey in a new, albeit short-lived, direction.

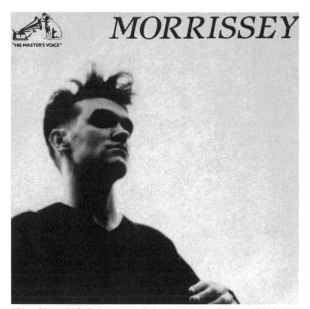

MORRISSEY

"Sing Your Life," the second single released from 1991's *Kill Uncle*.   *Author's collection*

Two other songs ("Pregnant for the Last Time" and "The Loop") continued with the rockabilly style, and his new backing band were all young, energetic rockabilly veterans.

The B-sides for "Sing Your Life" are "That's Entertainment" and "The Loop." It was released on 7″ vinyl, 12″ vinyl, and cassette single.

"Mute Witness"

"Mute Witness" is just like the Helen Keller story, except with more murder; it's a tale of a deaf-mute girl who witnesses an altercation between her parents. Coincidentally, "Mute Witness" is also the title of a 1996 horror movie.

"King Leer"

Although it is not the best Morrissey song, I would rather listen to it than read Shakespeare. It's not terrible, but it's not very Morrissey-esque. The lyrics are very plain and simple, lacking any of the usual Morrissey wit, and the rhyming is lazy. The only redeeming quality of "King Leer" is that it's better live.

"Found Found Found"

The heaviest song on *Kill Uncle*, "Found Found Found" is another mediocre song on a subpar album. This song is rumored to be about R.E.M.'s Michael Stipe.

"Driving Your Girlfriend Home"

"Driving Your Girlfriend Home" gets compared a lot to "There Is a Light That Never Goes Out." Of course, it's not as good as "There Is a Light That

Never Goes Out," but it's pretty damn good—it's clearly the best song on *Kill Uncle*. Its soft guitar strumming, Morrissey's dreamy crooning, and the haunting harmony vocals of Morrissey's best friend, Linder Sterling, give "Driving Your Girlfriend Home" a sweet, ethereal feel.

Fun fact: Morrissey did not get his driver's license until 1995, so driving anyone's girlfriend home would have been impossible for him in 1990.

"The Harsh Truth of the Camera Eye"

As *Kill Uncle*'s longest song, "The Harsh Truth of the Camera Eye" is exactly what the title states—it's Morrissey singing about looking bad in photos.

Oh, if only Photoshop were as widely available then as it is now!

Kill Uncle advertisement.   *Author's collection*

"(I'm) The End of the Family Line"

"(I'm) The End of the Family Line," "Will Never Marry," "Pregnant for the Last Time"—okay, we get it. Morrissey isn't the family type.

"(I'm) The End of the Family Line" is one of the better songs on *Kill Uncle* and one of my personal favorites. Maybe it's because of its delicate guitar work and truthful lyrics, or maybe it's because I, too, am the last of the family line and I get where he's coming from? Either way, "(I'm) The End of the Family Line" is a thoughtful and honest ballad about Morrissey's nonexistent need to breed.

"There's a Place in Hell for Me and My Friends"

Yet another *Kill Uncle* track that sounds better live than in the studio (e.g., as the B-side to "My Love Life" or on *The Tonight Show with Johnny Carson*). "There's a Place in Hell for Me and My Friends" is an okay end to an okay album. However, the song did have the honor of being performed on Morrissey's American television debut (*The Tonight Show*) in 1991.

16

London Is Dead

Your Arsenal

During the successful *Kill Uncle* tour, Morrissey realized that he liked performing as an actual front man again, with a real band that wasn't made up of studio musicians and friends. After spending six months on the road with newest line-up—Boz Boorer, Alain Whyte, Gary Day, and Spencer Cobrin—and feeling their chemistry, Morrissey decided to try them out in the studio.

Mark Nevin, guitarist and main composer for 1991's *Kill Uncle*, was under the impression that he would continue to work after corresponding with Morrissey during the *Kill Uncle* tour. When it came time to record the album, Morrissey chose to use songs composed by Boz Boorer and Alain Whyte after perform-ing Whyte's "We Hate It When Our Friends Become Successful" during the last leg of the tour. Mark Nevin did end up contributing two songs to *Your Arsenal*: open-ing track "You're Gonna Need Someone on Your Side" and torchy "I Know It's Going to Happen Someday."

Although Mark Nevin didn't have much to do with the recording of *Your Arsenal*, he did help Morrissey find a new producer, replac-ing Clive Langer and Alan Winstanley, who produced *Kill Uncle*. After striking out

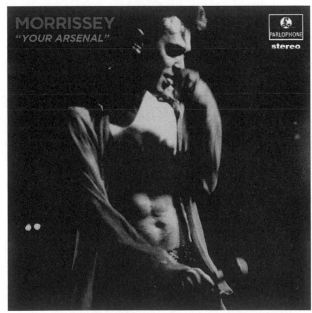

Morrissey's third solo album, 1992's *Your Arsenal*.
Author's collection

with John Cale and future Morrissey producer Tony Visconti, they decided to go glam and hired ex–David Bowie guitarist Mick Ronson.

In an interview with *Uncut* magazine from 2013, Morrissey speaks about why he chose Mick Ronson to produce *Your Arsenal*: "I was struck by the enormity of Mick's contribution to every record he'd played on—arrangements, incredible guitar, beautiful backing vocals, classical piano—he did it all, and he was northern and glamorous. He asked me what kind of LP I wanted to make, and I said, 'One people would listen to for a very long time,' and he said, 'Oh, all right then,' as if I'd asked him to put the cat out."

Because of this, most fans and critics refer to *Your Arsenal* as Morrissey's "glam album," and while it does have some glam rock moments, it's probably the most rock 'n' roll album Morrissey has ever done and the most

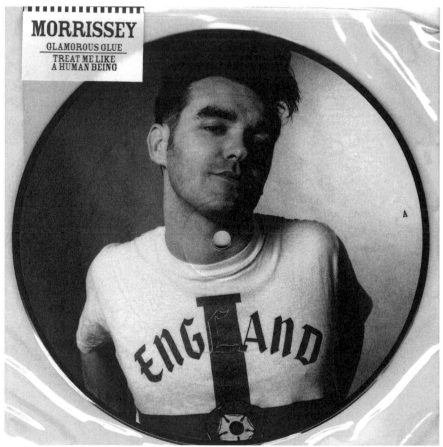

Although "Glamorous Glue" was never an original single from *Your Arsenal*, it was later released in 2011 as a single to promote the release of *Very Best of Morrissey*.

Author's collection

cohesive album he'd done until 2006's *Ringleader of the Tormentors. Your Arsenal* was released in July 1992 to excited reviews.

Rolling Stone had this to say about *Your Arsenal*: "*Your Arsenal* is the most direct—and outwardly directed—statement he's made since disbanding the Smiths. Buoyed by the conversational grace of his lyric writing, Morrissey rides high atop this album's rip-roaring guitar tide." The media weren't the only ones in love with the new album—fans were, too. Morrissey set the record in 1992 for selling out the Hollywood Bowl in twenty-three minutes for his October 21 and 22 shows, breaking the previous three-and-half-hour record set by the Beatles. It reached #4 on the UK charts and almost made it into the US Top 20 (coming in at #21). Morrissey also promoted the album to his US fan base by performing on *Saturday Night Live. Your Arsenal* was even

The B-side to the 2001 "Glamorous Glue" release.   *Author's collection*

nominated for a Grammy in the "Best Alternative Album" category in 1993, but sadly lost out to Tom Waits's *Bone Machine*.

"You're Gonna Need Someone on Your Side"

One of the only two tracks composed by former guitarist Mark Nevin, "You're Gonna Need Someone on Your Side" is a rocking start to an album full of strong material. It almost sounds theme song–esque in getting the listener pumped to hear the rest of the album. Mark Nevin wrote "You're Gonna Need Someone on Your Side" during the same period he penned "The Loop" and "Pregnant for the Last Time," and it shows—all three of those songs are scented with rockabilly goodness and provide the listener with an almost un-Morrissey-like good time.

"Glamorous Glue"

"Glamorous Glue" is the redheaded stepchild of *Your Arsenal* singles. It was one of the most popular songs on the album, yet wasn't picked to be released as a single back in 1992. It did get somewhat of a reprise—it was released in 2011 as a limited edition 7″ picture disc with the previously unreleased songs "Safe, Warm Lancashire Home" and "Treat Me Like a Human Being" (both from the *Viva Hate* sessions). Sadly, after its release in 2011, it charted at number #69, making it Morrissey's worst-charting single. It has the honor of having been performed on Morrissey's only appearance on *Saturday Night Live* (along with "Suedehead") and the honor of providing the world with one of Morrissey's best- and well-known sentiments: "London is dead." With its slide guitar and foot-stomping beat, "Glamorous Glue" is the best example of Mick Ronson's glam roots at work to give Morrissey a fresh sound.

"We'll Let You Know"

Yes, Morrissey—please let me know all about soccer hooligans. Oh, excuse me—FOOTBALL hooligans.

"We'll Let You Know" does just that—a song about why boys and men turn to violence to express their team loyalty. Morrissey likens his feelings to theirs—they're both generally good people, but something they're so passionate about causes them frustration, aggression, and pompous pride. Despite the topic, it's actually a beautiful song with soothing acoustic guitar and a rich tone that relaxes you. At the 2:44 mark, the term "your arsenal" is shouted, giving the album its title.

"The National Front Disco"

Morrissey thought it was a good idea to not include a lyric sheet in the *Your Arsenal* packaging. He wanted a "physical" album, one that assaulted your ears and not your eyes. Unfortunately, this idea backfired on him when he was accused of supporting the National Front party in England.

"The National Front Disco" is one of Morrissey's best songs—a soulful plea to a young man named David to resist the call of the far right conservatism of the National Front party. Instead of chastising him, Morrissey pities David for being so lost that he allows ignorant slogans like "England for the English" to brainwash him. But because of the lack of a lyric sheet, most listeners (albeit dumb listeners) couldn't read the lyrics in the context they were written: "England for the English" was originally written with quotes; hence, it was an example of what David was hearing and not what Morrissey was really saying. In a 1994 interview in *Select* magazine, Morrissey said of the National Front association: "I think that if the National Front were to hate anyone, it would be me. I would be at the top of the list."

This, combined with the "pro-Hooliganism" of "We'll Let You Know" and the "racist" undertones of "Bengali in Platforms" and "Asian Rut," started off what would be fifteen years of claims and accusations that Morrissey is "racist."

If he had only included a lyric sheet.

"Certain People I Know"

It's no secret about Morrissey's love for T. Rex—he and Johnny Marr wrote the Smiths' "Panic" as an homage to T. Rex's "Metal Guru." With Mick Ronson's glam rock pedigree and Boz Boorer's T. Rex love, it was only natural for a second homage to come about, and that song is "Certain People I Know." With a honky-tonk beat and style similar to T. Rex's "Ride a White Swan," Morrissey sings about how the behavior of his friends (and certain people he knows) influences his life, and how he shares what he has learned with others.

It was the last single to be released from *Your Arsenal*, charting at #35 on the UK chart. One of its B-sides, "Jack the Ripper," became a Morrissey cult favorite for its dark and sultry sound and lyrics about the most famous murderer of all time. A promotional version of this single made fun of its T. Rexiness by looking exactly like the T. Rex singles that were released by EMI the 1970s. "You've Had Her" is the other B-side. It was released on 7″ vinyl, 12″ vinyl, compact disc single, and cassette single.

"We Hate It When Our Friends Become Successful"

Haters gonna hate.

According to Morrissey, "We Hate It When Our Friends Become Successful" was written about the backstabbing music scene in Manchester. He admitted later on that it was his cheeky response to the success of the band James after they opened for the Smiths. Although the Smiths were clearly the more well-known band, James was more successful sales-wise.

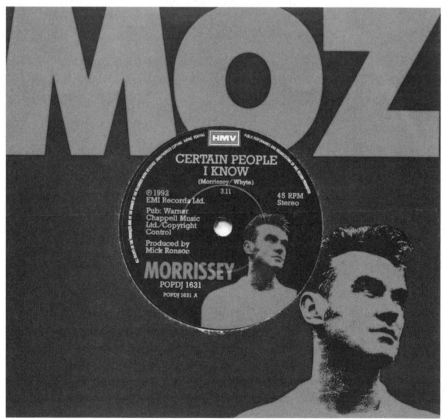

"Certain People I Know" was the last original single released from *Your Arsenal*. Because of its constant comparison to T. Rex's 1972 "Ride a White Swan," Morrissey released the single with a cover mimicking the style of the early T. Rex singles.   *Author's collection*

Morrissey and James were both scheduled to perform on ITV's *Amnesty International 30th Anniversary Special* in 1991, where Morrissey planned to perform "We Hate It When Our Friends Become Successful" as a playful jab at James, but unfortunately, James was removed from the schedule. James did get Morrissey back—during that summer's Glastonbury Festival, they took over Morrissey's spot after he had to cancel and opened with a cover of "We Hate It When Our Friends Become Successful."

"We Hate It When Our Friends Become Successful" was the first single released from *Your Arsenal* and rose to #17 on the UK chart. Live versions of "Suedehead," "I've Changed My Plea to Guilty," and "Pregnant for the Last Time" were the B-sides. It was released on 7″ vinyl, 12″ vinyl, compact disc single, and cassette single.

T. Rex's 1972 hit "Metal Guru."   *Author's collection*

"You're the One for Me, Fatty"

Most people (including myself) thought Morrissey was singing about guys who loved fat girls. But no, it's really about Madness's Cathal "Chas Smash" Smyth, who had gained a significant amount of weight since the band's heyday in the early 1980s. The title is a play on a 1971 B-side by the Marvelettes called "You're the One for Me, Bobby."

"You're the One for Me, Fatty" was the second single released from *Your Arsenal* and reached #19 on the UK chart. "Pashernate Love" and "There Speaks a True Friend" are the B-sides. It was released on 7″ vinyl, 12″ vinyl, compact disc single, and cassette single.

"Seasick Yet Still Docked"

Moody and dreamy lyrics is what Morrissey does best, and "Seasick Yet Still Docked" was the best example of that until 2006's "Life Is a Pigsty." A beautiful song due to Mick Ronson's acoustic guitar melody and the loneliness in Morrissey's voice, "Seasick Yet Still Docked" features lyrics that are somewhat ironic. During the recording of *Your Arsenal*, Mick Ronson was battling liver cancer, himself growing weaker and weaker but still able to work with Morrissey and the band. Sadly, Mick Ronson passed away April 1993.

"I Know It's Going to Happen Someday"

Yet another glam-ish song, "I Know It's Going to Happen Someday" is a slow and surprisingly optimistic song. Despite the shortness of the lyrics, Morrissey pleads with someone he obviously cares about not to lose faith. Because of its Bowie-esque sound, producer Mick Ronson (being the ex-Bowie guitarist he was) decided to add some moments of "Rock 'n' Roll Suicide," a song from David Bowie's 1972 album, *The Rise and Fall of Ziggy Stardust and Spiders from Mars* (an album that Ronson himself played on). After hearing his trademark sound on "I Know It's Going to Happen Someday," David Bowie decided to one-up Morrissey and record a cover of it. Bowie included it on his 1993 album, *Black Tie, White Noise*.

"Tomorrow"

"Tomorrow" is the final, but best-remembered, song from *Your Arsenal*, due to the popularity of its music video and biting lyrics. On "Tomorrow," Morrissey croons about how much he needs some physical attention, so much that his body aches for it. It's an unusual departure for Morrissey, but a welcome one to his fans. I know I was not the only one who melted when Morrissey asked, "Would you put your arms around me?"

"Tomorrow" was only released as a single in the United States, reaching #1 on the Billboard Hot Modern Tracks chart. Once again, "Pashernate Love" is a B-side for this single, as well as "Let the Right One Slip In." It was released on 12″ vinyl and compact disc single.

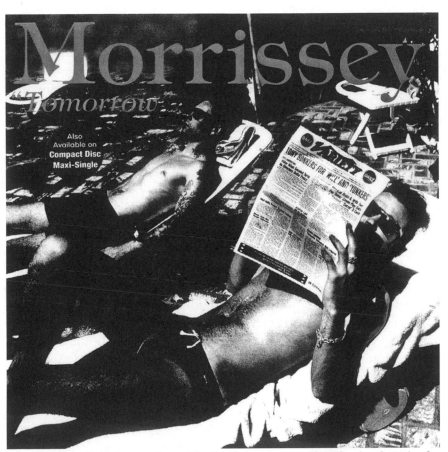

The "Tomorrow" single was released in the United States and easily wins the prize for "Sexiest Morrissey Cover."   *Author's collection*

17

Long May It Last

O ften referred to as Morrissey's perfect album, *Vauxhall and I* is a textbook example of rising to the occasion. The year 1992 proved to be a stellar one for Morrissey both commercially and personally, but 1993 proved otherwise. Three people close to Morrissey passed away in a short period of time, spiraling the singer into a deep depression. His trusted manager, Nigel Thomas, had a heart attack early into the year; Tim Broad (friend and video director) passed shortly after. The final blow was Mick Ronson, who finally succumbed to liver cancer in April of that year. After a period of healing, Morrissey decided to push forward on his fourth album.

Because of the sudden but not unexpected death of Mick Ronson (who was originally slated to produce the new album), Morrissey had to scramble to find someone else. He ended up with respected producer Steve Lillywhite. By 1993, Steve Lillywhite had quite the resume—past albums included *Boy*, *October*, and *War* by U2; Peter Gabriel's third self-titled album; *The Scream* by Siouxsie and the Banshees; and numerous albums by then-wife Kirsty MacColl. He had previously produced "Ask" for the Smiths and worked with Johnny Marr on the Talking Heads' *Naked* album as well, making him a comforting and familiar face for Morrissey to work with in this trying time.

Rumors about Morrissey's personal life exploded during and after the recording of *Vauxhall and I*. Jo Slee, Morrissey's personal assistant, resigned from her duties, and Morrissey replaced her with friend and companion Jake Walters. Since they were always together and doing things that teenage lovebirds do (like taking risqué photos and drawing on their skin with Magic Markers), rumors of their "homosexual" relationship made the rounds. It also didn't help that Jake received a "very special thanks" shout-out in the album credits, and that the title *Vauxhall and I* supposedly refers to Jake, since he grew up in South London, near Vauxhall. Fun fact: Vauxhall is also known for its gay-friendly lifestyle.

Despite his success with writing the majority of the tracks on 1992's *Your Arsenal*, Alain Whyte found himself in competition with guitarist Boz Boorer for Morrissey's songwriting attention. Morrissey did indeed use a majority of Whyte's songs for the final track listing for *Vauxhall and I*, but it was three of Boorer's contributions that were the strongest and most memorable tracks ("Now My Heart Is Full," "The More You Ignore Me, the Closer I Get," and "Speedway"). Their songwriting rivalry (albeit mostly friendly) would continue until 2009's *Years of Refusal.*

Vauxhall and I is an album about letting go and moving on. Songs such as "Used to Be a Sweet Boy," "Hold On to Your Friends," and "Now My Heart Is Full" speak volumes about dealing with one's parents, dealing with bad friends, and dealing with the future. Personally, I wouldn't say *Vauxhall and I* is Morrissey's best album, but I do say that's it is his most *personal* album, and a beautiful one at that. Every note of every song is rich with emotion, and never have Morrissey's lyrics been so painfully real and brutally honest. His last lyric in "Speedway" sums up the *Vauxhall and I* experience perfectly: "In my own sick way, I've always stayed true to you."

"Now My Heart Is Full"

"Now My Heart Is Full" is Morrissey's swan song to his past, full of gracious goodbyes and name-checking. It is a song about being at peace with one's self and in a happy place.

Yes, it really is a Morrissey song.

"Dallow, Spicer, Pinkie, Cubitt" are mentioned, a shout-out to the 1947 film *Brighton Rock.* There's also a shout-out to Patric Doonan, a British actor in such movies as *The Blue Lamp* and *The Cockleshell Heroes* (who ended up committing suicide by gassing himself to death). Morrissey sings this song as almost a relief—a relief from depression and a relief from youth (which were one in the same, according to Morrissey). With Morrissey singing about how his "heart is full," this was the first song to really start the Jake Walters rumors.

"Now My Heart Is Full" was released as a single in August 1994. The B-sides are "Moon River" and a live version of "Jack the Ripper." It was released on cassette single and compact disc single.

"Spring-Heeled Jim"

Like "The National Front Disco," "Spring-Heeled Jim" is another Morrissey song about a young lad choosing the wrong path in life. With dialogue samples from the 1958 documentary *We Are the Lambeth Boys*, "Spring-Heeled Jim" is yet another one of Morrissey's haunting hits. Fun fact: there is a mythical creature in England that many believe in named "Spring-Heeled Jack" that hops over fences and breathes fire.

"Billy Budd"

One of the first songs recorded for *Vauxhall and I*, "Billy Budd" tells the tale of Morrissey and a companion and how they're not accepted in today's society. "Billy Budd" is also the name of a Herman Melville novel and a 1960 movie starring Terence "General Zod" Stamp, one of Morrissey's favorite actors and Smith album cover model. Herman Melville also published a volume of poetry called *John Marr and Other Sailors*. Coincidence?

"Hold On to Your Friends"

Unfortunately, "Hold On to Your Friends" was Morrissey's poorest charting single (until 2011's rerelease of "Glamorous Glue"). In this cautionary tale about friendship and respect, Morrissey sings about how his trust was broken and how poorly he was treated by a "friend." Not to sound like a hater, but I can understand why this wasn't a great single—it was barely marketed, contained only "Moon River" as a B-side, and, frankly, it wasn't his best work. Of course it wasn't terrible, but certainly not one of his best ballads, nor the best song on *Vauxhall and I*.

"Hold On to Your Friends" was released in May 1994 and reached #47 on the UK chart. It was released on 7″ vinyl, 12″ vinyl, compact disc single, and cassette single.

"The More You Ignore Me, the Closer I Get"

A crowd favorite, "The More You Ignore Me, the Closer I Get" was the first single released from *Vauxhall and I*, reaching #8 on the UK chart and becoming Morrissey's first Top 10 single since 1989's "Interesting Drug." It was also the closest Morrissey came to really charting in the United States, hitting #45 on the Billboard Hot 100.

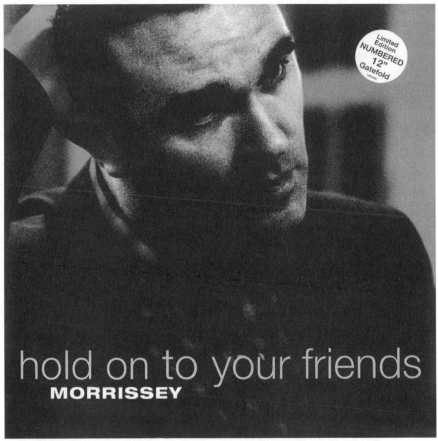

"Hold On to Your Friends" was the second single from 1994's *Vauxhall and I.*

Author's collection

Morrissey is unusually bold with his obsessiveness in "The More You Ignore Me, the Closer I Get," singing about stalking and taunting his subject. It's rumored that "The More Your Ignore Me, the Closer I Get" was written specifically about Mike Joyce and the court case against Morrissey and Johnny Marr, but that would be impossible considering "The More You Ignore Me, the Closer I Get" was released in 1994 and the court case didn't begin until 1996. Also strange is that this false information is referenced in the 2002 documentary *The Importance of Being Morrissey.*

"The More You Ignore Me, the Closer I Get" was released in February 1994, and the B-sides are "Used to Be a Sweet Boy" and "I'd Love To." It was released on 7″ vinyl, 12″ vinyl, compact disc single, and cassette single.

An advertisement for *Vauxhall and I* and the "The More You Ignore Me, the Closer I Get" single. As the ad points out, it was Morrissey's highest-charting single in the United States at the time. *Author's collection*

"Why Don't You Find Out for Yourself"

"Why Don't You Find Out for Yourself" is one of the most beautiful songs ever written about how terribly the music industry treats people. Originally it was written with more of a rock 'n' roll sound reminiscent of *Your Arsenal*, but producer Steve Lillywhite went with more of an ethereal sound with hints of richness. Morrissey's vocals were left untouched from the original version.

"I Am Hated for Loving"

I am hated for not loving this song.

"I Am Hated for Loving" is a nice, gentle song about Morrissey the Martyr. He's absolutely right, though—people hate him for no reason. Whenever Morrissey haters are asked why they hate, they usually don't have an answer. But in "I Am Hated for Loving," Morrissey accepts that he has haters and will continue to create music because he loves us. Thank you, Morrissey.

"Lifeguard Sleeping, Girl Drowning"

Certainly the most unusual song on *Vauxhall and I*, "Lifeguard Sleeping, Girl Drowning" is exactly what it sounds like it's about: a lifeguard who is irritated by a young woman being stupid out in the water and swimming against the tide, and who therefore can't nap in peace. Following in the footsteps of "In the Air Tonight" by Phil Collins, Morrissey paints a spooky picture of the last remaining breaths of a dying girl and her narcoleptic savior with guitarist Boz Boorer playing an eerie clarinet line over Morrissey tauntingly whispering the lyrics. Samples from the 1942 British movie *In Which We Serve* are mixed in with the song to complete its sinking feeling.

"Used to Be a Sweet Boy"

A precursor to 2006's "The Youngest Was the Most Loved," "Used to Be a Sweet Boy" tells a similar tale about parents needing to be responsible for their child's subpar upbringing.

"The Lazy Sunbathers"

As the only political song on *Vauxhall and I*, "The Lazy Sunbathers" is Morrissey's take on the rich people who do nothing to help the world, who just lie around in the sun and are concerned only with themselves. Between "Lifeguard Sleeping, Girl Drowning" and "The Lazy Sunbathers," all I want to do is head to the beach.

Fun fact: Because of the complicated music arrangement, Morrissey sang live with the band during the recording of this song. It is the only song on *Vauxhall and I* that was recorded this way.

"Speedway"

Where to start with this song?

"Speedway" is hands-down one of these best Morrissey songs ever. With thundering drums and motor-revving sound effects, Morrissey sings about not being a snitch and pledges his loyalty to whoever his partner in crime may be. The usual rumors about "Speedway" persist: it's about Johnny Marr, it's about Jake Walters, etc., but Morrissey has rebutted all claims to fame regarding its intended subject. Nevertheless, "Speedway" is truly the perfect end to an almost perfect album.

Speaking of truly, the Morrissey website True to You, which is run by uber-fan Julia Riley, borrows its name from the last few lines of "Speedway" ("In my own strange way, I've always been true to you").

18

You Don't Catch What I'm Saying

Southpaw Grammar

Southpaw Grammar was released in August 1995, reaching #4 on the UK chart. Like Morrissey's previous release *Vauxhall and I*, *Southpaw Grammar* was produced by Steve Lillywhite. But that's where the similarities end.

For the first time in Morrissey's career, he decided to make an album that focused more on the music and less on the lyrics. Not that the lyrics aren't amazing, but the songs on *Southpaw Grammar* feature a lot more experimentation, long solos and musical passages, and an extreme detail to sound. In typical Morrissey fashion, both the opening track ("The Teachers Are Afraid of the Pupils") and the closing track ("Southpaw") are dramatic and appropriate. They also both come in at over ten minutes due to their lush and moody musical arrangements.

Another first with this album is that it's the first to not have Morrissey's face on the cover. With his boxing fascination still in full effect, Morrissey chose to use a photo of American lightweight champion Kenny Lane. When it was time to reissue a remastered *Southpaw Grammar* in 2009, Morrissey's smug

The 2009 reissue of *Southpaw Grammar.*   *Author's collection*

mug graced the cover with a Bowie-esque font. This reissue featured four additional songs: "Nobody Loves Us," "Honey, You Know Where to Find Me," "You Should Have Been Nicer," and "Fantastic Bird." The playing order was also different than it was on the original release, with "The Boy Racer" as the first track and "Nobody Loves Us" finishing it out.

After the sentimental and soft sounds of *Vauxhall and I*, Morrissey decided that *Southpaw Grammar* needed to go in a completely different direction with a more rock 'n' roll sound.

"The Teachers Are Afraid of the Pupils"

Unlike the Smith's "The Headmaster Ritual," "The Teachers Are Afraid of the Pupils" represents the other side of the "English schools are terrible" argument—a tale of how teachers are helpless against the unruly students in the age of nonpunishment. The longest song on *Southpaw Grammar*, "The Teachers Are Afraid of the Pupils" is a swirling arrangement of drama due to the sampling of Dmitri Shostakovich's Symphony no. 5 in D Minor.

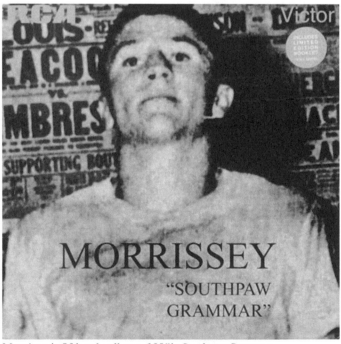

Morrissey's fifth solo album, 1995's *Southpaw Grammar*.

Author's collection

"Reader Meet Author"

Rumor has it that "Reader Meet Author" was written about Morrissey's encounter with journalist Julie Burchill. In 1994, she interviewed Morrissey for an article for the *Sunday Times* at her home, and she acted quite the fool by insulting Morrissey, asking questions that were too personal, and then lamented in the article about how terrible it was. If I were to meet Morrissey, I would just say "thank you" and wait to get snarky until after he left.

Because I have class.

"The Boy Racer"

"The Boy Racer" is the second single released from *Southpaw Grammar*, reaching #36 on the UK chart. Its poor charting power was due to the fact that the B-sides were live versions of older songs ("London," "Why Don't You Find Out for Yourself," "Billy Budd," and "Spring-Heeled Jim") and no new material. It's too bad, because "The Boy Racer" is one of the best songs on the album, and the most rocking. Morrissey nails this tale about a dumb, obnoxious "bro" type of guy who speeds around all day and thinks with his genitals.

"The Boy Racer" single was released on 7″ vinyl and compact disc single.

"The Operation"

Drum solos and Morrissey usually do not end up in the same sentence, but "The Operation" does indeed have a long and snappy drum solo. At least it is in the beginning, so it does not hold up the song. Before the recording of *Southpaw Grammar*, *Vauxhall and I* drummer Woodie Taylor was let go and *Your Arsenal*'s Spencer Cobrin was brought back to help perfect the harder sound Morrissey was looking for. Unfortunately, Spencer never got the chance to play his drum solo live, but audiences still got to hear it—Morrissey used it for his entrance music for his *Maladjusted* tour.

"Dagenham Dave"

"Dagenham Dave" is the first single from *Southpaw Grammar*, and despite its pop perfection, it only managed to hit #26 on the UK chart. Almost a twin to the male character in "The Boy Racer," "Dagenham Dave" is also an idiot, albeit not a macho one, and the girl he is dating leaves him by the end of the song. The cover of the single features English football manager

Terry Venables (who was born in Dagenham). Fun fact: Sandie Shaw was also born in Dagenham!

The B-sides to "Dagenham Dave" are "Nobody Loves Us" and "You Must Please Remember." It was released on 7″ vinyl and compact disc single.

"Do Your Best and Don't Worry"

The weakest song on the album, "Do Your Best and Don't Worry" was a last-minute addition to *Southpaw Grammar*. It's another song with heavy drums courtesy of Spencer Cobrin, and Morrissey chose this song to open on the *Southpaw Grammar* tour to set the rocking mood.

"Best Friend on the Payroll"

Despite the shortness of lyrics and long musical bridges, "Best Friend on the Payroll" is a cautionary tale about not letting just anyone shack up with you. Supposedly ex-assistant and rumored paramour Jake Walters is the subject of this song since he and Morrissey were roommates for a short

"Dagenham Dave" was the first single from 1995's *Southpaw Grammar*.
Author's collection

time during the *Vauxhall and I* period. The line "I turn the music down, but I don't know why—this is my house" makes you think Jake is whom Morrissey is referring to, but I think anyone would get sick of listening to the New York Dolls nonstop.

"Southpaw"

"Southpaw" is, in my opinion, one of the most beautiful songs Morrissey has ever written and is one of my favorite songs. A perfect end to a perfect album, "Southpaw" starts off hard and rocking, but smooths out and takes you away to Morrisseyland. Like 99 percent of his songs, "Southpaw" has some autobiographical notes, especially regarding Morrissey's positive relationship with his mother. If "The Teachers Are Afraid of the Pupils" gets you excited for what is to come on *Southpaw Grammar*, "Southpaw" rewards your listening efforts with its graceful guitar, hypnotizing percussion, and lush lyrics.

19

Ready with Ready Wit

Maladjusted

T he biggest problem with *Maladjusted* is that it's not as good as Morrissey's other albums. People hated this album when it came out—it was "boring" and "bland." But when you listen to it in hindsight, it is actually pretty decent album. The melodies are there and the lyrics just as bitingly sharp, but the one negative thing about *Maladjusted* is that it sounds dated. It has that late '90s sound and look—a mix of frat boy rock and pop punk. When I listen to *Maladjusted*, it instantly takes me back to 1997—I had graduated high school that year and spent the summer publishing a zine and record shopping. I would hear *Maladjusted* (especially the song "Alma Matters") every time we'd be at any given Tower Records, and KROQ sure played the hell out of it. *Maladjusted* may not be his best album, but it's certainly not his worst.

Despite the acclaim for 1994's *Vauxhall and I* and the "meh-claim" for 1995's *Southpaw Grammar*, 1996 was a crappy year for Morrissey. Leaving the David Bowie tour and the drama with the Mike Joyce court case did nothing to inspire him. An EP was planned for early 1996 and was to be produced by the Clash's Joe Strummer, but Morrissey canceled it suddenly. After signing to Mercury Records, Morrissey decided it was time and proceeded to make a new studio album.

Maladjusted was released in August 1997 to lukewarm reviews. Despite reaching #8 on the UK chart and having a Top 20 single ("Alma Matters"), it sold poorly and was hailed as a failure by both fans and Morrissey himself. To avenge this disappointment, Morrissey rereleased *Maladjusted* in 2009 with all-new packaging with a better cover photo and removed two of the original songs while adding the B-sides. The newer *Maladjusted* is a more cohesive album and resembles Morrissey's original vision.

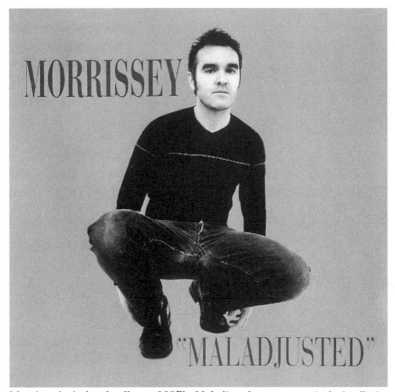

Morrissey's sixth solo album, 1997's *Maladjusted*.   *Author's collection*

"Maladjusted"

A thundering start to an album, reminiscent of *Southpaw Grammar*'s open-ing track, "The Teachers Are Afraid of the Pupils," "Maladjusted" starts the album rocking with its semi-autobiographical lyrics and shredding guitar. "Maladjusted" has the honor of being the only Morrissey song that shares its title with the album. Dialogue from actor Anthony Newley from the 1955 movie *The Cockleshell Heroes* is sampled in the beginning.

"Alma Matters"

Released as the first single from *Maladjusted*, "Alma Matters" reached #16 on the UK chart, making it Morrissey's third-highest-charting single of the '90s and his first Top 20 single since 1994's "The More You Ignore Me, the Closer I Get." Inspired by favorite author Shelagh Delaney, Morrissey crafted the line "It's my life to ruin my own way" from Delaney's 1958 play, *A Taste of Honey*.

The B-sides for the "Alma Matters" single are "Heir Apparent" and "I Can Have Both." It was released on 7″ vinyl, compact disc single, and cassette single.

"Ambitious Outsiders"

"Ambitious Outsiders" was Morrissey's first choice for the title of this album, but with *Maladjusted*, I think he made a wise choice. With its faux orchestral sound and controversial lyrics regarding pedophilia, "Ambitious Outsiders" is often regarded as one of the worst songs on *Maladjusted*.

The 2009 reissue of *Maladjusted*.   *Author's collection*

"Trouble Loves Me"

Easily the best song on *Maladjusted*, "Trouble Loves Me" is one of the, if not the, best Morrissey ballads ever. Dramatic piano intertwines with Morrissey's desperate crooning about not being able to get a break. "Trouble Loves Me" should have been a single release purely because it represents the classic Morrissey sound and solid writing.

"Papa Jack"

Yet another Morrissey tune about how crappy and fickle showbiz is. Still on his boxing kick, Morrissey chose to name this song after Jack "Papa Jack" Johnson. That tidbit of information is the most interesting thing about this song. Even Morrissey thought the song was boring—when *Maladjusted* was rereleased in 2009, he intentionally left it off.

"Ammunition"

Certainly not the worst song on *Maladjusted*, but certainly not the best. Out of all the songs on this album, "Ammunition" is the most dated, with its trendy '90s radio-friendly sound.

"Wide to Receive"

"Wide to Receive" was the first Morrissey song written by drummer Spencer Cobrin. Having taken up the piano the year before, Spencer took up song-writing and submitted several songs for album consideration. "Wide to Receive" was the only song chosen, and even then it almost didn't make the cut—it replaced the Boz Boorer–penned "I Can Have Both." Spencer would have better luck with the 2009 rerelease of *Maladjusted*: two of his previous B-sides ("Lost" and "Now I Am a Was") were included.

"Roy's Keen"

Roy's keen?

More like Roy's meh . . .

"Roy's Keen" was Morrissey's twenty-third single and made it to #42 on the UK chart, just shy of the Top 40. Its shortcomings are something of fodder—Morrissey and his band recorded a performance of "Roy's Keen" in anticipation of appearing on "Top of the Pops," but unfortunately the single never topped the pop, leaving the footage unaired until 2003. A play on the name of former Manchester United footballer Roy Keane, "Roy's Keen" was never a fan favorite or even a Morrissey favorite; he acknowledged his embarrassment by the song in an interview with *Hot Press* in 2008. "Roy's Keen" is the second song that was intentionally left off of the 2009 *Maladjusted* reissue.

"Lost" and "The Edges Are No Longer Parallel" are the B-sides to "Roy's Keen," although 99.9 percent of all Morrissey fans would have preferred "Lost" as the single. It was released on 7″ vinyl, 12″ vinyl, compact disc single, and cassette single.

"Roy's Keen" was the second single released from 1997's *Maladjusted*. It is the only Morrissey single to not be included on an album reissue (2009's *Maladjusted* reissue).   *Author's collection*

"He Cried"

Another of Morrissey's late '90s delights, "He Cried" is a mid-tempo tale of not being needed. It also shares its name with a song by the 1960s girl group the Shangri-Las.

"Sorrow Will Come to You in the End"

One of my favorite songs on *Maladjusted*, "Sorrow Will Come to You in the End" is nothing but Morrissey bitching about losing the 1996 court case to Mike Joyce. It is so bitter and slanderous, it was left off of the original UK versions of *Maladjusted* for fear of libel action (it was eventually released on the 2009 reissue). With its crazy carnival-like strings and Morrissey's powerful reciting of threats/lyrics, "Sorrow Will Come to You in the End" is the highlight of *Maladjusted*.

"Satan Rejected My Soul"

But I thought "there's a place in hell" for him and his friends?

Well, I guess not, because Satan rejected his soul.

"Satan Rejected My Soul" is the last single from *Maladjusted* and his last release until 2004's *You Are the Quarry*. Unlike "Roy's Keen," "Satan

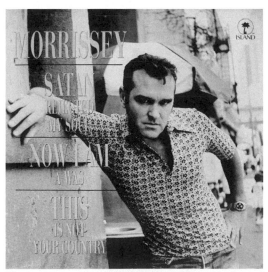

"Satan Rejected My Soul" was the final single released from 1997's *Maladjusted*. It would be Morrissey's last official release until 2004's *You Are the Quarry*.

Author's collection

Rejected My Soul" got into the Top 40 on the UK chart by making it to #39. Morrissey brings his classic glam sound back as he bemoans Satan not wanting him and not being accepted into Heaven. Of course Heaven doesn't want him, because "Heaven knows" he's "miserable now."

"Now I Am a Was" and "This Is Not Your Country" are the B-sides to "Satan Rejected My Soul." It was released on 7″vinyl, 12″vinyl, compact disc single, and cassette single.

20

Come Back to the Charts

You Are the Quarry

We all know that absence makes the heart grow fonder, so by the time *You Are the Quarry* was released, people were crazy with the Moz Fever. There was a seven-year time period between *Maladjusted* and *You Are the Quarry*, so people had time to forget the bad and reminiscence about the good. Up until then, Morrissey was releasing albums every one to two years, so there were always some new Morrissey tracks to look forward to. But during that seven-year period, there were absolutely zero releases because Morrissey wasn't signed to a label—his contract was annulled when his previous label (PolyGram) was taken over. So Morrissey did what any rock star without a label did—moved to Los Angeles, toured when he felt like it, and took the time to regroup and reevaluate.

After a resurgence of interest in the Smiths in the early 2000s, Morrissey finally signed to Attack/Sanctuary Records and got the band back together. Although they returned to Hookend, Morrissey's favorite studio, he decided to go a different route and picked Jerry Finn to produce his album. Finn, known for producing harder-sounding bands like Green Day and Blink-182, was an odd choice, but Morrissey felt it was a smart move to go in a different direction.

"America Is Not the World"

As much as I love Morrissey, I find it somewhat hypocritical that he wrote "America Is Not the World" while living in America.

Que sera, I guess.

As the opening track of *You Are the Quarry*, "America Is Not the World" does not have the typical Morrissey flair of earlier album opening tracks. But it does reintroduce new and old Morrissey fans to the singer's views about meat consumption and gluttonous Americans.

"Irish Blood, English Heart"

As the first single released from *You Are the Quarry* and his first single released in seven years, "Irish Blood, English Heart" is a roaring rock anthem reminiscent of Morrissey's *Your Arsenal* days. Despite being officially released in 2004, "Irish Blood, English Heart" has a much older history. It was originally recorded and released in 1998 by Alain Whyte and the band Johnny Panic and the Bible of Dreams as a song titled "Not Bitter, but Bored." Morrissey created his own lyrics and melody, giving it the typical Morrissey bite and witticisms.

"Irish Blood, English Heart" criticizes historical English figure Oliver Cromwell, political parties, and the never-ending problems between England and Ireland. It debuted at #3 on the UK chart, #4 on the Billboard Hot 100 Singles chart, and #36 on the Modern Rock chart. Its B-sides are "It's Hard to Walk Tall When You're Small," "Munich Air Disaster," and

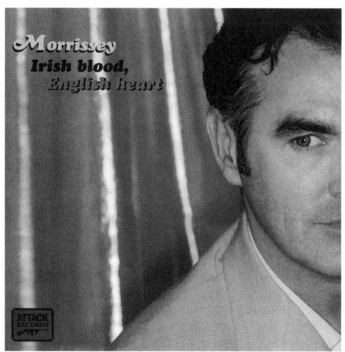

"Irish Blood, English Heart" was the first single from 2004's *You Are the Quarry.*   *Author's collection*

"The Never-Played Symphonies." It was released on 7″ vinyl, 12″ vinyl, and compact disc single.

"I Have Forgiven Jesus"

"I Have Forgiven Jesus" was the fourth and final single from *You Are the Quarry*, reaching #10 on the UK chart in December 2004. What's a Christmas season without a song about Jesus? Morrissey preaches in this song about the Catholic Fear: whatever you do that's good never makes up for the bad. To get you pumped for your upcoming religious experience, "I Have Forgiven Jesus" starts with some serious organ, and then Morrissey chimes in to croon you up to Heaven.

Out of the four singles released from *You Are the Quarry*, "I Have Forgiven Jesus" has the weakest selection of B-sides: "No One Can Hold a Candle to You," "The Slum Mums," and "The Public Image." Morrissey may have forgiven Jesus, but I don't think I can forgive Morrissey for those B-sides. It was released on 7″ vinyl and compact disc single.

"Come Back to Camden"

"Come Back to Camden" is one of the more interesting tracks on *You Are the Quarry* if only for its scandalous whispers. Rumor has it that "Come Back to Camden" is a wistful memory of former personal assistant/photographer/paramour Jake Walters. Morrissey and Jake cohabitated in Camden in the mid-1990s. Because of the "maybe" feelings about the "maybe" subject, "Come Back to Camden" is the only song from *You Are the Quarry* to have never been performed live, even on the *You Are the Quarry* tour to promote the album. Now that Morrissey's *Autobiography* has cleared the air (somewhat) about what went on between the two of them, "Come Back to Camden" needs to come back to the set list.

"I'm Not Sorry"

The best use of underwater sonar equipment since *The Hunt for Red October*, "I'm Not Sorry" is one of the hidden gems of *You Are the Quarry*. The pinging from the sonar machine and the dreamy beach-y guitar sound give Morrissey's lyrics about his lack of remorse an underwater theme. It sounds weird, but it works—Morrissey realizes he's drowning in stubbornness but can't bring himself to settle for just anyone to rescue him from his loneliness.

"The World Is Full of Crashing Bores"

Despite its lackluster album love, "The World Is Full of Crashing Bores" has been a tour favorite since it was first performed live in 2002. Not the best song on *You Are the Quarry*, but easily not the worst.

"How Can Anybody Possibly Know How I Feel"

Often regarded as the "It should have been a B-side" track of *You Are the Quarry*, "How Can Anybody Possible Know How I Feel" is yet another gripey post–court case Morrissey jam. Easily the weakest song on the album, it should have been called "How Can Anybody Listen to This Crap?"

"First of the Gang to Die"

I am probably the only Morrissey fan who doesn't care for this song. But don't worry, all of the other 10,386,547 Morrissey fans LOVE this song and make up for my sour-puss attitude.

"First of the Gang to Die" was the second single released from *You Are the Quarry*, reaching #6 on the UK chart, and for the first time since 1989, Morrissey had two Top 10 hits in a row. After debuting at #12 on the Billboard Singles Sales chart, its success brought "Irish Blood, English Blood" back to the chart for a week. It was also the third-highest-charting single of his career and remained on the charts for seven weeks. It was obviously a fan favorite then, and Morrissey has continued to perform it live on every tour since 2002.

"My Life Is a Succession of People Saying Goodbye," "Teenage Dad on His Estate," and "Mexico" are the B-sides to "First of the Gang to Die." It was released on 7″ vinyl, 12″ vinyl, and compact disc single.

"Let Me Kiss You"

"Let Me Kiss You" was the third single from *You Are the Quarry* and a sultry one at that. When this song is performed live in concert, Morrissey's shirt comes off and the crowd begins to fight, and everyone becomes heated.

That's what this song does to you.

Morrissey's seventh solo album, 2004's *You Are the Quarry*.
Author's collection

Yet another Morrissey tale of feeling ugly yet yearning for love, "Let Me Kiss You" was originally written for Nancy Sinatra and her 2004 self-titled album (released on Morrissey's Attack label). Morrissey did double duty, providing backing vocals on Nancy's version and recording his own version for *You Are the Quarry*. Both singles were released on October 11, 2004, in the UK in a friendly race to see who would chart higher. Morrissey's version came in at #8, while Nancy's did okay at #46.

The B-sides for "Let Me Kiss You" are "Don't Make Fun of Daddy's Voice," "Friday Morning" (one of my personal favorites), and "I Am Two People." It was released on 7″ vinyl and compact disc single.

"All the Lazy Dykes"

Morrissey's anthem of support for the lesbians of the world, "All the Lazy Dykes" calls to all of the closeted and out lesbians to be strong and to be themselves. The Palms Bar, a local Los Angeles lesbian (say that five times fast!) bar, was Morrissey's inspiration for "All the Lazy Dykes" since it was near his home. The Mulholland Dam was also not too far from his Hollywood home, but "All the Lazy Dams" didn't have the right ring to it.

"I Like You"

Yet another song that is rumored to be about Johnny Marr, "I Like You" was performed live in concert starting in 2002, two years prior to the release of *You Are the Quarry*.

"You Know I Couldn't Last"

As the closing track of *You Are the Quarry*, "You Know I Couldn't Last" explores a new Morrissey. An older and wiser Morrissey. One who recognizes that despite the fanatical fan base, his star will eventually fall. After his seven-year hiatus, "You Know I Couldn't Last" is a tongue-in-cheek reminder that although sometimes down, Morrissey will never be out.

Taking its title from the deathbed letter of Warhol gang member Candy Darling ("Did you know I couldn't last?"), it also is the only songwriting contribution ever from on-and-off bass player Gary Day.

21

Every Second of My Life, I Only Live for You

Ringleader of the Tormentors

After the successful comeback that was *You Are the Quarry*, Morrissey kept the hit train a-rolling with his eighth studio album, *Ringleader of the Tormentors*—his third #1 album and biggest since 1994's *Vauxhall and I.*

Unlike with past albums, Morrissey decided to record *Ringleaders of the Tormentors* at Forum Music Village in Rome, Italy, instead of his usual choice of the Hookend studio back in England. After previous attempts

Morrissey's eighth solo album, 2006's *Ringleader of the Tormentors.*

Author's collection

to self-produce the album failed, Morrissey recruited Tony Visconti to take over the recording of the album. Visconti, who has worked with such legends as David Bowie, T. Rex, Sparks, and Iggy Pop, brought his wealth of rock knowledge to Rome and, with the help of soundtrack god Ennio Morricone, an Italian children's choir, and the Roman vibe, produced one of Morrissey's best solo albums.

"I Will See You in Far Off Places"

With its unusual exotic sound, "I Will See You in Far Off Places" continues the tradition of being a strong album opening track. Written as a response to the invasion of Iraq in 2003, "I Will See You in Far Off Places" is one of Morrissey's stronger political sentiments despite the dreamy musical arrangement.

"Dear God Please Help Me"

"Dear God Please Help Me" was quite the pearl-clutcher when *Ringleader of the Tormentors* was released. A pretty graphic take on a clandestine homosexual encounter in Rome, it threw Morrissey fans and critics into a tizzy due to the realism of the lyrics. Morrissey has refuted the idea that the song is autobiographical.

Ennio Morricone, the famous Italian composer who has written music for numerous Italian movies, collaborated with producer Tony Visconti to bring a sensuous yet haunting sound to "Dear God Please Help Me"—so sensual that, when played live, the audience becomes visually heated (as if you're not heated up enough just being at a Morrissey concert).

Marianne Faithfull recorded a version of "Dear God Please Help Me" for her two–compact disc edition of her 2008 album, *Easy Come, Easy Go.*

"You Have Killed Me"

Do you love Italy?

Morrissey does!

"You Have Killed Me" was the first single released from *Ringleader of the Tormentors*, reaching #3 on the UK chart, #1 on the Hot 100, and #45 on the Modern Rock chart. Creating a tribute to his temporary home, Morrissey name-checks Italian screen heroes such as Pier Paolo Pasolini, Anna Magnani, and Luchino Visconti, although most people mistakenly think he's singing about *Ringleader of the Tormentors* producer Tony Visconti. Because of this, Morrissey will sometimes put a "Tony" before the "Visconti" while performing it live in concert.

The B-sides for "You Have Killed Me" are "Good Looking Man About Town," "Human Being," and "I Knew I Was Next." It was released on 7″ vinyl and compact disc single.

"The Youngest Was the Most Loved"

Easily one of the best songs on *Ringleader of the Tormentors*, "The Youngest Was the Most Loved" was the second single released, and it reached #14 on the UK chart and #11 on the Hot 100 Singles chart. The downloadable US single of "The Youngest Was the Most Loved" also came with a special video for fifth generation iPods. With an angelic children's choir countering Morrissey's take on a good boy gone bad, "The Youngest Was the Most Loved" is the only Morrissey song about receiving too much love.

Interestingly enough, "The Youngest Was the Most Loved" is another instance where the B-sides almost surpass the original single. "If You Don't

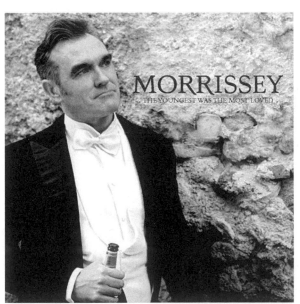

"The Youngest Was the Most Loved" was the second single released from 2006's *Ringleader of the Tormentors*. This single is also known for its superior selection of B-sides.

Author's collection

Like Me, Don't Look at Me," "Ganglord," and "A Song from Under the Floorboards" are all great B-sides, with "Ganglord" becoming a concert set list staple. It was released on 7″ vinyl and compact disc single.

"In the Future When All's Well"

"In the Future When All's Well" was the third single released from *Ringleader of the Tormentors*, reaching #7 on the UK chart. Its B-sides are "Christian Dior" and live versions of "I'll Never Be Anybody's Hero Now" and "To Me You Are a Work of Art." It was released on 7″ vinyl and compact disc single.

"The Father Who Must Be Killed"

For whatever reason, "The Father Who Must Be Killed" became one of the least-performed songs from *Ringleader of the Tormentors*. With its sweet children's chorus in the background and Morrissey's sage advice to a girl about killing her father front and center, "The Father Who Must Be Killed" is one of the more solid songs on the album.

"Life Is a Pigsty"

As much as I champion Morrissey's rock 'n' roll stuff, his over-the-top gut wrenchers are legendary. "Life Is a Pigsty" reminds me of "Late Night, Maudlin Street." Both are filled with lots of emotion and lots of warbling. But at least Morrissey is aware of his constant cries for love—the opening line of "Life Is a Pigsty" says it all: "It's just the same old S.O.S."

Because of its dramatic and moody music arrangement, "Life Is a Pigsty" is always a fan favorite when played live in concert.

"I'll Never Be Anybody's Hero Now"

Yet another song about Morrissey not feeling appreciated, despite having millions of fans worldwide. It's a perfectly good song and perfectly typical Morrissey.

"On the Streets I Ran"

Another song about Morrissey dying. It has been performed live only fourteen times.

"To Me You Are a Work of Art"

Yay! Morrissey finally found someone to love him!

With its raw and honest sentiments, "To Me You Are a Work of Art" is a fine vehicle for Morrissey to express his newly discovered love for other human beings.

"I Just Want to See the Boy Happy"

"I Just Want to See the Boy Happy" was the fourth and final single released from *Ringleader of the Tormentors* and was surprisingly more well received than the previous single, reaching #17 on the UK chart. Its B-sides are "Sweetie-Pie" and live versions of "I Want the One I Can't Have," "Speedway," and "Late Night, Maudlin Street." It was released on a compact disc single, 7" vinyl, 12" vinyl, and picture disc.

"At Last I Am Born"

Like with "The Youngest Was the Most Loved," "At Last I Am Born" features a charming children's choir that compliments Morrissey's rich voice. It is also the only *Ringleader of the Tormentors* track to be written by keyboardist Michael Farrell.

"At Last I Am Born" is Morrissey's cry of spiritual awakening and a shedding of his Catholic guilt, making it an appropriate, but not typically strong, Morrissey album finale.

22

You're Gonna Miss Me When I'm Gone

Years of Refusal

Years of Refusal is Morrissey's ninth studio album, reaching #3 on the UK chart. If *Ringleader of the Tormentors* is Morrissey's "happy and in love" album, then *Years of Refusal* is his "just got dumped" album. Almost all of the songs have negative themes: death, suicide, depression, and disappearing from life. Behind-the-scenes events regarding *Years of Refusal* only enhanced the gloominess of the album.

Morrissey's *Greatest Hits* album was due to be released in February 2008, and *Years of Refusal* was set to follow in September. Despite being successful in the UK, *Greatest Hits* sold poorly in the US due to mishandled promotion by his label, Decca. For *Years of Refusal*, he decided to drop Decca in favor of Polydor for his UK distribution and Lost Highway for his US distribution. This was the biggest setback for *Years of Refusal*, pushing it past its September 2008 due date to a February 2009 launch. Two other misfortunes also didn't help: Morrissey had to find a new manager, and then producer Jerry Finn unexpectedly passed away in August 2008 from a brain hemorrhage almost immediately after finishing the album. But despite these setbacks, *Years of Refusal* was released in February 2009 to positive reviews and accolades.

Everybody loves a cute baby, and the cover baby on *Years of Refusal* is no exception. His name is Sebastian Browne, and he belongs to Charlie Browne, Morrissey's tour manager. Here's another fun fact: the cover photo for *Years of Refusal* was shot by none other than "Morrissey paramour" Jake Walters! *Years of Refusal* continues the tradition of having just as much drama behind the scenes as on the actual album.

"Something Is Squeezing My Skull"

Only Morrissey can make taking antidepressants sound like fun.

"Something Is Squeezing My Skull" was the second single released from *Years of Refusal* and reached #46 on the UK chart. With Morrissey's admission of having taken antidepressants in the past, you could safely assume this song is autobiographical. But it's not a "downer"; "Something Is Squeezing My Skull" is a hard-rocking opening track that has the traditional Morrissey wit. One of the best moments on the entire album is when he clarifies the brand name of a medication with this simple lyric: "Diazepam (that's Valium)."

I guess his insurance only covers generics.

The B-sides for "Something Is Squeezing My Skull" are live versions of "This Charming Man," "Best Friend on the Payroll," and "I'll Keep Mine Hidden." It was released on two different compact disc singles and on 7″ vinyl. There are two different covers for this single, but both feature Morrissey posing at the Johnny Ramone memorial in the Hollywood Forever cemetery.

Morrissey and the ghost of Johnny Ramone advertise *Years of Refusal* and the upcoming *Swords* compilation. This image was also used as the cover of the "Someone Is Squeezing My Skull" single.   *Author's collection*

"Mama Lay Softly on the Riverbed"

Rumors persist that Morrissey had written "Mama Lay Softy on the Riverbed" about Virginia Woolf because she committed suicide by drowning herself in a river. But it can't be true.

Virginia Woolf never had any children.

"Black Cloud"

Guitar legend Jeff Beck makes an appearance on this track. Other than that, this song should have been called "Lack Cloud."

"I'm Throwing My Arms Around Paris"

"I'm Throwing My Arms Around Paris" was the first single released from *Years of Refusal*, reaching #21 on the UK chart. One of the better songs from the album, this track has Morrissey crooning his little black heart out about the City of Lights. To continue the Europe theme, Morrissey has stated (albeit jokingly) that "I'm Throwing My Arms Around Paris" was supposed to be his entry into the 2007 Eurovision Song Contest.

When released, this single caused quite a stir due to the nearly naked photo of Morrissey and his band, with 7″vinyl singles perched strategically over their seven inches. Speaking of singles, the B-sides of "I'm Throwing My Arms Around Paris" are "Because of My Poor Education," "Shame Is the Name," and a live version of "Death of a Disco Dancer." It was released on two different compact disc singles and on 7″vinyl.

"All You Need Is Me"

Originally released as a single of the 2008 *Greatest Hits* compilation and reaching #24 on the UK chart, "All You Need Is Me" received a second life by being included on *Years of Refusal*.

The B-sides for "All You Need Is Me" are "Children in Pieces," "My Dearest Love," and "Drive-In Saturday." It was released as a compact disc single and two different 7″vinyl versions.

"When I Last Spoke to Carol"

A haunting song about a woman who is obsessed with Morrissey, "When I Last Spoke to Carol" has the honor of almost having had Herb Alpert record its horn parts. Morrissey inquired about getting the trumpet master, but it unfortunately never came together.

"That's How People Grow Up"

Another single that was released in conjunction with his 2008 *Greatest Hits*, "That's How People Grow Up" is a pretty awesome song that reached #14 on the UK chart. With an intro by his screeching chanteuse, Kristeen Young, and the pulsating accordion part by guitarist Boz Boorer, "That's How People Grow Up" is easily the best song on *Years of Refusal*.

Its B-sides are live versions of "The Boy with the Thorn in His Side," "Why Don't You Find Out for Yourself" (another song made great live by Boz's accordion), and "The Last of the Famous International Playboys." It was released as a compact disc single and two different 7″ vinyl versions.

"One Day Goodbye Will Be Farewell"

Performed in concert before appearing on *Years of Refusal*, "One Day Goodbye Will Be Farewell" is definitely better live, and Morrissey knows

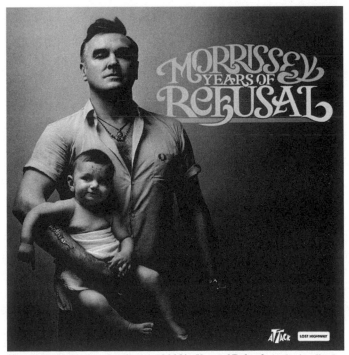

Morrissey's ninth solo album, 2009's *Years of Refusal*. *Author's collection*

HB0329	GENADM GA2 23	MP3PKG EHB0329

Morrissey stops in Boston on his 2009 Tour of *Refusal*.   *Author's collection*

this—that's why it's usually last on the set list. The crowd goes nuts when this tale of Morrissey's eventual flame-out starts up, and that's when the majority of stage invasions start. When performed on the 2014 tour, members of the crowd took it upon themselves to hug him, tackle him, and throw him down in a chokehold. If these stage antics continue, one day goodbye will really be farewell for Morrissey.

"It's Not Your Birthday Anymore"

First he wished us an "Unhappy Birthday." Now he wants to take it away from us altogether.

I guess someone hates getting older.

"It's Not Your Birthday Anymore" is an okay song—Morrissey definitely hits some high notes in this song about cruelty and submission.

"You Were Good in Your Time"

"You Were Good in Your Time" is the weirdest song on *Years of Refusal* (and in Morrissey's entire catalog), but that's what makes it so good. I really like it because it has a '70s sound and vibe to it. Slightly different, yet keeping with the theme of *Viva Hate*'s "Little Man What Now," "You Were Good in Your Time" tells the tale of someone who's at the end of his showbiz career and then dies. And Morrissey really emphasizes the dying part by cutting out of the song, letting the sparse music and background noise continue on for a few more minutes.

Samples from the 1937 French film *Pépé le Moko* start the song off, instantly giving it the creepy feeling Morrissey was aiming for. And it worked—"You Were Good in Your Time" definitely is a chilling, yet witty, look at fame and death.

"Sorry Doesn't Help"

Yet another Morrissey song that is "rumored" to be about the 1996 court case. Morrissey should put together a compilation and call it *Tough Justice: Songs About the Court Case*. The song was performed live only during the *Refusal* tour.

"I'm OK by Myself"

After writing songs about not being loved, Morrissey finally decided, nine solo studio albums later, that he's now okay by himself. I doubt that, because if he were really okay without being loved, there wouldn't have been a tenth album. "I'm OK by Myself" is a lackluster finish to a mediocre album.

23

You Are the Soldier

World Peace Is None of Your Business

On July 14, 2014, in the United Kingdom and July 15 in the United States, Morrissey released his tenth solo album, *World Peace Is None of Your Business*. It was recorded during the winter of 2014 at Studios La Fabrique in Saint-Rémy de Provence, France, and was preceded by a brief US tour rife with Morrissonian-type cancellations and just a little bit of drama (make that a whole lot of drama).

World Peace Is None of Your Business was Morrissey's first studio recording since the warmly received *Years of Refusal* in 2009. Recording started in February 2014 and wrapped up in March 2014 as a part of a two-album deal with Capitol Music through its Harvest Records label.

For the recording of *World Peace Is None of Your Business*, Morrissey brought in renowned producer Joe Chiccarelli, who has produced albums by Oingo Boingo, Frank Zappa, My Morning Jacket, Counting Crows, the Shins, Elton John, the White Stripes, U2, and Beck, among others. He also added keyboard player Gustavo Manzur, along with some new touches like flamenco guitars and mariachi horns.

World Peace is None of Your Business as an album finds Moz in a bitter place. There is not a lot of his usual playful, tongue-in-cheek narration here, and although his voice has held out well, the fifty-five-year-old Morrissey's silky effortless baritone does not sound quite as silky or as effortless this time around.

Of course, what would Morrissey be without a bit of controversy (and do not say "Robert Smith with better hair")?

Morrissey took a jab at his label, Harvest and Capitol Music, when he thanked his fans for making real videos of material from *World Peace Is None of Your Business*. He began by graciously thanking three individuals for making videos, and soon it turned into a barbed jab at the record company, complaining that the release was given no promotion.

Morrissey's tenth solo album, 2014's *World Peace Is None of Your Business.*
Author's collection

Subsequently he was dropped from Harvest/Capitol and is now without a label (again). Harvest/Capital have also (at the time I write this) taken all digital formats of *World Peace Is None of Your Business* offline. I understand it is kind of a "tit-for-tat" situation, but why would Harvest/Capitol get rid of something that will bring in business and make money? At first I thought Morrissey might have been overreacting, but maybe he was right to doubt the qualifications of his label.

"World Peace Is None of Your Business"

"Each time you vote, it supports the process," Morrissey bitches in the opening majestic title track. It is Morrissey-as-George-Carlin-meets-Timothy-Leary ("Turn on, tune in, and drop out"). Or as George Carlin used to say, "Don't blame me, I didn't vote!" Coming from the usually socially conscious, politically active Morrissey, the lyric reflects his world-weariness.

On May 13, 2014, Morrissey released "World Peace Is None of Your Business" as a digital-only single. The track was met with positive reviews from fans and critics alike and reached #83 on the UK charts. A spoken word video for "World Peace Is None of Your Business" was also released on the same day, featuring Morrissey reciting the lyrics and pretending to play the piano. Nancy Sinatra brings him a suitcase unfortunately filled with flowers and the lyrics to "World Peace Is None of Your Business." I was really hoping the suitcase was filled with cocaine, because I would love to see Morrissey and Nancy do a few rails and sing "Jackson."

"Neal Cassady Drops Dead"

"Neal Cassady Drops Dead" is a noisy, punchy track with some great Morrissey lyrics: "Everyone has babies, babies full of rabies, rabies full of scabies, Scarlet has a fever, Ring is full of ringworm," Morrissey growls as a flamenco guitar peeks into the mix. "Neal Cassady Drops Dead" is one of the better songs on the album, with its sharp, biting lyrics and strong guitar riffs.

"I'm Not a Man"

Did I mention that Joe Chiccarelli engineered the late Frank Zappa's *Joe's Garage (Parts One and Two)*? Good. Let me also mention that at eight minutes, "I'm Not a Man" is a bit drawn out.

But I still love it. In typical Morrissey fashion, he sings about how he hates being a disgusting man, bitching about all of the disgusting things men do, like eating Beefaroni, getting prostate cancer, and wearing wifebeaters. Moz delves further into his earnest beliefs, but this has been said more succinctly in "Meat Is Murder." The song winds down with bloodcurdling screams, drowning out my own.

"Istanbul"

"Istanbul" grinds along to Morrissey's tale of a father identifying his dead son's body. It's *Midnight Express* gone bad, set to a banging beat. Great song!

In an interview for the OZY website, producer Joe Chiccarelli comments on the making of "Istanbul": "Morrissey wanted to evoke the feeling of the hectic and chaotic streets of the city of Istanbul, so he used a cigar-box guitar, a lap steel guitar, and a complicated and busy drum rhythm, plus an actual gong as percussion, as well as vocal samples from a field recording taken in the streets of Istanbul by guitarist Jesse Tobias."

"Istanbul" is actually my favorite song on *World Peace Is None of Your Business* because of that reason. I love it because it does make you feel like you are in Istanbul, while keeping a 1970s sound and vibe. It was the second single released from *World Peace Is None of Your Business*, and it, too, came with a promo video with Morrissey reciting the lyrics. It was also released as a digital-only single.

"Earth Is the Loneliest Planet"

"Earth Is the Loneliest Planet" was the third single released from *World Peace Is None of Your Business*. A promotional video for "Earth Is the Loneliest Planet" was released on the same date, and it featured Morrissey, once again, doing a spoken word version while standing on top of the Capitol Records building. And guess what? Pamela Anderson is up there with him, so I guess he is technically not lonely anymore.

"Earth Is the Loneliest Planet" was also released as a digital-only single.

"Staircase at the University"

Like "The Headmaster Ritual" and "The Teachers Are Afraid of the Students," "Staircase at the University" is a classic Morrissey tale of how shitty school can be, when a student's academic failures lead to suicide.

"The Bullfighter Dies"

Tejano horns fittingly enough signal the intro to "The Bullfighter Dies," Morrissey's fourth and final single released from *World Peace Is None of Your Business*, and it is a cheery number where Morrissey cites Spanish locations and roots for the bull to kill the brave bullfighter. As with the other three singles from *World Peace Is None of Your Business*, Morrissey made a promotional spoken word video for "The Bullfighter Dies."

"The Bullfighter Dies" was also released as a digital-only single.

"Kiss Me a Lot"

Next up is an '80s-sounding "Kiss Me a Lot," a joyous tune that bounces along with trumpets, castanets, and more flamenco guitars thrown in for good measure. Morrissey has always appreciated his Latino fans, and throughout this album he lovingly acknowledges them with these touches. And I know that I (and all his other fans) would not mind kissing him "a lot."

"Smiler with Knife"

"Smiler with Knife" is beatnik prose Morrissey-style: a reassuring welcome to a murderer. I feel I should snap my fingers at its conclusion. I'm sure Neal Cassady would approve of this song.

It is rumored that the title "Smiler with Knife" was taken from the 1939 novel *The Smiler with a Knife*, written by Nicholas Blake.

"Kick the Bride Down the Aisle"

"Kick the Bride Down the Aisle" is an angry rant that comes off a bit nasty. Perhaps it missed the mark, or perhaps sarcasm doesn't translate as well when you are fifty-five. Well, what do we expect? The man said he "will never marry."

"Mountjoy"

In the sparse acoustic "Mountjoy," Morrissey opens with "The joy brings many things. It cannot bring you joy." And he later laments, "We all lose." It is a pensive piece that continues the bitterness and pessimism that permeates the album.

"Oboe Concerto"

"Oboe Concerto" brings the set to a close and sums up Morrissey's feelings: "The older generation have tried, sighed, and died which pushes me to their place queue, round, rhythm goes round, round, round rhythm of life goes round." To drive home a point, an oboe—an instrument from the days of Morrissey's parents—squeals and contorts as the song builds momentum.

24

Good Night and Thank You

Compilations and Live Albums

Beethoven Was Deaf (1993)

B *eethoven Was Deaf* was Morrissey's first live album released as a solo artist. Most of the tracks were recorded at the Paris Zenith on December 22, 1992, but a few tracks were recorded two days earlier at the London Astoria. It reached #13 on the UK chart.

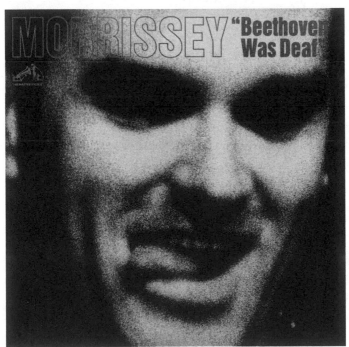

Beethoven Was Deaf, Morrissey's first live album as a solo artist.

Author's collection

The track listing for *Beethoven Was Deaf*:

1. "You're the One for Me, Fatty"
2. "Certain People I Know"
3. "The National Front Disco"
4. "November Spawned a Monster"
5. "Seasick Yet Still Docked"
6. "The Loop"
7. "Sister I'm Poet"
8. "Jack the Ripper"
9. "Such a Little Thing Makes Such a Big Difference"
10. "I Know It's Going to Happen Someday"
11. "We'll Let You Know"
12. "Suedehead"
13. "He Knows I'd Love to See Him"
14. "You're Gonna Need Someone on Your Side"
15. "Glamorous Glue"
16. "We Hate It When Our Friends Become Successful"

Live at Earls Court (2005)

Live at Earls Court was Morrissey's second live release, reaching #18 on the UK chart. Unlike *Beethoven Was Deaf*, all of *Live at Earls Court* was indeed performed live at Earls Court during the *You Are the Quarry* tour in front of 17,183 people. Released shortly after the *Who Put the M in Manchester?* DVD, it shares a lot of the same style and same vibe since they were both performances on the same tour. Unlike with *Beethoven Was Deaf*, a single was released from *Live at Earls Court*: the "There Is a Light That Never Goes Out"/"Redondo Beach" split.

The track listing for *Live at Earls Court*:

1. "How Soon Is Now?"
2. "First of the Gang to Die"
3. "November Spawned a Monster"
4. "Don't Make Fun of Daddy's Voice"
5. "Bigmouth Strikes Again"
6. "I Like You"
7. "Redondo Beach"
8. "Let Me Kiss You"

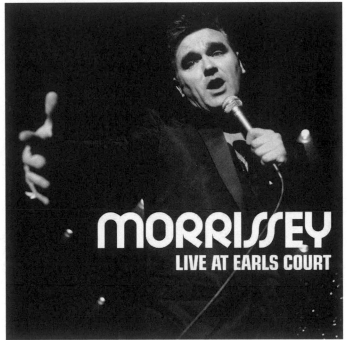

Live at Earls Court, Morrissey's second live album.　*Author's collection*

9.　"Munich Air Disaster 1958"
10.　"There Is a Light That Never Goes Out"
11.　"The More You Ignore Me, the Closer I Get"
12.　"Friday Mourning"
13.　"I Have Forgiven Jesus"
14.　"The World Is Full of Crashing Bores"
15.　"Shoplifters of the World Unite"
16.　"Irish Blood, English Heart"
17.　"You Know I Couldn't Last"
18.　"Last Night I Dreamed That Somebody Loved Me"

Bona Drag (1990)

Bona Drag was originally planned to be Morrissey's second album. After the success of *Viva Hate* hitting #1 on the charts, four Top 10 singles, and the over-enthusiastic reception at the Wolverhampton Civic Hall concert, Morrissey was feeling pretty good (and confident) about his next album. He

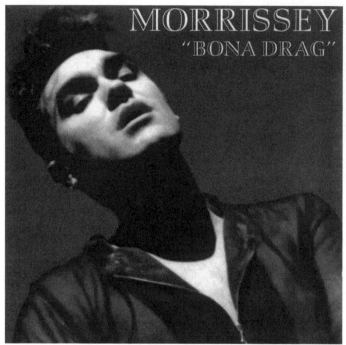

Bona Drag, Morrissey's first compilation as a solo artist.
Author's collection

still lacked a proper band, with previous collaborator Stephen Street opting not to work with him and ex-Smiths Mike Joyce and Craig Gannon out because of their pending lawsuits against Morrissey. Only ex-Smith Andy Rourke remained on board (due to settling with Morrissey out of court).

Morrissey recruited producers Clive Langer and Alan Winstanley to work on *Bona Drag* and brought back *Viva Hate*'s drummer, Andrew Paresi, and new guitarist Kevin Armstrong. Once again, Morrissey's favorite recording studio, Hookend, was used to record the new album.

In between *Viva Hate* and *Bona Drag*, Morrissey recorded "Ouija Board, Ouija Board" as his highly anticipated first single. Before the November 1989 release of "Ouija Board, Ouija Board," Morrissey and the band managed to record a couple of songs (such as "Piccadilly Palare") for *Bona Drag*. Unfortunately, when "Ouija Board, Ouija Board" was released, it failed to reach the Top 10 on this UK chart (his first not to do so as a solo artist), and all the critics hated it. Morrissey became depressed and kept to himself, refusing to finish the album. Whatever songs that were completed became singles and B-sides.

Morrissey's label, EMI, released *Bona Drag* in October 1990 as a compilation of Morrissey's first seven singles and their B-sides. Surprisingly to Morrissey (but not the rest of the world), it was a hit—reaching #9 on the UK chart and becoming, some say, a bigger and better album than *Viva Hate*. With his spirits lifted, he decided to move forward with an official second album, 1991's *Kill Uncle*.

Bona Drag is truly a great album and the only album that non–Morrissey fans actually like, due to its poppyness, addicting melodies, and the fact that it is incredibly easy to sing along to.

"Piccadilly Palare"

As the only "official" single released from *Bona Drag*, "Piccadilly Palare" tells the tale of a northern boy running away from home and being lured into the seedy underbelly of London, complete with intonations of male prostitution. Morrissey in later years has stated his disdain for this song, but I think it is pretty good, with one of my favorite Morrissey lines and the dramatic way he sings it ("So why do you smile when you think about Earls Court? But you cry when you think of all the battles you've fought and lost?").

Because of Clive Langer and Alan Winstanley's previous work with the band Madness, some of Kevin Armstrong's guitar riffs were replaced with obnoxious piano parts, and they even employed Madness singer Suggs to give the song a real "life on the streets" sound with him speaking in the background. Overall, it is a pretty decent opener and a better song than Morrissey remembers.

"Piccadilly Palare" reached #18 on the UK chart. The B-sides to "Piccadilly Palare" are "Get Off the Stage" and "At Amber." It was released on 7″ vinyl, 12″ vinyl, cassette single, and compact disc single.

"Interesting Drug"

"Interesting Drug" is Morrissey's attempt to connect Margaret Thatcher and her regime to working-class drug abuse. And then he makes the video for "Interesting Drug" about animal rights. I think the only interesting drugs were the ones Morrissey was on when he came up with the idea for all of this.

A light and poppy song about drug abuse, "Interesting Drug" reached #9 on the UK chart, making it Morrissey's last Top 10 hit until 1994. Good

CHARTS

45s   NETWORK UK TOP 50   LPs

		45s	
1	3	SOMETHING'S GOTTEN HOLD OF MY HEART	Marc Almond featuring Gene Pitney (Parlophone)
2	6	LOVE TRAIN	Holly Johnson (MCA)
3	4	CUDDLY TOY	Roachford (CBS)
4	2	THE LIVING YEARS	Mike And The Mechanics (WEA)
5	3	YOU GOT IT	Roy Orbison (Virgin)
6	10	THAT'S THE WAY LOVE IS	Ten City (Atlantic)
7	7	WAIT	Robert Howard & Kym Mazelle (RCA)
8	(—)	THE LAST OF THE FAMOUS INTERNATIONAL PLAYBOYS	Morrissey (HMV)
9	5	SHE DRIVES ME CRAZY	Fine Young Cannibals (London)
10	20	MY PREROGATIVE	Bobby Brown (MCA)
11	35	LOVE CHANGES EVERYTHING	Michael Ball (Really Useful)

	LPs	
(—)	TECHNIQUE	New Order (Factory)
(—)	MYSTERY GIRL	Roy Orbison (Virgin)
1	THE LEGENDARY ROY ORBISON	Roy Orbison (Telstar)
3	LIVING YEARS	Mike And The Mechanics (WEA)
23	THE MARQUEE – 20 LEGENDARY YEARS	Various (Polydor)
15	ANCIENT HEART	Tanita Tikaram (WEA)
2	THE INNOCENTS	Erasure (Mute)
7	WATERMARK	Enya (WEA)
5	ANYTHING FOR YOU	Gloria Estefan & Miami Sound Machine (Epic)
4	GREATEST HITS	Fleetwood Mac (Warner Brothers)
6	THE PREMIERE COLLECTION – THE BEST OF ANDREW LLOYD WEBBER	Various (Really Useful Records)
(—)	AFTER THE WAR	Gary Moore (Virgin)

"The Last of the Famous International Playboys" (featured on *Bona Drag*) at #8 on the UK chart in February 1989.   *Author's collection*

friend and colleague Kirsty MacColl lent her angelic voice for the backing vocals, making "Interesting Drug" a sweet song . . . about drug abuse.

The B-sides for "Interesting Drug" are "Such a Little Thing Makes Such a Big Difference" and a live version of "Sweet and Tender Hooligan." It was released on 7″vinyl, 12″vinyl, cassette single, and compact disc single.

"November Spawned a Monster"

A fan favorite (and a Morrissey personal favorite), "November Spawned a Monster" was a controversial hit, due to its topic of disabled people having feelings and how the public reacts to them. Morrissey is pretty confrontational in this song—asking listeners if they would kiss the disabled wheelchair girl on the mouth and if they are willing to accept that she is human and needs to be loved (just like everybody else does). "November Spawned a Monster" is basically Morrissey's *Elephant Man.*

Mary Margaret O'Hara (sister to *SCTV*'s Catherine O'Hara) provided the sounds of the "monster spawning" during the middle of the song. Because her sounds were considered "scary and grotesque," *Top of the Pops* and certain radio DJs would fade "November Spawned a Monster" out before it got to the spawning part. Do you know what really is scary and grotesque? Paying forty dollars for the 2010 *Bona Drag* vinyl reissue.

The B-side for "November Spawned a Monster" is "He Knows I'd Love to See Him." It was released on 7″ vinyl, 12″ vinyl, cassette single, and compact disc single.

"Will Never Marry"

Just like "Late Night, Maudlin Street" before it and "Seasick Yet Still Docked" after it, "Will Never Marry" is second in line when it comes to Morrissey's "weepers." I am sure I cannot be the only Morrissey fan who has used the lines from this song to turn away potential suitors. With its lush orchestration and Morrissey dramatically dropping the last syllable from many of the words to stretch out his loneliness, "Will Never Marry" is a great song for us spinster Morrissey fans.

"Will Never Marry" is the B-side to "Everyday Is Like Sunday."

"Such a Little Thing Makes Such a Big Difference"

"Such a Little Thing Makes Such a Big Difference" is Morrissey's homage to the 1974 Sparks hit "Never Turn Your Back on Mother Earth." Just like with the Smiths' "Still Ill," "Such a Little Thing Makes Such a Big Difference" searches for the connection between one's body and mind and how "most people keep their brains between their legs." Morrissey also gets beat down with a bicycle chain for "only singing." Yeah, I do not know how to connect the two either.

"Such a Little Thing Makes Such a Big Difference" is the B-side to "Interesting Drug."

"The Last of the Famous International Playboys"

I asked a friend of mine (and fellow Morrissey fan) what his favorite Morrissey solo song was, and he answered with "The Last of the Famous International Playboys." When I inquired why, his answer was: "I like it because I learned something from it. I never knew who the Krays were until I heard it, and it encouraged me to read up and learn more about them."

I think most non-English people first heard about the Krays while listening to "The Last of the Famous International Playboys." Ronnie and Reggie Kray were twin gangster brothers who controlled East London in the 1950s and 1960s and were finally caught and arrested in 1968. They were sentenced to life in jail, with Ronnie dying in jail in 1995 and Reggie dying out of jail in 2000. In "The Last of the Famous International Playboys," Morrissey sings the tale of a young man who, due to the glorification of the Kray twins, yearns to be a gangster (or "international playboy").

For the recording of "The Last of the Famous International Playboys," Morrissey ditched his *Viva Hate* recording band and recruited Mike Joyce, Andy Rourke, and Craig "The Fifth Smith" Gannon for a quasi–Smiths reunion of sorts. What resulted was a bass-heavy and stompingly great song that is one of the highlights of *Bona Drag*. Seriously, whenever "The Last of the Famous International Playboys" comes on, everyone goes "Oh shit!" and starts moving to the song. Don't believe me? Just try it and thank me and Morrissey and the Krays for putting you in a good mood.

The cover for the "The Last of the Famous International Playboys" single is unique for its lack of a photo of an old movie star or Morrissey's adult face, but instead has a picture of Morrissey at age six, climbing a tree. He might not have been an international playboy then, but he's a boy nonetheless.

"The Last of the Famous International Playboys" reached #6 on the UK chart. The B-sides are "Lucky Lisp" and "Michael's Bones." It was released on 7″ vinyl, 12″ vinyl, cassette single, and compact disc single.

"Ouija Board, Ouija Board"

I admit it, I was not a fan of this song when I first listened to it (see the introduction), but it has grown on me, and I think it has grown on other listeners, too, due to the fact that it was not widely received when first released as a single in 1989, but it had a kick-ass video that still resonates with people today.

"Ouija Board, Ouija Board" tells the tale of Morrissey trying to reconnect with an "old female friend" via the Ouija board. During the recording of "Ouija Board, Ouija Board" at the Hookend studio, Morrissey and the band actually used a Ouija board to try to communicate with the ghosts that supposedly haunted the studio. Morrissey should have asked the Ouija board if the song would be a hit. Sorry Morrissey—the glass points to "No."

Due to the public backlash over "Ouija Board, Ouija Board," Morrissey refused to perform it live until 2002. Despite the critics hating it, it did not do too poorly on the charts (reaching #18 on the UK chart) when you compare it to other Morrissey singles. I think the Ouija board should have told him to "G-E-T O-V-E-R I-T."

The B-sides to "Ouija Board, Ouija Board" are "Yes I Am Blind" and "East West." It was released on 7″ vinyl, 12″ vinyl, and compact disc single.

"Hairdresser on Fire"

My friend and hairdresser Brian gets called "Hairdresser on Fire" a lot due to his hatred of Morrissey. But for someone who hates Morrissey so, he sure rocks the same sideburns as Moz.

"Hairdresser on Fire" is about Morrissey's gratitude for and worship of his hairdresser and how much power any hairdresser wields over his or her clients. As someone obviously obsessed with his hair, Morrissey is eternally grateful that his "hairdresser on fire" was able to get him an appointment.

"Hairdresser on Fire" almost made it onto *Viva Hate*—EMI really liked the song and pushed for it to be added, but Morrissey and producer Stephen Street pushed back, having already decided on their track listing.

"Hairdresser on Fire" is the B-side to "Suedehead."

"Everyday Is Like Sunday"

See "It Was a Good Lay: *Viva Hate.*"

"He Knows I'd Love to See Him"

"He Knows I'd Love to See Him" is a mellow jam, but it is loaded with meaning. Some say that the "he" in the title refers to Johnny Marr (like a million other Morrissey solo songs), and that lines in the song refer to Morrissey's days growing up in gloomy old Manchester (like another million other Morrissey solo songs), but the most interesting part of this song is when he refers to being interrogated, because that really did happen. After *Viva Hate* was released, the Special Branch (England's version of the FBI) interrogated him and searched his house due to his anti-Thatcher lyrics in "Margaret on the Guillotine." After realizing Morrissey was not a threat, they then proceeded to ask him for his autograph.

Mary Margaret O'Hara makes another appearance by providing the backing vocals on "He Knows I'd Love to See Him." It is the B-side to "November Spawned a Monster."

"Yes I Am Blind"

Working on this book has made me blind.

"Yes I Am Blind" is another Morrissey "weeper" (although not as good as "Will Never Marry"). It was written by ex-Smith bassist Andy Rourke, but he never played on it (Morrissey recruited session bassist Matthew Seligman to help out). "Yes I Am Blind" tells the tale of a man (probably Morrissey) who sees himself in a young man and finally can admit to his shortcomings.

"Yes I Am Blind" is admittedly not one of my favorite songs on *Bona Drag*. During an uncanceled 2014 concert I attended, Morrissey performed "Yes I Am Blind" live. During those few minutes, I also wished I were deaf.

"Yes I Am Blind" is the B-side to "Ouija Board, Ouija Board."

"Lucky Lisp"

"Lucky Lisp" is one of my favorite Morrissey songs. And yes, it is because I have a lisp, although I really would not call it lucky.

"Lucky Lisp" is about Morrissey telling a friend that he will be granted fortune and fame due to his "lucky lisp." If only it were true.

"Lucky Lisp" is the B-side to "The Last of the Famous International Playboys."

"Suedehead"

See "It Was a Good Lay: *Viva Hate*."

"Disappointed"

"Disappointed" is a surprising fan favorite, due to its now-required audience participation. A typical Morrissey tale of loneliness, drinking, and performing on stage, "Disappointed" takes on an almost biographical vibe, with

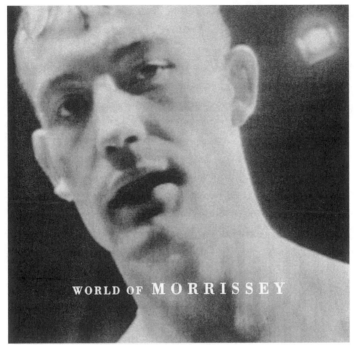

World of Morrissey, Morrissey's second compilation.   *Author's collection*

Morrissey still being in the dumps about the reception and performance of the "Ouija Board, Ouija Board" single.

When the song is performed live, the audience automatically cheers "YAY" after Morrissey sings the line "This is the last song I will ever sing," but then GROANS after the following line of "No, I've changed my mind again."

The line "Goodnight and thank you" ends "Disappointed" and *Bona Drag* in general. Although it technically cannot be considered a "studio album," *Bona Drag* really made a memorable mark on Morrissey's recorded history and is worlds better than any other compilation he has released. Morrissey usually has a cantankerous relationship with any record label he is signed to, but in the case of *Bona Drag*, the label ultimately did him (and his fans) a favor.

World of Morrissey (1995)

World of Morrissey was released in February 1995, reaching #15 on the UK chart. Morrissey's intention with this album was to mimic the style of the *The World Of* series released by Decca in the 1960s and 1970s. Despite leaving the "The" from the title, Morrissey got everything else on par with the old Decca releases: an album with a few hits, a few B-sides, a few live gems, but overall, nothing spectacular. With the live version of "Jack the Ripper" and "Whatever Happens, I Love You" being the exceptions in the rehashed mish-mash, *World of Morrissey* should have been titled *World of Meh*.

"Whatever Happens, I Love You"

"Whatever Happens, I Love You" is a great opener for this mediocre album. With Morrissey singing about the end of a relationship, he actually sounds a little stalker-ish with his declarations of love. Guitarist Boz Boorer whips out his clarinet to give "Whatever Happens, I Love You" a dizzying dramatic sound. Morrissey had never performed the song in the United States until the 2007 *Greatest Hits* tour.

"Whatever Happens, I Love You" is the B-side to 1995's "Boxers."

"Billy Budd"

See "Long May It Last: *Vauxhall and I.*"

"Jack the Ripper"

Whenever I mention "Jack the Ripper" to my friends, the first and most obvious thing they answer is "Link Wray?"

I need a new group of friends.

"Jack the Ripper" is Morrissey's take on the gruesome prostitute killings that traumatized the poor people of Whitechapel, England, back in 1888. The story of Jack the Ripper is legendary, and only a legend like Morrissey could do it any justice. Despite its dour topic and scary undertones, "Jack the Ripper" is actually kind of a sexy song. With lyrics such as "Crash into my arms—I want you. You don't agree, but you don't refuse" and "And if it's the last thing I ever do—I'm gonna get you," you get a little turned on, even though it is about a serial killer.

"Jack the Ripper" was also the first song that was written for Morrissey by guitarist Boz Boorer. It was attempted to release "Jack the Ripper" as a post–*Your Arsenal* single, but unfortunately it was relegated to a B-side for the 1992 "Certain People I Know" single. It remains a crowd favorite and always gets an extremely positive reaction when performed live.

"Have-A-Go Merchant"

Another typical Morrissey song about the English working class, "Have-A-Go-Merchant" tells the tale of a loud and drunk jerk who is too busy drinking and starting fights to pay any attention to his daughter. A rumor persists that "Have-A-Go Merchant" was written in regards to Natalie Merchant, singer for 10,000 Maniacs, because the band had covered Morrissey's "Everyday Is Like Sunday" as the B-side to their 1993 "Candy Everybody Wants" single. I highly doubt that is the case—sometimes I wish these rumormongers would "have a go" at starting some decent rumors.

"Have-A-Go Merchant" is the B-side to 1995's "Boxers."

"The Loop"

"The Loop" is the best rockabilly-esque song that Morrissey and his band have ever recorded and performed. It is dark and twangy, focusing mainly on the music, since Morrissey does not provide a whole lot of lyrics. Still, what he does sing is poignant—telling a friend that he will always be there for him ("I'm still right here, where I always was") and he can always be reached ("So one day when you're bored, by all means call me"). When performed live, "The Loop" is sped up and played faster, rocking the roof off of the place, and puts any "real" rockabilly band to shame.

"The Loop" is the B-side to 1991's "My Love Life."

"Sister I'm a Poet"

"Sister I'm a Poet" is about a person who is an outsider among his peers and is obsessed with true crime stories, and it has an obvious biographical tone, since we all know that Morrissey was the loner and weirdo of his neighborhood while growing up, although from what I have learned, his sister, Jacqueline, seemed pretty cool and understanding of her little brother's "weirdness."

"Sister I'm a Poet" is one of the only Morrissey solo songs that sounds exactly like a Smiths leftover. I find that funny considering this was one of the early Morrissey solo songs that Mike Joyce, Andy Rourke, and Craig "The Fifth Smith" Gannon did not play on.

"Sister I'm a Poet" is the B-side to 1988's "Everyday Is Like Sunday."

"You're the One for Me, Fatty"

See "London Is Dead: *Your Arsenal.*"

"Boxers"

Do you feel like crying? Then listen to "Boxers."

A lush-sounding tune about a washed-up boxer who is still a hero to his nephew, "Boxers" has always been an underrated Morrissey song. Morrissey sounds great, the band sounds great, and it really is a sweet story (and accompanying video). To lend it an authentic feel, a sample of BBC ringside commentator Reg Gutteridge is used and real boxer Cornelius Carr is the star of the "Boxers" music video.

"Boxers" was supposed to be released on a four-song EP along with "Have-A-Go Merchant," "Whatever Happens, I Love You," and "Sunny." Instead, they released "Boxers" as regular single and saved "Sunny" for its own single release later that year.

The B-sides for "Boxers" are "Have-A-Go Merchant" and "Whatever Happens, I Love You," and it reached #23 on the UK chart. It was released on 7″ vinyl, 12″ vinyl, cassette single, and compact disc single.

"Moon River

See "I Take the Cue: Cover Songs."

"My Love Life"

"My Love Life" is Morrissey's eleventh single, released in 1991, reaching #29 on the UK chart. It was the last song recorded with his *Viva Hate/Kill Uncle* musicians, but the single erroneously credits Boz Boorer, Alain Whyte, Spencer Cobrin, and Gary Day as the participating musicians.

"My Love Life" tells the story of a man (probably Morrissey) who wants to be included in a polyamorous relationship because he loved one half of the relationship so much, he would take anything over nothing. It was originally planned to be a B-side to 1991's "Sing Your Life," but Morrissey, the producers, and the record label all agreed it was strong enough to be its own single.

The B-sides for "My Love Life" are "I've Changed My Plea to Guilty," "There's a Place in Hell for Me and My Friends," and "Skin Storm." It was released on 7″ vinyl, 12″ vinyl, cassette single, and compact disc single.

"Certain People I Know"

See "London Is Dead: *Your Arsenal.*"

"The Last of the Famous International Playboys"

See the previous entry, *Bona Drag.*

"We'll Let You Know"

See "London Is Dead: *Your Arsenal.*"

"Spring-Heeled Jim"

See "Long May It Last: *Vauxhall and I.*"

Suedehead: The Best of Morrissey (1997)

Suedehead: The Best of Morrissey is a compilation album that contains the usual assortment of Morrissey hits but also has some unexpected jams, like his cover of the Jam's "That's Entertainment" and "Interlude," his duet with Siouxsie Sioux.

Interesting note: EMI, the label that released *Suedehead: The Best of Morrissey*, as well as *Beethoven Was Deaf* and *World of Morrissey*, deleted all three of these albums from its catalog, although *World of Morrissey* is available in MP3 format on Amazon.com for some reason. But do not worry—Amoeba probably has some used copies of all three albums for sale.

The track listing for *Suedehead: The Best of Morrissey*:

1. "Suedehead"
2. "Sunny"
3. "Boxers"
4. "Tomorrow"
5. "Interlude"
6. "Everyday Is Like Sunday"
7. "That's Entertainment"
8. "Hold On to Your Friends"
9. "My Love Life"
10. "Interesting Drug"
11. "Our Frank"

12. "Piccadilly Palare"
13. "Ouija Board, Ouija Board"
14. "You're the One for Me, Fatty"
15. "We Hate It When Our Friends Become Successful"
16. "The Last of the Famous International Playboys"
17. "Pregnant for the Last Time"
18. "November Spawned a Monster"
19. "The More You Ignore Me, the Closer I Get"

My Early Burglary Years (1998)

My Early Burglary Years is an American release and a pretty good one at that—it compiles mostly B-sides and cuts from *Southpaw Grammar*. The highlight of *My Early Burglary Years* is the live version of Morrissey's cover of T. Rex's "Cosmic Dancer."

"Sunny"

"Sunny" was released as its own single after being kicked off of the "Boxers" single. That was fine—"Sunny" was definitely a strong enough song to get its own release, although it only reached #42 on the UK chart. A tale about a group of friends torn apart by heroin addiction, it has the usual wistful and introspective feel that only Morrissey can bring to a subject like drug addiction.

Although Morrissey's 1995 album *Southpaw Grammar* was released by RCA, 1995's "Sunny" was released on the Parlophone label. The B-sides for "Sunny" are "Black-Eyed Susan" and "A Swallow on My Neck." It was on 7″ vinyl, cassette single, and compact disc single.

"At Amber"

Previously known as "The Bed Took Fire," "At Amber" is a weird Morrissey song. Once again, Morrissey writes about a disabled friend, but in "At Amber," he is staying at the Sands Hotel in Las Vegas and calls "Amber" to tell her about the miserable time he is having (only Morrissey could have a miserable time in Las Vegas). Amber gets his ass in check by reminding him that at least he has full use of his arms and legs and is not wheelchair-bound.

Touché, Amber.

"At Amber" was originally scheduled to be the B-side for the "Interesting Drug" single, but Morrissey dropped it due to lack of interest. He brought it back from the dead while working on *Bona Drag*. "At Amber" was eventually released as a B-side to "Piccadilly Palare."

"Cosmic Dancer"

See "I Take the Cue: Cover Songs."

"Nobody Loves Us"

"Nobody Loves Us" was intended to be included on 1995's *Southpaw Grammar* but was left off of the original release. It was welcomed back for the 2009 rerelease of *Southpaw Grammar*, taking its place as the final track.

"Nobody Loves Us" sounds similar to 1997's "Alma Matters" (both written by guitarist Alain Whyte), and once again, Morrissey writes about how he is the "King of Misfits." Not cool Misfits, like Glenn Danzig, but the loners and weirdoes of the world.

"Nobody Loves Us" is the B-side to "Dagenham Dave."

"A Swallow on My Neck"

Despite the double entendre in its title, "A Swallow on My Neck" is a song about tattoos, according to Morrissey. During the recording and release of *Vauxhall and I*, Morrissey went through a tattoo phase. Pictures of tattoos or people with tattoos (both real and fake) appeared all over the marketing and promotional material for *Vauxhall and I* and its singles, including photos of Morrissey with the word "honey" drawn around his nipple, a stomach with the word "MOZ" sprawled across it (and the O is charmingly set to go around the belly button), and—you guessed it—hand-drawn swallows! Except they are on the hands of Morrissey's confidante and assistant, Jake Walters, and not on his neck.

"A Swallow on My Neck" is one of the Morrissey-and-Jake-Walters-rumor songs, since it is about Morrissey developing "feelings" for a man who gives him a swallow tattoo on his neck. Why a swallow? Swallow tattoos on hands usually indicate that someone is a good fighter (with fast, bird-like hands). When the swallow tattoo is on your neck, I can only imagine.

"A Swallow on My Neck" was originally planned to be the B-side to "Hold On to Your Friends," but it ended up being the B-side to "Sunny."

"Sister I'm a Poet"

See *World of Morrissey*.

"Black-Eyed Susan"

"Black-Eyed Susan" was one of the first songs recorded and considered for 1994's *Vauxhall and I*, but it was put aside and dragged back out to be used as a B-side to 1995's "Sunny." It gets its name from the 1829 Douglas William Jerrold play, although it does not have anything in common with the nautical theme of the play. Yet another dumb rumor exists about "Black-Eyed Susan" really being about Siouxsie Sioux and what happened regarding the Morrissey and Siouxsie duet, "Interlude," but that would be impossible, since "Black-Eyed Susan" was originally recorded back in 1993 and "Interlude" was recorded and released in 1994.

"Michael's Bones"

"Michael's Bones" is your typical Morrissey fare—the dead body of a young man is discovered and he never experienced love. But the rumored backstory is pretty interesting.

The "Michael" in "Michael's Bones" is actually Michael Ryan, a twenty-seven-year-old loner and firearms collector (two words that always seem to go together) who shot up his town of Hungerford, England, in 1987. After killing sixteen people (including his mother), he barricaded himself in a school. He then turned the gun on himself after the police surrounded the school, and his body and brains laid splattered in a classroom. It seems to me that one can make an honest assessment and agree that "Michael's Bones" is about Michael Ryan.

But the Morrissey connection doesn't stop there! The Smiths' 1987 single "Stop Me If You Think You've Heard This One Before" was released shortly after the Hungerford massacre, but received little radio airplay due to the BBC declaring the song "insensitive" due to the "And plan a mass murder" lyric.

"Michael's Bones" is the B-side to 1989's "The Last of the Famous International Playboys."

"I'd Love To"

I remember a million years ago I was dating a guy with sideburns who was the one who really got me into Morrissey. I picked up the compact disc single of "The More You Ignore Me, the Closer I Get" and instantly fell in love with its B-side, "I'd Love To."

"When we get married, I would like to have 'I'd Love To' as the song we first dance to," I mentioned to him.

"No. That song it stupid," he answered.

After that, I realized I'd love to dump him.

"I'd Love To" is a dreamy and ethereal song, much like the Smiths' "Last Night I Dreamt That Somebody Loves Me." Morrissey sings about how he is in love and yearns for that person and it is tearing him apart, ultimately accepting the fact that it will never happen.

Because the majority of Morrissey songs are about loneliness, not being loved or accepted, and being miserable, people often forget that he is capable of writing something about love and on the other end of the misery spectrum. And when he does, Morrissey brings it, and "I'd Love To" is a perfect example of that.

"Reader Meet Author"

See "You Don't Catch What I'm Saying: *Southpaw Grammar*."

"Pashernate Love"

Not one of Morrissey's greatest songs, "Pashernate Love" was the first song that guitarist Alain Whyte submitted to Morrissey, and Morrissey liked it enough to record it. It was also the first song that his new *Kill Uncle* band (Boz Boorer, Spencer Cobrin, Gary Day, and Alain Whyte) performed live on stage.

"Pashernate Love" is the B-side to 1992's "You're the One for Me, Fatty."

"Girl Least Likely To"

Written by both Morrissey and Andy Rourke, "Girl Least Likely To" is Morrissey's true thoughts about a female friend of his for whom, even though she believed she was destined for success, Morrissey (and others) knew it was not meant to be. Unfortunately for Morrissey, the friend realized that he was singing about her and became angry with him (I guess she was not as clueless as everyone believed her to be).

"Girl Least Likely To" is the B-side to "November Spawned a Monster"— and a boring B-side at that.

"Jack the Ripper"

See *World of Morrissey*.

"I've Changed My Plea to Guilty"

One of Morrissey's finest torch songs, "I've Changed My Plea to Guilty" is Morrissey singing his heart out, begging to be put in jail because he is just so exhausted by all of the emotions he is feeling. He feels that a life locked up in loneliness is the safest way to live. The creepy opening and closing muffled sounds were taken from the 1963 Skeeter Davis song "The End of the World."

"I've Changed My Plea to Guilty" is the B-side to 1991's "My Love Life."

"The Boy Racer"

See "You Don't Catch What I'm Saying: *Southpaw Grammar*."

"Boxers"

See *World of Morrissey*.

The Best of Morrissey (2001)

It pains me to say this because I am a big fan of Rhino Records, but this is a very basic "best of" collection of Morrissey songs. If you are looking to buy a greatest hits collection because you need to be schooled on some Morrissey hits because you might score with a Morrissey fan, then this is the album for you.

The track listing for *The Best of Morrissey*:

1. "The More You Ignore Me, the Closer I Get"
2. "Suedehead"
3. "Everyday Is Like Sunday"

4.   "Glamorous Glue"
5.   "Do Your Best and Don't Worry"
6.   "November Spawned a Monster"
7.   "The Last of the Famous International Playboys"
8.   "Sing Your Life"
9.   "Hairdresser on Fire"
10. "Interesting Drug"
11. "We Hate It When Our Friends Become Successful"
12. "Certain People I Know"
13. "Now My Heart Is Full"
14. "I Know It's Going to Happen Someday"
15. "Sunny"
16. "Alma Matters"
17. "Hold On to Your Friends"
18. "Sister I'm a Poet"
19. "Disappointed"
20. "Tomorrow"
21. "Lost"

Greatest Hits (2008)

I did not buy this album.

Why?

Because I already own *You Are the Quarry* and *Ringleader of the Tormentors*!

The title "Greatest Hits" is misleading—sure, they are great. And sure, they are technically hits. But of fifteen tracks, eight are from *You Are the Quarry* and *Ringleader of the Tormentors*, four are hits from previous albums, one was not even a hit, and two are brand-new tracks that would eventually end up on *Years of Refusal*! That is some ballsy Babe Ruth stuff—calling two unheard tracks "greatest hits" before they are even properly released. *Greatest Hits* also includes a bonus disc with a performance from the Hollywood Bowl and a delicious pic of Morrissey's naked butt in the gatefold.

The music nerd in me would also like to point out that not all of the songs on *Greatest Hits* were, in fact, his biggest hits. "In the Future When All's Well" reached #17, and "I Just Want to See the Boy Happy" reached number #16—whereas "Interesting Drug" reached #9, and "November Spawned a Monster" hit #12, and they are NOT included on the album. *Greatest Hits* made it to #5 on the UK chart but only #178 on the US chart.

That is because we know our hits.

The track listing for *Greatest Hits*:

1. "First of the Gang to Die"
2. "In the Future When All's Well"
3. "I Just Want to See the Boy Happy"
4. "Irish Blood, English Heart"
5. "You Have Killed Me"
6. "That's How People Grow Up"
7. "Everyday Is Like Sunday"
8. "Redondo Beach"
9. "Suedehead"
10. "The Youngest Was the Most Loved"
11. "The Last of the Famous International Playboys"
12. "The More You Ignore Me, the Closer I Get"
13. "All You Need Is Me"
14. "Let Me Kiss You"
15. "I Have Forgiven Jesus"

Swords (2009)

Swords is a compilation of B-sides from, once again, the *You Are the Quarry* and *Ringleader of the Tormentors* years. But unlike *Greatest Hits*, *Swords* is actually really good, because a lot of his B-sides from that period are better than the actual singles. "Ganglord," "My Dearest Love," and especially "Friday Mourning" are all phenomenal examples of what should have been hit singles.

Swords reached #55 on the UK chart and was released with a bonus compact disc, *Live in Warsaw*.

"Good Looking Man About Town"

With its sitar sounds and pumping beat, "Good Looking Man About Town" has a little bit of a Bollywood-ish sound, much like "I Will See You in Far Off Places," the opening track to 2006's *Ringleader of the Tormentors*. "Good Looking Man About Town" is a twist on the usual Morrissey rhetoric of "I am human and I need to be loved" by having Morrissey tell the nerdy hero that he needs to get over himself if he ever wants to be loved. Maybe years of listening to his own music has finally changed Morrissey's outlook on life?

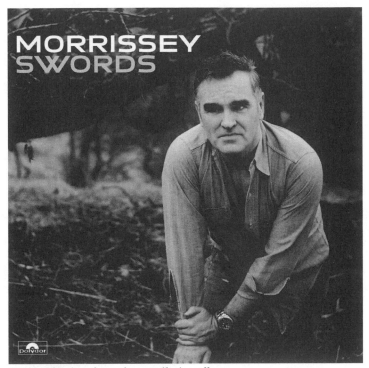

Swords, Morrissey's tenth compilation album.

Author's collection

"Good Looking Man About Town" is the B-side to "You Have Killed Me."

"Don't Make Fun of Daddy's Voice"

I'd rather make fun of this song.

"Don't Make Fun of Daddy's Voice" is not one of Morrissey's best. I remember when he was touring (and actually showing up to the concerts) around 2004 through 2006, and I saw him quite a few times. He would always whip this one out, and you could just tell that the audience did not dig it (like the "Meat Is Murder" slaughterhouse footage, it encouraged fans to visit the restroom or grab another beer). I also feel that the band did not like playing it, either—while attending one of the 2007 Pasadena Civic Auditorium shows, Morrissey made a gesture with his hand to the band to "speed it up." The band continued at the pace they were playing.

Like 2004's "Irish Blood, English Heart," "Don't Make Fun of Daddy's Voice" was originally recorded and released in 1998 by Alain Whyte's side project, Johnny Panic and the Bible of Dreams, under the name "Paranoia." Morrissey kept the original music and added his own lyrics.

"Don't Make Fun of Daddy's Voice" is the B-side to 2004's "Let Me Kiss You."

"If You Don't Like Me, Don't Look at Me"

I like "If You Don't Like Me, Don't Look at Me" a lot, but unfortunately, there's nothing interesting to write about. Morrissey sings about his problem with people looking at him.

"If You Don't Like Me, Don't Look at Me" is the B-side to 2006's "The Youngest Was the Most Loved."

"Ganglord"

"Ganglord" is one of the best B-sides Morrissey has ever recorded and instantly became a fan favorite. In the vein of "First of the Gang to Die," "Ganglord" is another saga about the dangerous gang life in Los Angeles. Morrissey sings about being in a life of crime with the Los Angeles Police Department constantly after him, and his only hope is the local "ganglord" to get him out of the mess he is in.

When performed live, Morrissey has fun with the song and changes up the lyrics, from the boring "But what they really mean to say is get yourself back to the ghetto" to "But what they really mean to say is get your fat ass back to the ghetto."

When I first heard him sing that line live, I was all, "Did he really just sing 'fat ass'?" And when I realized he did, I liked the song even more, and the crowd agrees with me, making "Ganglord" one of the most rambunctious and fun live songs he performs.

"Ganglord" is the B-side to 2006's "The Youngest Was the Most Loved."

"My Dearest Love"

If you listen to "My Dearest Love" and "Unbelievable" by EMF, they sound unusually similar, due the hard-driving piano and thumping bass that drives both of those songs. But that is where the similarities end—"My Dearest

Love" is a heartfelt plea by Morrissey to his "dearest love" to take him and make him happy. And only Morrissey would use the word "grotesquely" in a love song.

"My Dearest Love" was produced by award-winning composer Gustavo Santaolalla, who composed the soundtrack to the 2005 movie *Brokeback Mountain*. It is also the B-side to 2009's "All You Need Is Me."

"The Never-Played Symphonies"

To me, "The Never-Played Symphonies" is a total snoozer of a song, but maybe it is supposed to be, since it is about Morrissey on his deathbed, being pathetic and regretting not having had enough sex while he was still able. Morrissey's favorite poet, John Betjeman, made a similar sentiment on his deathbed in 1984 about "not having enough sex" while he was fit and able.

"The Never-Played Symphonies" is the B-side to 2004's "Irish Blood, English Heart."

"Sweetie-Pie"

Like most of the other songs written and recorded for 2006's *Ringleader of the Tormentors*, "Sweetie-Pie" is about Morrissey being in love. That being said, "Sweetie-Pie" is a truly terrible Morrissey song (maybe even his worst song ever?). It was originally written by keyboardist Michael Farrell as a nice, normal ballad, but Morrissey decided to "go crazy" with it and make something different. On the Internet, they refer to him doing this as "Golden Lighting it" because of Morrissey's famous incident of messing with (and messing up) the Smiths' 1986 B-side "Golden Lights" to make it sound more "weird," thereby ruining the perfectly fine original recording. And to make it worse, Morrissey has his protégé, Kristeen Young, warbling throughout the song. What gives?

"Sweetie-Pie" is the B-side to 2006's "I Just Want to See the Boy Happy."

"Christian Dior"

"Christian Dior" is the only song for 2006's *Ringleader of the Tormentors* that was written by guitarist Boz Boorer, but sadly, it only ended up as a B-side. Morrissey compares himself to famous fashion designer Christian Dior because they both have such incredible work ethic and put so much into their craft that they didn't get to enjoy life. Maybe for Morrissey, but from what I've read about Christian Dior, he led a pretty great life with lots of partying, traveling, and sex. And he was still able to churn out groundbreaking clothing and cosmetics.

Morrissey is just a lightweight.

"Christian Dior" is the B-side to 2006's "In the Future When All's Well."

"Shame Is the Name"

For not being an interesting song, "Shame Is the Name" has a lot of interesting "fun facts," such as:

- Fun Fact #1: Chrissie Hynde of the Pretenders guest sings on "Shame Is the Name."
- Fun Fact #2: Morrissey's pet dog at the time was actually named Shame.
- Fun Fact #3: François Truffaut's masterpiece *The 400 Blows* (*Les Quatre Cents Coups*) is sampled in "Shame Is the Name." The sample is of a schoolboy making fun of another schoolboy who is named Mauricet, and when pronounced, it sounds like he's saying "Morrissey." Pretty clever, Moz!

"Shame Is the Name" is the B-side to 2009's "I'm Throwing My Arms Around Paris."

"Munich Air Disaster 1958"

"Munich Air Disaster 1958" is not your typical Morrissey "I want to die" BS. It is actually pretty profound and poignant, although a slight bit morbid. "Munich Air Disaster 1958" tells the true-life tale of the 1958 Manchester United football team and their trip back from the European Cup game in Belgrade. After stopping for fuel in Munich, their plane crashed after its third attempt to take off, killing twenty-one passengers on board, including players, coaches, managers, and journalists. Morrissey sings about how lucky they were and how he wishes he could have died in the prime of his life, when he was young, skinny, and good-looking.

Anyone who has seen a recent Morrissey concert (and a recent shirt stained with his boob sweat) would agree with his sentiments.

"Munich Air Disaster 1958" is the B-side to 2004's "Irish Blood, English Heart."

"I Knew I Was Next"

Morrissey and *Ringleader of the Tormentors* producer Tony Visconti clearly picked the best songs to go on *Ringleader of the Tormentors*, because like "Sweetie-Pie," "I Knew I Was Next" is really blah. Did you know that everyone hates Morrissey? No? Than listen to "I Knew I Was Next" and 586 of his other songs.

"I Knew I Was Next" is the B-Side to 2006's "You Have Killed Me."

"It's Hard to Walk Tall When You're Small"

"It's Hard to Walk Tall When You're Small" was written by ex-drummer Spencer Cobrin back in 1997, originally for a B-side for *Maladjusted*, but was quickly shelved by Morrissey. In 2004, it was dug out and rerecorded, making it considerably heavier than Cobrin's original ballad.

"It's Hard to Walk Tall When You're Small" is the B-side to 2004's "Irish Blood, English Heart."

"Teenage Dad on His Estate"

"Teenage Dad on His Estate" is a perfectly lovely Morrissey song—sweetly melodic, almost with a 1960s girl-group melancholy feel. Rich bored dads versus young junkie dads, "Teenage Dad on His Estate" is one of the better B-sides from the *You Are the Quarry* period.

"Teenage Dad on His Estate" is the B-side to 2004's "First of the Gang to Die."

"Children in Pieces"

"Children in Pieces" is a really awkward Morrissey song that just does not "go." It is pretty hard-rocking, but it is about such an important and sensitive topic—the sexual and physical abuse of Irish children that attended state-run industrial schools that were controlled by the evil Catholic Church's Christian Brothers! Morrissey name-checks it all in "Children in Pieces," so much that I didn't have to do much research to get what he was singing about (but I researched it anyway). Morrissey can't give us a somber song for a somber topic, yet we get a somber song about him not getting laid ("The Never-Played Symphonies").

"Children in Pieces" is the B-side to 2009's "All You Need Is Me." It was produced by award-winning composer Gustavo Santaolalla.

"Friday Mourning"

No matter how I feel about Morrissey's other crappy B-sides, this one makes up for it all. Seriously, when I first heard it, I felt all swoony and in love with Morrissey again. "Friday Mourning" is about Morrissey calling it quits—he's serious this time, guys. Do not leave the house lights on because he is NOT

At KROQ is Morrissey's only EP (extended play) album.   *Author's collection*

coming back. He is going to kill himself and everyone (friends, bosses, teachers . . .) will be glad he is gone because he is a loooooser.

"Friday Mourning" is so lush-sounding, yet torchy at the same time. Morrissey nails his singing—you really believe that he is finally going to kill himself and you kind of agree with him, because he sounds so sure and mature about it.

"Friday Mourning" is the B-side to 2004's "Let Me Kiss You."

"My Life Is a Succession of People Saying Goodbye"

I think the title of this song explains it all.

"My Life Is a Succession of People Saying Goodbye" is the B-side to 2004's "First of the Gang to Die."

"Drive-In Saturday"

See "I Take the Cue: Cover Songs."

"Because of My Poor Education"

Despite looking "bookish," Morrissey never went to college, so now he blames his lack of higher learning for no one loving him.

"Because of My Poor Education" is the B-side to 2009's "I'm Throwing My Arms Around Paris."

At KROQ (1991)

Morrissey's *At KROQ* is a three-song EP that was released in 1991 in support of his *Kill Uncle* tour. The best part of this EP is the hidden track—it is over eight minutes of fans crazed with "Moz-teria" calling in to DJ Richard Blade's voicemail, leaving messages of love for Morrissey. What can I say? We Angelenos love Morrissey!

The track listing for *At KROQ*:

1. "There's a Place in Hell for Me and My Friends"
2. "My Love Life"
3. "Sing Your Life"
4. "The Hidden Track"

A bumper sticker for Morrissey's 1991 visit to the KROQ studio.   *Author's collection*

Very Best of Morrissey (2011)

Very similar to the previously released *Suedehead: The Best of Morrissey*, *Very Best of Morrissey* features releases spanning from 1988 to 1995. It only reached #80 on the UK charts, probably because people were sick of buying Morrissey hits compilations. This album does contain a bonus DVD of assorted remastered Morrissey videos, which is a nice-to-have.

To help promote *Very Best of Morrissey*, "Glamorous Glue" was rereleased as a single, only reaching #69 on the UK chart, making it Morrissey's worst charting single ever.

The track listing for *Very Best of Morrissey*:

1.   "The Last of the Famous International Playboys"
2.   "You're Gonna Need Someone on Your Side"
3.   "The More You Ignore Me, the Closer I Get"
4.   "Glamorous Glue"
5.   "Girl Least Likely To"
6.   "Suedehead"
7.   "Tomorrow"
8.   "Boxers"
9.   "My Love Life"
10. "Break Up the Family"
11. "I've Changed My Plea to Guilty"
12. "Such a Little Thing Makes Such a Big Difference"

13. "Ouija Board, Ouija Board"
14. "Interesting Drug"
15. "November Spawned a Monster"
16. "Everyday Is Like Sunday"
17. "Interlude"
18. "Moon River"

Under the Influence (2003)

Fans were pissed when *Under the Influence* was released.

Actually, only stupid fans were pissed when it was released.

Toutcd as "the first Morrissey release in six years," *Under the Influence* features NO music actually made by Morrissey and/or the Smiths. It is exactly

—VERY BEST OF —
MORRISSEY
· THE REMASTERED CLASSIC HITS · RARE PHOTOS ·
· PREVIOUSLY UNRELEASED VERSIONS AND LIVE PERFORMANCES ·
· THE REMASTERED VIDEOS ON DVD ·
DELUXE CD + DVD · HEAVYWEIGHT VINYL · DOWNLOAD
amazon.co.uk   **OUT NOW**   MAJOR RECORDS

An advertisement for 2011's *Very Best of Morrissey.*

Author's collection

what it sounds like—songs that have influenced Morrissey. But people still bought it—people who obviously could not read—and complained. If they would have bought it and liked it for what it was, they would have had a great compilation to listen to—Morrissey picked some gems like "Arts and Crafts Spectacular" by Sparks, "So Little Time" by Diana Dors, "Great Horse" by Tyrannosaurus Rex (a.k.a. T. Rex), and "Judy Is a Punk" by the Ramones.

Morrissey donated his proceeds from *Under the Influence* to the People for the Ethical Treatment of Animals.

25

The Never-Played Symphonies

Miscellaneous Songs and B-sides

"Fantastic Bird"

Morrissey tries to go a little sci-fi with this ditty, singing about a space ship (the "Fantastic Bird") and how it will carry his significant other into space. Kind of a different topic for Morrissey, but I enjoyed it because it was something different for a change. Although it was recorded around 1992 to become a potential B-side to "Certain People I Know," it was then slated to be released on 1995's *Southpaw Grammar*. It was cut from that album, too, and would finally be released on the 2009 *Southpaw Grammar* reissue.

I guess "Fantastic Bird" really was lost in outer space.

"Get Off the Stage"

Morrissey never gets to live this one down.

"Get Off the Stage" is the B-side to 1990's "Piccadilly Palare." It is about aging rockers who just don't know when to quit—more specifically, the Rolling Stones. In a 1990 interview with Nick Kent for *The Face* magazine, Moz has this to say about old timers:

> I find it frightening, but not for challenging reasons. It's frightening because it symbolizes the state of music in America. If you look at the top ten albums of the moment you'll find the Rolling Stones, Bob Dylan, Neil Young, Eric Clapton, Grateful Dead, and I find that horrifying. There's a song on this album that has the Rolling Stones in mind because I've been so disgusted by their most recent comeback that I no longer find it sad or pitiful, I just feel immense anger that they don't just get out of the way. You open papers in this country, and

every day there's the obligatory picture of, y'know, Mick-with-bags-at-the-airport, or Keith saying he's completely normal now. They just won't move away! The song is called "Get Off the Stage."

Mick Jagger was forty-six when "Get Off the Stage" was released. So what was Morrissey doing when HE was forty-six?

It was 2005—*You Are the Quarry* was a big hit in 2004, and he was still riding that comeback wave, touring, and working on 2006's *Ringleader of the Tormentors*. So if he would have listened to his own advice, none of that would have even happened. (Side note: Although it is hypocritical, I do agree with him about the Rolling Stones. They should have hung it up after *Undercover* in 1983.)

"Happy Lovers at Last United"

"Happy Lovers at Last United" is Morrissey's tale about hooking two friends up and then becoming a bitter third wheel. It was originally supposed to be a B-side to "Everyday Is Like Sunday," but Morrissey decided to cut it. It ended up on the 2010 reissue of *Bona Drag*.

"Heir Apparent"

"Heir Apparent" is Morrissey's tale of a Manchester homecoming and a young lad who reminds him of himself. He warns him of the dangers of the music biz in London, yet finds himself to be jealous of the youth's naïveté. Although "Heir Apparent" is one of the better tracks that was recorded during the 1997 *Maladjusted* sessions, it was denied its place on the final track listing. But "Heir Apparent" made its return on the 2009 reissue of *Maladjusted*.

"Honey, You Know Where to Find Me"

"Honey, You Know Where to Find Me" is Morrissey's attempt at playing it cool when he runs into a past love at the local pub. Originally written by Alain Whyte during the *Vauxhall and I* sessions, it was scrapped by Morrissey, but then brought back for the *Southpaw Grammar* sessions—but with Boz Boorer's music! But it was still scrapped until it resurfaced on the 2009 *Southpaw Grammar* reissue. Of all of the scrapped tracks that found their way onto the reissue, "Honey, You Know Where to Find Me" is my favorite—Morrissey's lyrics are indeed smooth like honey, and the beat drives just enough to keep the song flowing.

"I Can Have Both"

"I Can Have Both" is Morrissey's tale about discovering that it is okay to be bisexual, and that it is nice to have a choice. Morrissey has obviously been okay with it for years now, or at least since 1981, when he disclosed to pen pal Robert Mackie that he and his girlfriend Annalisa were in fact bisexual. "I Can Have Both" delves a little deeper, disclosing memories of being a young boy and being told to choose one or the other. But once he realizes he has a choice in sexual partners, his life opens up.

"I Can Have Both" is another song that was cut from the track listing for 1997's *Maladjusted*, but it resurfaced on the 2009 reissue.

"I Know Very Well How I Got My Name"

"I Know Very Well How I Got My Name" is the B-side to 1988's "Suedehead." Another song about his separation from Johnny Marr, "I Know Very Well How I Got My Name" is an autobiographical song purely for its anecdotal lyrics regarding "A child in a curious phase" turned into "A man with sullen ways." A line later in the song references "A thirteen-year-old who dyed his hair gold"—that was Morrissey, who admitted to bleaching his hair to look Bowie-esque.

Viva Hate guitarist Vini Reilly released an unreleased version of "I Know Very Well How I Got My Name" titled "I Know Very Well How I Got My Note Wrong"—his flubbed note really stood out in such a delicate song, so his other band, the Durutti Column, released his mistake as a free single in 1989.

"Journalists Who Lie"

"Journalists Who Lie" is the B-side to 1991's "Our Frank." After critics tore apart the "Ouija Board, Ouija Board" single, Morrissey became all butt-hurt and wrote "Journalists Who Lie" as a response.

It was also the last song written by co-writer Stephen Street, but was recorded after he and Morrissey quit working together. Morrissey's recording is totally different from the Street demo that was left, and in later years, Morrissey would disown "Journalists Who Lie," declaring it one of the worst songs he's ever recorded.

"Let the Right One Slip In"

In my introduction, I stated that Gene Simmons of KISS and Morrissey do not have anything in common. But I was wrong.

Both KISS and Morrissey had their own condoms for sale.

I know what you're thinking—when you think of having sex, you don't think about Morrissey. But on the merch table for his 1999 and 2000 tour, he had condoms for sale that were printed with

Let the right one slip in
Morrissey

For a B-side, "Let the Right One Slip In" has quite a bit going for it (besides the condoms). It is actually a pretty decent B-side and one of the first songs written by guitarist Alain Whyte, and it has the honor of being the title of a pretty bad-ass vampire book, 2004's *Let the Right One In.*

"Let the Right One Slip In" is the B-side to 1992's "Tomorrow" and appears on the 1997 reissue of *Viva Hate* and the 2010 reissue of *Bona Drag.*

"Lifeguard on Duty"

Morrissey is visiting a pool and asks the lifeguard to protect him from the bad things in life, like getting beat up and spit upon. It was one of the first songs recorded for 1988's *Viva Hate*, but all parties involved in the recording agreed that it wasn't a very strong song, and it was cut. Morrissey would finally get a lifeguard to save him when he wrote and recorded "Lifeguard Sleeping, Girl Drowning" for 1994's *Vauxhall and I.*

"Lifeguard on Duty" appears on the 2010 reissue of *Bona Drag.*

"My Life Is a Succession of People Saying Goodbye"

"My Life Is a Succession of People Saying Goodbye" is the B-side to the 2004 "First of the Gang to Die" single. Morrissey is sad that people are leaving him—some are actually getting up and leaving and some are actually dying, and "My Life Is a Succession of People Saying Goodbye" is just a rehashing of his feelings of abandonment. Morrissey's lyrics also inform us (once again) that life is boring and has nothing to more to offer than luxury items, like "money, jewelry, and flesh."

I think I'll take the money.

"Noise Is the Best Revenge"

"Noise Is the Best Revenge" is the B-side to the 2005 "There Is a Light That Never Goes Out"/"Redondo Beach" split single. It was recorded live in 2004 for a BBC Radio 2 session with Janice Long and is another song in a long line of songs that are rumored to about the Court Case. I think it is about what the title implies—by still making "noise," a.k.a. music, Morrissey is extracting revenge on all of the critics and haters that have bashed him throughout his career. Or maybe his neighbors are really rude and he gets back at them by blasting Lou Reed's *Metal Machine Music?*

Fun fact: Morrissey's nephew, Johnny Dwyer, named his band Noise Is the Best Revenge.

"Now I Am a Was"

"Now I Am a Was" is the B-side to 1997's "Satan Rejected My Soul," and its lyrics are somewhat . . . normal? "Now I Am a Was" is Morrissey's tale of his feelings about a relationship falling apart and blaming himself for the cause of the breakdown. Yes, it is the typical Morrissey "I am so miserable" fare, but the lyrics suggest that he has matured, and although the breakup is painful, he understands why it happened. But still—"Now I Am a Was" is a crappy B-side to a crappy single, and was the end of a crappy year for Morrissey.

"Oh Well, I'll Never Learn"

"Oh Well, I'll Never Learn" is the forgettable B-side to 1988's "Suedehead." Some say it sounds very Velvet Underground-y; others do not say anything at all. Did I mention that this is a very forgettable song? It is clearly not his best work, thereby making sense that it was relegated to a B-side.

"Please Help the Cause Against Loneliness"

"Please Help the Cause Against Loneliness" is Morrissey's satirical plea to people to obviously help the cause against loneliness. Morrissey had asked Sandie Shaw to come down to the studio to record some backing vocals for the song. After not liking how it was turning out (and not thinking it was going to be a hit), he gave the song to Sandie Shaw to record and release. And so she did, releasing her own version of "Please Help the Cause Against

Sandie Shaw's 1988 single "Please Help the Cause Against Loneliness," originally written by Morrissey.   *Author's collection*

Loneliness" in 1988 (with Morrissey musicians Andrew Paresi and Kevin
Armstrong backing her). Unfortunately, the single failed to chart, proving
that Morrissey was right in discarding it for his own album.

The demo for "Please Help the Cause Against Loneliness" appears on
the 2010 reissue of *Bona Drag*.

"Pregnant for the Last Time"

Despite the fact that Morrissey said he "will never marry" and that he is "the
end of the family line," he surprisingly knows a lot about being knocked up.
"Pregnant for the Last Time" tells the tale of a girl who finds herself with
one up the stump after meeting someone new. But Morrissey sings about all
the problems that come from being with child—craving "chips with cream,"
having to buy "tiny stripe socks," and having "corned beef legs." One of the
wittiest songs Morrissey has ever penned, "Pregnant for the Last Time" is

the Morrissey anthem for all the single mothers, just like Beyoncé's "Single Ladies" is the anthem for . . . well, you know.

Fun fact: His new "rockabilly band" (Spencer Cobrin, Gary Day, and Alain Whyte) is featured in the video, but did not actually record "Pregnant for the Last Time"—that was *Kill Uncle* collaborators Mark Nevin, Andrew Paresi, Jonny Bridgwood (who would end up taking Spencer Cobrin's place in 1994), and new-to-the-band Boz Boorer on guitar.

Originally written to be included on the never-recorded rockabilly EP in 1990, "Pregnant for the Last Time" was salvaged and released as a single in 1991, reaching #25 on the UK chart. The B-sides for "Pregnant for the Last Time" are "Skin Storm," "Cosmic Dancer," and "Disappointed."

"The Public Image"

"The Public Image" is the B-side to 2004's "I Have Forgiven Jesus." Morrissey sings about how he is pretty much all image and not a human. This goes against everything he has preached to us about being human and needing to be loved.

"The Public Image" is a pretty good B-side, and the lyrics are pretty sharp, but the music is kind of soft. Originally slated to be included on 2004's *You Are the Quarry* but cut at the last minute, I can see why it was not included.

Morrissey does have an image to uphold.

"The Slum Mums"

"The Slum Mums" is the B-side to 2006's "I Have Forgiven Jesus." I wonder if Morrissey watches the television show *Maury* when he is on his tour bus, because the lyrics to "The Slum Mums" sound a lot like the guests on any given episode of *Maury* ("Six filthy children from six absent fathers . . ."). "The Slum Mums" is a really harsh view of the lives of poor people and how they live, and probably one of the best examples of the "Curmudgeon Morrissey" that people have been speaking of in recent years. I hope his next song is called "Get Off My Lawn."

"There Speaks a True Friend"

"There Speaks a True Friend" is the B-side to 1992's classic "You're the One for Me, Fatty." It's based on one of Morrissey's favorite movies, *The Killing of Sister George.* The subject of "There Speaks a True Friend" was actually a real friend of Morrissey's who had resigned from the friendship after harsh words were never made right. A potential song to be included on *Your Arsenal,* "There Speaks a True Friend" did not make the cut and was destined to be a B-side.

"This Is Not Your Country"

"This Is Not Your Country" is the B-side to 1997's "Satan Rejected My Soul." "This Is Not Your Country" was originally titled "Belfast" and dealt with the pre–Good Friday Agreement troubles in Northern Ireland. Morrissey disapproved of how the media in the United Kingdom covered the situation and the situation in general—the British Army was there and occupying with their soldiers and machinery. Morrissey felt that someone had to stick up for the Irish, and so he did with "This Is Not Your Country."

"Tony the Pony"

"Tony the Pony" is the B-side to "Our Frank," and there's nothing remark-able about it, which made it perfect fodder for 1991's *Kill Uncle.* But this tale of woe about drunk Tony and his shitty home life was cut from the album and relegated to a B-side.

"Tony the Pony" did make a version of *Kill Uncle*—Sire Records was responsible for releasing it here in the United States and added it to end of the album. Morrissey was upset about the addition because he did not consent to it.

"You Must Please Remember"

"You Must Please Remember" that "You Must Please Remember" is the B-side to 1995's "Dagenham Dave," since the song is quite forgettable. I even forgot that this song about Morrissey's dark past existed until I was researching this book.

"You Should Have Been Nice to Me"

One of the first songs recorded (and then dumped) for 1995's *Southpaw Grammar,* "You Should Have Been Nice to Me" is a total snoozer, and it is very obvious why it was originally left off the album (it reappeared on the

2009 reissue of *Southpaw Grammar*). Morrissey whines about how a significant other treats him like shit. He is absolutely right—the significant other should have been nicer, because then we would have be spared this song.

"You've Had Her"

"You've Had Her" is the B-side to 1992's "Certain People I Know." It is one of the first songs Boz Boorer wrote for Morrissey and another in a long line of unremarkable B-sides from his early solo career.

26

Ganglords

Record Labels and Website Wars

Attack Records

Attack Records was Morrissey's "vanity" label from 2004 until 2007. After Morrissey signed with Sanctuary Records, they let him choose a label from the many they had swallowed up over time. Attack Records was originally a reggae-only label that was created in the 1960s out of North London and fell under Trojan Records. Some of the acts on Attack Records were Gregory Isaacs, Dave and Ansel Collins, and Bob & Marcia (whose song "Young, Gifted, and Black" was a personal favorite of Morrissey).

Morrissey didn't care about making any money from any of the albums released on Attack Records—he just wanted to release "good records." Most of the Attack releases occurred in 2004 (although a couple of singles were released in 2006), with those releases being by artists who were near and dear to his heart, such as:

- *Morrissey Presents: The Return of the New York Dolls—Live from Royal Festival Hall 2004* by the New York Dolls (2004)
- *Nancy Sinatra* by Nancy Sinatra (2004)
- *Let Me Kiss You* (single) by Nancy Sinatra (2004)
- *Seize the Day* by Damien Dempsey (2004)
- *Lonely Planet Boy* by Jobriath (2004)
- *I Love a Good Fight* (single) by Jobriath (2004)
- *Born That Way* (single) by James Maker and Noko 440 (2004)
- *Worry Young* (single) by Remma (2004)
- *Kill the Father* (single) by Kristeen Young (2006)
- *London Cry* (single) by Kristeen Young (2006)

Jobiath's posthumous compilation, *Lonely Planet Boy*, was released
in 2004 on Attack Records.   *Author's collection*

Morrissey also released three of his albums on the Attack Records/
Sanctuary Records label, 2004's *You Are the Quarry*, 2005's *Live at Earls
Court*, and 2006's *Ringleader of the Tormentors*. In 2007, Attack Records/
Sanctuary Records was purchased by Universal, putting Morrissey under
their Decca label.

Decca

Decca is a record label that was THE label to be on if you were an English
rock band—Decca was home to the Rolling Stones, Small Faces, Them,
and Morrissey favorites Marianne Faithfull, Anthony Newley, David Bowie,
Kenneth Williams, Twinkle, and Billy Fury.

While Morrissey was signed to Sanctuary Music Group/Attack Records,
Universal Music Group purchased the label, therefore taking over Morrissey
and his contract. Universal Music Group decided to put Morrissey on the
appropriate Decca label (which they also owned). Morrissey was excited and
told the press, "I am delighted to be part of the Decca and Polydor family,

and am very excited about the new singles and albums we are going to do together in 2008."

Decca released his 2008 *Greatest Hits* album, but it sold poorly in the United States, making Morrissey renegotiate his contract. Then, 2009's *Years of Refusal* was released in the United States under Lost Highway, an affiliated imprint of Universal Music Group. Although Morrissey was still technically on the Decca label, Polydor was the label that issued *Years of Refusal* and the *Swords* compilation. His contract with Decca ended after the release of *Swords*.

EMI Records

The Smiths (and Morrissey in general) have a long and sordid past with EMI Records (but not as sordid as with Rough Trade). The Smiths were unhappy with Rough Trade regarding the release of their 1986 album, *The Queen Is Dead*. They signed with EMI shortly after that, although they wouldn't be recording for them until their contract with Rough Trade was fulfilled with the release of their 1987 album, *Strangeways, Here We Come*. The Smiths broke up before *Strangeways, Here We Come* was released and certainly before anything was recorded with EMI Records. EMI Records stood by a clause in their contract that stated they were owed something, so it was up to either Morrissey or Johnny Marr to record an album for them. Morrissey accepted the challenge and hastily came up with 1988's *Viva Hate*, which ended up being a phenomenal album and big hit for him and EMI Records, proving that Morrissey was skilled enough and worthy of a career as a solo artist. Morrissey as a solo artist continued to record under EMI Records until 1995.

EMI was also responsible for recording an early Smiths demo—a friend of Johnny Marr worked for EMI Records and hooked them up with studio time in 1982.

HMV (His Master's Voice)

HMV was Morrissey's first record label as a solo artist, starting with the release of 1988's *Viva Hate* and ending with the live album *Beethoven Was Deaf* in 1993. Like Attack Records, HMV (and Nipper the Dog) was a defunct label owned by EMI Records that Morrissey took a shine to and asked if his albums could be released under that label (making him the only recording artist on that label). HMV was the first in a long line of vintage record labels that Morrissey would resurrect to release his albums.

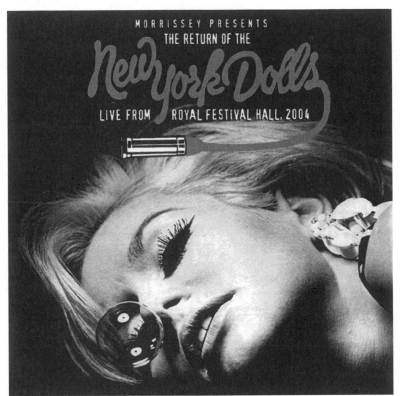

Morrissey Presents: The Return of the New York Dolls—Live from Royal Festival Hall 2004 was released in 2004 on Attack Records.   *Author's collection*

Parlophone

After leaving HMV, but still being under contract with EMI Records, Morrissey was moved to the Parlophone label (which was under the EMI Records umbrella) in 1994. At first he was not too happy about it, because there were other boring bands alongside him (like Radiohead), but then he became okay with it after realizing that some of his favorite artists (Cilla Black, David Bowie, and actress Joan Sims) all had released albums on Parlophone. His 1994 album, *Vauxhall and I*, was the only original studio album he released on Parlophone, but his 1995 compilation, *World of Morrissey*, and five singles ("The More You Ignore Me, the Closer I Get," "Hold On to Your Friends," "Interlude," "Boxers," and "Sunny") were released while on the Parlophone label. In 1995, he left Parlophone and was signed over to BMG, where he brought back the RCA Victor label for his *Southpaw Grammar* album.

RCA Victor

Morrissey was on the BMG record label in 1995 for his *Southpaw Grammar* album and its singles. Like with Decca and HMV, he insisted on BMG releasing his album on their defunct RCA Victor label. They even brought back the vintage RCA logo from the 1970s. Fun fact: BMG had no record of the '70s logo—Morrissey lent their graphics department one of his Lou Reed records so they could copy it.

David Bowie (who was originally on RCA Victor in the '70s) also was signed to the new RCA Victor to release his *1.Outside* album. Because of this, David Bowie asked Morrissey to tour with him to support both albums. It ended badly, with Morrissey leaving the tour after ten concerts.

Morrissey left RCA Victor after *Southpaw Grammar*'s release and the ill-fated tour.

Rough Trade

Rough Trade was the Smiths' only label (at least in the United Kingdom)—they released their first single, "Hand in Glove," in 1983 and everything until their posthumous live album, *Rank*, in 1987. Although originally thrilled and grateful to be given the chance by label head Geoff Travis, Morrissey and the Smiths became wary and critical of how they were being handled (especially Morrissey).

Rough Trade first started life as a record store in Notting Hill in 1976 (specializing in imports, punk, and reggae) and then became a label and distributor, with bands like Cabaret Voltaire, the Fall, the Raincoats, Stiff Little Fingers, and Morrissey's favorite, the Monochrome Set, on their roster. Although the Smiths had approached Manchester's Factory Records and EMI Records with their demo, Rough Trade seemed like the right fit for them.

The Smiths were the big act Rough Trade was waiting and hoping for, since acts that had previously been on their label (Aztec Camera, Orange Juice, and Scritti Politti) had all scored hits and become bigger after they'd left Rough Trade. That is why Rough Trade signed the Smiths to a long contact, which was always a bone of contention with Morrissey.

After an unauthorized remix of "This Charming Man" was released without the label consulting any of the Smiths, the band was upset and felt betrayed. To keep an eye on Geoff Travis and Rough Trade, the Smiths moved to London in 1984 to remain close to them. Rough Trade continued to jerk the Smiths around—releasing singles sporadically and not picking

 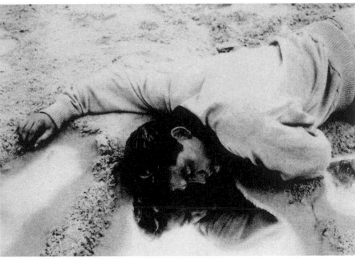

"Hand in Glove" was the Smiths' first release on Rough Trade Records.   *Author's collection*

the right singles to release. Still, for a small indie label, Rough Trade did the Smiths okay—they had a #1 album (*Meat Is Murder*) and eight Top 20 singles. But that wasn't good enough for the Smiths (especially Morrissey).

The Smiths signed with EMI Records in 1986 but were still going to fulfill their contract with Rough Trade by recording and releasing one last album (1987's *Strangeways, Here We Come*). But since the Smiths broke up shortly after the recording of *Strangeways, Here We Come*, Morrissey himself released an album, fulfilling the Smiths' obligation to EMI Records and establishing himself as a solo artist.

Rough Trade disbanded and declared bankruptcy in 1991 (Morrissey and Johnny Marr purchased the rights to the Smiths' catalog from Rough Trade and then sold it to Warner Brothers) but then bounced back in 2000 by signing hot new bands like the Libertines and the Strokes.

Morrissey-Solo.com

Morrissey-Solo.com is the "other" website, the site that does not get the support of Morrissey. But as much as I like True-to-You.net, I like the fact that Morrissey-Solo.com is an objective forum that posts the good and the bad about Morrissey. The owner and creator of Morrissey-Solo.com, David Tseng, does seem a little harsh sometimes, but I support his quest for freedom of speech regarding Morrissey. USA! USA! USA!

Morrissey was okay with Morrissey-Solo.com for a while, especially during his late '90's/early 2000s exile to Los Angeles. Because he was not on a label (and no social media really existed at the time), there really was not a source for information about Morrissey (whether he was playing some shows, working on new stuff, etc.). Morrissey-Solo.com was the place to get all that, plus connect with other rabid Morrissey fans (or just rabid people in general).

In 2003, Morrissey turned against Morrissey-Solo.com and sent them a "cease and desist" letter because they chose to run a story about Morrissey not paying some of his tour personnel. The story was never proven to be true (or false), but that ended any kind of warm and fuzzy feelings between Morrissey and David Tseng.

But wait—it gets better!

In 2014, a man named Bradley Steyn, who worked security for Morrissey, claimed that Morrissey tried to hire him to "hurt" David Tseng! Morrissey has denied this and states the following in a statement posted on True-to-You.net: "The very idea that I would ask a complete stranger (Bradley Steyn) to physically attack David Tseng surely cannot register with any sane person as being likely. As mildly irritating as David Tseng may be, he is not someone who troubles me enough to even bother with."

I do not believe that Morrissey hired this Steyn guy to kill David Tseng, because seriously—why would he have the need to hire anyone when he could get a couple of thugs to do it? Even Tseng, when interviewed about the claim, did not really seem to believe it was true. I guess that is the price you pay for the freedom to post links to other articles about Morrissey on your website.

True to You

True-to-You.net is the closest thing that Morrissey has to an "official" website. Started as a fanzine in 1994 by the world's biggest Morrissey fan, Julia Riley, True-to-You.net then became a web presence in 2000, bringing Morrissey fans the most up-to-date information about Morrissey. Although there have been websites run by his record labels, they have been more about his albums than about Morrissey personally. He does have an official Facebook page, but once again, it seems like it is run by his label and management. Morrissey only communicates personally with Julia and True-to-You.net—and it is usually an "official statement" about some controversy he is embroiled in or about some miscommunication regarding a situation he is involved in. Sometimes he will ask Julia to post fun stuff, like lists of favorites, and he will answer questions from True-to-You.net readers. I have always wanted to write in and ask him if he would consider doing a cover of "Billion Dollar Babies" with Alice Cooper (with Morrissey singing the Donovan part).

There are some fans who are haters and are jealous of Julia's relationship with Morrissey, and then there are some who accuse True-to-You.net of not being objective enough and "kissing ass" by pandering to Morrissey. Even if it is true, True-to-You.net serves as some sort of authentic social media relationship with Morrissey.

Julia Riley continues to be Morrissey's biggest fan by attending every concert (she has been to every Morrissey concert since 1992). He shows his appreciation by giving her a heads-up and a shout-out every night from the stage.

27

Get Off the Stage

Wolverhampton Civic Hall, England (December 22, 1988)

Wolverhampton is technically Morrissey's first solo show, yet it is also technically the last Smiths show. Confused? I was too.

Because the breakup of the Smiths was so quick, a farewell show was never planned or performed even though Morrissey felt like they owed their fans a proper goodbye. During the recording of the B-sides for "Everyday Is Like Sunday" and "Suedehead" in December 1988, Morrissey decided to throw a surprise concert to symbolize a transition from his time in the Smiths to his new solo career.

Morrissey decided on Wolverhampton because "it wasn't London and it wasn't Manchester."

The concert was announced on December 19, four days before it was scheduled to be held at the Wolverhampton Civic Hall. Guess what—it was also free admission to anyone who was wearing a Smiths or Morrissey T-shirt! People started to make their way to sleepy Wolverhampton in droves, camping out in line just to guarantee entrance to the show. But like most things in life, their place in line was not guaranteed due to the number of line jumpers and gate crashers. Despite room for only fifteen hundred concert goers, nearly three thousand fans showed up, causing a scene of chaos and "Moz-teria." When Morrissey and the band showed up in a stylish old 1940s bus, the waiting crowd got even crazier.

Morrissey's set only lasted about thirty minutes, with him and the band agreeing not to perform any Smiths songs that had been performed live with Johnny Marr. With that leaving pretty much just songs from *Strangeways, Here We Come*, the Smiths/solo set consisted of "Stop Me If You Think You've Heard This One Before," "Disappointed," "Interesting Drug," "Suedehead,"

"The Last of the Famous International Playboys," "Sister I'm a Poet," "Death at One's Elbow," and "Sweet and Tender Hooligan." The crowd, of course, went nuts at the sight of Morrissey and bombarded the stage throughout the performance, making it hard for Morrissey to even sing. Despite the uniqueness of the circumstances of this concert, it was indeed a proper farewell for what was left of the Smiths and a proper look into the future of what to expect from Morrissey's solo career.

Dublin National Stadium, Dublin (April 27, 1991)

For Morrissey's first concert as a solo artist and his first time on tour in more than four years, tickets sold out in just forty-seven minutes. Positively reviewed in the press everywhere, Morrissey was on top of his game, although the band still needed more time to grasp the songs. The crowd was wild with excitement and provided Morrissey with the welcome he had earned and deserved.

San Diego Sports Arena, San Diego (May 30, 1991)

Morrissey's first solo American tour was launched in San Diego. The first of a tradition of crazy Southern California concerts, San Diego was a great beginning to the *Kill Uncle* tour. Although a fan was hurt when she was pushed off the stage by security, the fans were excited and "wide to receive" Morrissey's inaugural performance.

Great Western Forum, Los Angeles (June 2, 1991)

Fourteen thousand tickets were sold out in a record fourteen minutes! This show started off as a typical Southern California Morrissey concert—lots of cheering and singing, sideburns, and fans rushing the stage. But then BAM! David Bowie joined Morrissey on stage for a duet on "Cosmic Dancer." Morrissey, the band, and the fans went nuts, making this concert an event of legendary status.

Southern California was ready for Morrissey. News outlets broadcast stories and interviews with Morrissey, and he and the band made an appearance on *The Tonight Show with Johnny Carson* before his performance at the Forum.

On June 2, 1991, Morrissey became an honorary Angeleno.

Starplex, Dallas (June 17, 1991)

Because of the craziness of the fans and the tightness of the band, Morrissey released the footage of this concert as the 1992 *Live in Dallas* home video. It was never professionally recorded or intended to be released, but after Morrissey saw the raw security footage, he decided that it had to be seen by everyone because it perfectly showed the chaos and charm of a Morrissey performance.

UCLA Pauley Pavilion, Los Angeles (November 1, 1991)

The crowd was unusually unruly the evening of November 1, and Morrissey helped encourage it. After inviting the crowd to come up on stage, Morrissey was warned by UCLA management to tone it down. Morrissey asked the crowd to settle down, but after the excitement of hearing his new song ("We Hate It When Our Friends Become Successful"), the crowd rushed even harder, and Morrissey and band were taken off stage and the rest of the show canceled. Fans were mad—chairs were thrown, fire alarms pulled, and merchandise stolen. After everything was said and done, forty-eight fans were injured during the riot. Because of this incident, venues throughout the rest of the tour were wary and overly strict about stage antics.

Madstock, Finsbury Park, London (August 8, 1992)

Madness was reuniting, and to celebrate, they threw a festival with numerous bands on the bill. Originally Morrissey was only to perform on Sunday, August 9, but he was added to the Saturday lineup after tickets were already sold. Because of the lack of Morrissey fans at the Saturday performance and the majority of the people there for Madness, the crowd became unruly. To make matters worse, Morrissey had a photo of a skinhead as his backdrop and waved the Union Jack flag around while performing. The crowd began to heckle and throw items at Morrissey, causing him to walk off the stage after nine songs. This is the event that really set fire to the "Morrissey is racist" rumors and was featured quite prominently in the *New Musical Express* and local news stories. Morrissey also declined to play the second night of Madstock.

Hollywood Bowl, Hollywood (October 10 and 11, 1992)

Thirty-five thousand tickets went on sale for these two shows on August 8, and they sold out in twenty-three minutes, breaking the previous record set by the Beatles.

Coachella Valley Music and Art Festival, Indio, California (October 9, 1999, and April 17, 2009)

Morrissey was one of the headliners of the inaugural Coachella Valley Music and Art Festival in 1999, performing in front of a crowd of fifty thousand in the blazing desert sun. His performance of "November Spawned a Monster" was featured in the 2006 documentary *Coachella*. Morrissey was invited back for the tenth anniversary of the festival, performing the first night ahead of

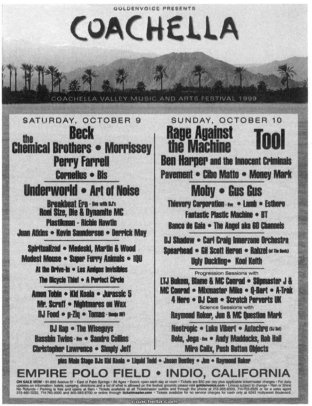

Morrissey's appearance at the first Coachella Valley Music and Arts Festival in 1999.   *Author's collection*

fellow vegetarian Paul McCartney. When an intense BBQ smell assaulted him during the performance of "When I Last Spoke to Carol," Morrissey uttered the following famous line that is still quoted today: "I can smell burning flesh and I hope to God it's human."

Morrissey left the stage, stating that the smell of burning animals was making him sick. Despite the BBQ aroma, Morrissey was able to come back on stage and finish the rest of his set.

MEN Arena, Manchester, May 22, (2004)

Although Morrissey had not performed in Manchester in twelve years, he decided to celebrate his forty-fifth birthday there with a grand performance. Eighteen thousand tickets for the concert were sold out in ninety minutes, and it was quite the homecoming for Morrissey—*You Are the Quarry* was at #2 on the charts, "Irish Blood, English Heart" was #3 on the Singles chart, and he looked and felt great.

Meltdown Festival 2004, Royal Festival Hall, London (June 11, 2004)

The Meltdown festival is an annual music and arts showcase that was created in 1993. Held in London at the South Bank Centre, what makes the Meltdown festival unique is that a different artist or musician is picked each year to select the acts and build a desirable program. Morrissey was chosen as the 2004 curator.

Morrissey himself played three times during the festival. His chosen acts were Sparks (who played both *L'il Beethoven* and *Kimono My House* in their entirety), Nancy Sinatra, Loudon Wainwright III, Jane Birkin, Cockney Rejects, Damien Dempsey, Gene, James Maker and Noko 440, Ennio Marchetteo, Lypsinka, the Ordinary Boys, the New York Dolls, Alan Bennett, the London Sinfonietta, and Linder Sterling. Ari Up of the Slits and the Libertines were also scheduled, but had to back out at the last minute. Maya Angelou and Bridgette Bardot were invited to perform at the Morrissey-curated 2004 Meltdown festival, but both declined.

The newly reunited New York Dolls played twice during the festival, with the second performance recorded and released as 2004's *Morrissey Presents: The Return of the New York Dolls*. Footage of their reunion and the days leading up to it are featured in the 2005 documentary *New York Doll*.

Morrissey picked his favorite bands, such as Sparks and the New York Dolls, to play his Meltdown festival in 2004.   *Author's collection*

Austin Music Hall, Austin (March 16, 2006)

Morrissey made his first appearance at SXSW. The crowd was receptive and Morrissey was in a playful mood. Keyboardist Michael Farrell played "Deep in the Heart of Texas" on the piano between "Life Is a Pigsty" and "Trouble Loves Me" to keep the mood light. Despite being "cool," many of the people in the crowd sang along with real and faux Texan pride.

BBC Radio Theatre (February 11, 2009)

To promote *Years of Refusal*, Morrissey decided to give a free concert that would be broadcast on BBC Radio 2. The remaster of *Southpaw Grammar* was due to be released around the same time, and because of that, Morrissey performed "Reader Meet Author" and, for the first time ever, "Best Friend on the Payroll."

Morrissey performed at the legendary Hollywood High in March 2013. The performance was released in theaters and on DVD/Blu-ray as *Morrissey: 25: Live.*   *Author's collection*

Hollywood High School, Hollywood (March 2, 2013)

Despite canceling most of his concerts this tour, Morrissey managed to pull himself together to perform his sold-out show at the Staples Center and this quickly arranged gig at the legendary Hollywood High School. This concert ended up being released on DVD and Blu-ray as *Morrissey: 25: Live* (2013 would mark Morrissey's twenty-fifth year being a solo artist). *Morrissey: 25: Live* made it to theaters in the US and UK, including IMAX 3D during the summer of 2013.

28

Because We Must

I t is a hard job to open up for Morrissey.

No one wants to see you. The crowd arrives late or spends their time drinking out in the lobby. And the ones who are there just want to see Morrissey.

Then they start to chant: MORRISSEY—MORRISSEY—MORRISSEY.

But you do it anyway. You get your band members together, you get your gear together, and you get your hopes and dreams together.

Some bands made it big, some bands made it work, and some bands barely made it.

Even if you hate Morrissey, you gotta give the man this—he's a touring machine. Sure, he's canceled some shows, but when you compare it to the number of shows he has performed, they're just a drop in the bucket. But because he tours and tours, there are quite a few opening bands. Most of them were one-night stands, but there are a few that managed to actually go on "tour" with him.

Bradford, Morrissey's First Concert/The Smiths' Farewell Concert (1988)

The so-called heirs to the Smiths' throne, Bradford is a five-piece band from Blackburn, England. With their sweet melodic sound and nontraditional indie pop look, they were an obvious choice to open for Morrissey's solo debut concert in Wolverhampton, England. Morrissey enjoyed their sound so much, he covered their 1988 single "Skin Storm." Bradford's debut album, *Shouting Quietly*, was produced by Smiths producer Stephen Street and released on his Foundation label.

Phranc, *Kill Uncle* Tour (1991)

Phranc is a Los Angeles–based singer-songwriter best known for meshing punk rock and folk music and for her androgynous look. She opened for Morrissey on most of his *Kill Uncle* tour (United States and abroad), but had to suddenly leave the tour when her brother was shot and killed back in Los Angeles. She rejoined the tour shortly after that and continued to play her style of smart and frank (or is it phrank?) folk rock.

Gallon Drunk, *Your Arsenal* Tour (1992)

Gallon Drunk is an English alternative band that opened up for Morrissey for the first leg of his American tour. With the songs from *Your Arsenal* being lighter in nature, Gallon Drunk's darker, edgier sound was a great compliment. After this tour and two full-length albums, Gallon Drunk's front man, James Johnston, joined the ultimate dark, edgy band: Nick Cave and the Bad Seeds.

Big Sandy and His Fly-Rite Boys, *Your Arsenal* Tour (1992)

With Morrissey's *Kill Uncle* tour and album having more of a rockabilly feel, it was slightly surprising that he selected Big Sandy and His Fly-Rite Boys to open for him on the second leg of his American tour. After catching

Gallon Drunk opens for Morrissey.   *Author's collection*

Big Sandy and His Fly-Rite Boys supported Morrissey during this leg of the American *Your Arsenal* tour in 1992.

Author's collection

their show one night in Los Angeles, Morrissey approached Big Sandy in the men's room and asked if they would go on tour with him. Big Sandy said yes, and they left the next day.

Marion, Boxers Tour (1995)

Marion is another band that has toured with Morrissey that was considered to be "the next Smiths," but real success eluded them until they broke up in 1999. This band is what started the "Morrissey Curse"—bands that Morrissey loves and takes on tour, but never become famous.

The Smoking Popes, *Maladjusted* Tour (1997)

The Smoking Popes are an American pop punk band that gained Morrissey's respect and attention with their second full-length release, 1994's *Born to Quit*. In a 2010 *New Musical Express* article, Morrissey picked *Born to Quit* as one of his thirteen favorite albums. Calling it "the most loveable thing I'd heard in years," Morrissey demonstrated his loyalty by playing "Midnight Moon," the first song on *Born to Quit*, during intermission on the first American leg of the *Maladjusted* tour. Audience members got to hear it performed live when the Smoking Popes joined the second leg of the tour.

The Killers, *You Are the Quarry* Tour (2004)

I remember the first time I heard the Killers.

I was in Tower Records (remember them?) to buy *You Are the Quarry* the day it was released. After grabbing my copy and heading toward the register, I heard "Somebody Told Me" playing overhead. At that time in my life, I was too cool for new music. But it was pretty catchy, and I thought it had a unique sound, so I made a mental note to find out who it was.

The Killers opened for Morrissey during his warm-up gigs before officially starting the *You Are the Quarry* tour, and shortly after headlined their own tour. They also opened up for him in Chicago later that year.

David Johansen, *You Are the Quarry* Tour (2004)

I'm sure teenage Morrissey never imagined that David Johansen would share the same stage as him, let alone open a concert for him. But it happened in 2004 on the *You Are the Quarry* tour. Just like the Killers, David opened up for Morrissey on some warm-up gigs at the Apollo Theater in New York. Later in 2004, David Johansen would join ex–band members Sylvain Sylvain and Arthur Kane to reunite the New York Dolls at the Meltdown festival, which was organized by Morrissey.

Damien Dempsey, *You Are the Quarry* Tour (2004)

Damien Dempsey is an Irish singer-songwriter who has been lauded for his insightful lyrics regarding life in past and present Ireland. Before he opened for Morrissey, he opened for Sinead O'Connor in 2002 and 2003 and for Bob Dylan on the Irish leg of his 2004 tour. Morrissey became a fan and took liking to him, inviting Damien to open for him on the European leg and American leg of the tour. Morrissey signed Damien to his Attack label and released his album *Seize the Day*.

Tiger Army, Tour of the Tormentors (2006)

Tiger Army is an acclaimed psychobilly band that has the honor of being the first opening band that was dismissed from a Morrissey tour. There are rumors galore as to why they were kicked off: Morrissey didn't like their "vibe," Morrissey didn't like that they smoked, Morrissey didn't like them eating meat on the tour, Tiger Army didn't like the sound crew, Tiger Army got a better audience reception than Morrissey—whatever the real case may be, only Morrissey and Tiger Army know what went down. They supported Morrissey on the American warm-up dates and the British leg of the tour.

Kristeen Young, Tour of the Tormentors (2006)

Morrissey discovered Kristeen Young while recording his *Ringleader of the Tormentors* album—while visiting producer Tony Visconti in the studio, he viewed a video of Kristeen Young performing and thought she was great. He then invited her to open up for him, taking the place of Tiger Army. She finished off the *Tour of the Tormentors* and proceeded to open up for him on the 2007 *Greatest Hits* tour.

Halfway through that tour, Kristeen herself was dismissed for responding inappropriately to hecklers in the crowd (she made a joke about Morrissey's oral sex skills). Morrissey must not have been that offended because he invited her back to open for him on his 2011 tour.

Other Bands That Opened for Morrissey (Usually Just Once or Twice)

- The Would-Be's (*Kill Uncle* tour)
- Melissa Ferrick (replacing Phranc for part of the *Kill Uncle* tour)
- The Johnson Family (*Kill Uncle* tour)
- The Planet Rockers (*Kill Uncle* tour)
- The Zip Guns (*Your Arsenal* tour)
- Jet Black Machine (*Your Arsenal* tour)
- The Well-Oiled Sisters (*Your Arsenal* tour)
- Kirsty MacColl and Shane McGowan (*Your Arsenal* tour)
- McAlmont (Boxers tour)
- Elcka (*Southpaw Grammar* tour)
- El Vez (*¡Oye Esteban!* tour)
- Sack (*¡Oye Esteban!* tour)
- Micro (*¡Oye Esteban!* tour)
- Konstantinos B (*¡Oye Esteban!* tour)
- Shrinking Violet (*¡Oye Esteban!* tour)
- Sigh (*¡Oye Esteban!* tour)
- Lovesick (*¡Oye Esteban!* tour)
- The Cultivators (*¡Oye Esteban!* tour)
- Promise Ring (*¡Oye Esteban!* tour)

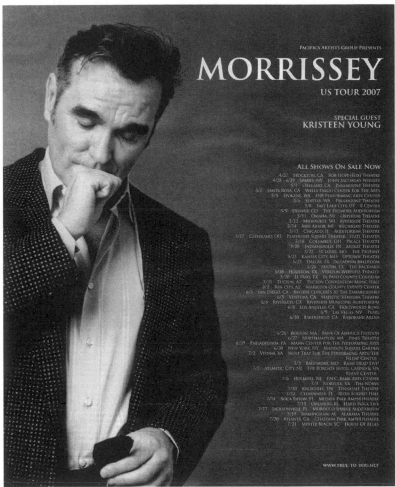

Morrissey toured the United States in support of his 2007 *Greatest Hits* album. Surprisingly enough, none of the concerts were canceled on this leg of the tour.

Author's collection

- Verbow (*¡Oye Esteban!* tour)
- Hawksley Workman (*¡Oye Esteban!* tour)
- Red Bank (*¡Oye Esteban!* tour)
- The Sheila Divine (*¡Oye Esteban!* tour)
- Black Beetle (*¡Oye Esteban!* tour)
- Phantom Planet (*¡Oye Esteban!* tour)
- King Cheetah (unnamed 2002 tour)
- Jumbo (unnamed 2002 tour)
- Los Jaguares (unnamed 2003 tour)

- Elefant (*You Are the Quarry* tour)
- The Shins (*You Are the Quarry* tour)
- Dios (*You Are the Quarry* tour)
- Franz Ferdinand (*You Are the Quarry* tour)
- The Dead 60s (*You Are the Quarry* tour)
- The Dears (*You Are the Quarry* tour)
- Nancy Sinatra (*You Are the Quarry* tour)
- James Maker (*You Are the Quarry* tour)
- PJ Harvey (*You Are the Quarry* tour)
- Remma (*You Are the Quarry* tour)
- The Boyfriends (Tour of the Tormentors)
- Sons and Daughters (Tour of the Tormentors)
- Girl in a Coma (*Greatest Hits* tour)
- Noise Is the Best Revenge (*Greatest Hits* tour)
- The New York Dolls (*Greatest Hits* tour)
- Red Cortez (Tour of Refusal)
- The Courteeners (Tour of Refusal)
- Doll and the Kicks (Tour of Refusal)
- Flats (unnamed 2011 tour)
- Brother (unnamed 2011 tour)
- Mona (unnamed 2011 tour)
- All the Young (unnamed 2011 tour)
- The Heartbreaks (unnamed 2011 tour)
- Patti Smith (unnamed 2013 tour)
- Tom Jones (unnamed 2014 tour)

29

Back to the Old House

Morrissey for Home Viewing

I t's no secret about Morrissey's love of old movies, and when you watch his music videos, you can see where that love shines through. Always a little dramatic, always with a little thought, Morrissey's video compilations and live concert footage have always been more than your typical promotional release.

VHS Releases

Hulmerist (1990, released on DVD in 2004)

Released when "Moz-teria" was at its peak, *Hulmerist* (named after Hulme, the district of Morrissey's first childhood home) showcases seven short films/videos and concert footage of his first quasi-solo concert on December 22, 1988, in Wolverhampton, England (quasi-solo meaning he performed both Morrissey solo and the Smiths songs, but had Johnny Marr–less Smiths as his backing band).

The video listing is as follows:

1. "The Last of the Famous International Playboys"
2. "Sister I'm a Poet"
3. "Everyday Is Like Sunday"
4. "Interesting Drug"

MORRISSEY
"HULMERIST"
The
first
Video
Collection

DIGITALLY MASTERED

The last of the Famous International Playboys
Everyday is like Sunday
Interesting Drug
Suedehead
Ouija Board, Ouija Board
November Spawned a Monster

PLUS BONUS TRACK
Sister I'm a Poet and specially edited footage from the celebrated Civic Hall Wolverhampton concert in 1988

Hulmerist was Morrissey's first video compilation as a solo artist.

Author's collection

5.   "Suedehead"
6.   "Ouija Board, Ouija Board"
7.   "November Spawned a Monster"

Live in Dallas (1992, released on DVD in 2000)

Never meant to be released, it was released commercially after Morrissey reviewed the security footage and liked its raw, unbiased look at what a real Morrissey concert was really like: the crazed fans rushing the stage, the thumping beat of his new rockabilly-ish band, and Morrissey in all of his big-head-of-hair-and-no-chest-hair prime.

The set list is as follows:

1.   "The Last of the Famous International Playboys"
2.   "Interesting Drug"
3.   "Piccadilly Palare"
4.   "Trash" (New York Dolls cover)
5.   "Sing Your Life"
6.   "King Leer"
7.   "Asian Rut"
8.   "Mute Witness"
9.   "November Spawned a Monster"
10. "Will Never Marry"
11. "Angel, Angel, Down We Go"
12. "There's a Place in Hell for Me and My Friends"
13. "That's Entertainment"
14. "Our Frank"
15. "Suedehead"
16. "Everyday Is Like Sunday"

The Malady Lingers On (1992, released on DVD in 2004)

The second compilation of videos released by Morrissey, most of the songs are from his 1992 album, *Your Arsenal* (with the exception of "My Love Life," "Sing Your Life," and "Pregnant for the Last Time").

The video listing is as follows:

1.   "Glamorous Glue"
2.   "Certain People I Know"
3.   "Tomorrow"

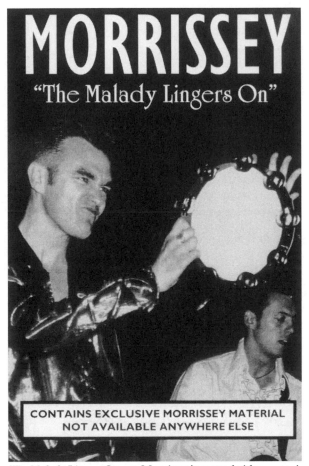

The Malady Lingers On was Morrissey's second video compilation. *Author's collection*

4. "We Hate It When Our Friends Become Successful"
5. "My Love Life"
6. "You're the One for Me, Fatty"
7. "Sing Your Life"
8. "Pregnant for the Last Time"

Introducing Morrissey (1996, released on DVD in 2014)

Yet another look at the revelry of a typical Morrissey concert. Back on his native soil, this concert shows a slightly matured Morrissey, full of sideburns and sass. As with most Morrissey concerts, this one begins with a short black-and-white film showing several Morrissey-important landmarks with the singer himself making a cameo.

The set list is as follows:

1.   "Billy Budd"
2.   "Have-a-Go Merchant"
3.   "Spring-Heeled Jim"
4.   "You're the One for Me, Fatty"
5.   "The More You Ignore Me, the Closer I Get"
6.   "Whatever Happens, I Love You"
7.   "We'll Let You Know"
8.   "Jack the Ripper"
9.   "Why Don't You Find Out for Yourself"
10. "The National Front Disco"
11. "Moon River"
12. "Hold On to Your Friends"
13. "Boxers"
14. "Now My Heart Is Full"
15. "Speedway"

Introducing Morrissey was Morrissey's second concert film. It had only been available on VHS until 2014 when it was officially released on DVD.   *Author's collection*

DVD Releases

¡Oye Esteban! (2000)

True story: I bought a DVD player just so I could watch this DVD. And that's when DVD players were expensive!

Released in 2000, *¡Oye Esteban!* is a compilation of Morrissey videos from throughout his solo career. It's kind of a weird compilation—it doesn't include all of his previously released videos (like "Ouija Board, Ouija Board" and "Sister I'm a Poet"), yet it has a rare, hardly seen promo video for "Seasick Yet Still Docked." Despite this, it is still a great compilation for newbie fans to watch and learn about all that is Morrissey, and it's a great refresher course for the Morrissey Expert.

I don't have the DVD player anymore, but you know I still have the DVD!

The video listing is as follows:

1. "Everyday Is Like Sunday"
2. "Suedehead"
3. "Will Never Marry"
4. "November Spawned a Monster"
5. "Interesting Drug"
6. "The Last of the Famous International Playboys"
7. "My Love Life"
8. "Sing Your Life"
9. "Seasick Yet Still Docked"
10. "We Hate It When Our Friends Become Successful"
11. "Glamorous Glue"
12. "Tomorrow"
13. "You're the One for Me, Fatty"
14. "The More You Ignore Me, the Closer I Get"
15. "Pregnant for the Last Time"
16. "Boxers"
17. "Dagenham Dave"
18. "The Boy Racer"
19. "Sunny"

Who Put the M in Manchester? (2005)

This DVD showcases a Morrissey concert hat trick: it was the first official concert date of his comeback *You Are the Quarry* tour, it was his Manchester homecoming (it was the first time he had played Manchester in twelve years), and it was his forty-fifth birthday! Unlike *Live in Dallas* and *Introducing Morrissey*, this live concert DVD is professionally shot with lots of bonus non-concert footage (such as audience interviews and Manchester scenery) and actually has DVD extras.

My favorite part of the DVD? Morrissey's performance of "Jack the Ripper"—it's filmed in both color and black and white (for dramatic purposes), and he sings it so hauntingly beautifully. He ends the concert with "There Is a Light That Never Goes Out," and it's a perfect description of Morrissey's career at that point.

Who Put the M in Manchester? was filmed at Morrissey's forty-fifth birthday concert in Manchester, documenting his triumphant return to his hometown.   *Author's collection*

The set list is as follows:

1. "First of the Gang to Die"
2. "Hairdresser on Fire"
3. "Irish Blood, English Heart"
4. "The Headmaster Ritual"
5. "Subway Train" (New York Dolls cover) and "Everyday Is Like Sunday"
6. "I Have Forgiven Jesus"
7. "I Know It's Gonna Happen Someday"
8. "How Can Anybody Possibly Know How I Feel?"
9. "Rubber Ring"
10. "Such a Little Thing Makes Such a Big Difference"
11. "Don't Make Fun of Daddy's Voice"
12. "The World Is Full of Crashing Bores"
13. "Let Me Kiss You"
14. "No One Can Hold a Candle to You" (Raymonde cover)
15. "Jack the Ripper"
16. "A Rush and a Push and the Land Is Ours"
17. "I'm Not Sorry"
18. "Shoplifters of the World Unite"
19. "There Is a Light That Never Goes Out"

DVD Extras

Move Festival 2004

1. "First of the Gang to Die"
2. "I Have Forgiven Jesus"
3. "Everyday Is Like Sunday"
4. "There Is a Light That Never Goes Out"
5. "Irish Blood, English Heart"

Music Videos

1. "Irish Blood, English Heart"
2. "First of the Gang to Die" (UK version)
3. "First of the Gang to Die" (US version)
4. "I Have Forgiven Jesus"

25: Live (2013, also available on Blu-ray)

Despite a year of illness, Morrissey managed to get it together to enough to throw an impromptu gig at Hollywood High the day after his sold-out show at the Staples Center in Los Angeles. To mark this momentous occasion, he decided to use the footage from this concert to make a new concert film. *25: Live* was released both in theaters and on DVD/Blu-ray. The sound quality is amazing, it's crisp and clear, the band is tight, and Morrissey sounds wonderful. I almost bought tickets to this show, but I was afraid he was going to cancel (he was sick through much of 2013). After viewing this show, I was mad that I didn't.

The set list is as follows:

1. "Alma Matters"
2. "Ouija Board, Ouija Board"
3. "Irish Blood, English Heart"
4. "You Have Killed Me"
5. "November Spawned a Monster"
6. "Maladjusted"
7. "You're the One for Me, Fatty"
8. "Still Ill"
9. "People Are the Same Everywhere"
10. "Speedway"
11. "The Joke Isn't Funny Anymore"
12. "To Give (The Reason I Live)" (Frankie Valli cover)
13. "Meat Is Murder"
14. "Please, Please, Please Let Me Get What I Want"
15. "Action Is My Middle Name"
16. "Everyday Is Like Sunday"
17. "I'm Throwing My Arms Around Paris"
18. "Let Me Kiss You"
19. "The Boy with the Thorn in His Side"

30

Everything They've Seen on the Moving Screen

Morrissey's Music Videos

"No. We want to bypass the whole video market. I think it's something that's going to die very quickly. I want to herald the death of that. I think it has nothing whatsoever to do with music, and I want to get back to total music."

—Morrissey, after being asked if the Smiths plan on making a video for their first two singles

S ays the man who made a music video of him humping a rock! For someone who hated videos so much, he sure made some great ones. Granted, all people while young say stupid things, and he may have truly believed that at that time. But with MTV and other video programs becoming the next big addiction, Morrissey knew that eventually he would have to jump on the video bandwagon.

On the flip side, after MTV really stopped being MTV and music videos were delegated to YouTube and iTunes, Morrissey's music videos stopped being "creative" and started being more "functional." I get that records need to be sold, but when the man responsible for a great video like "Ouija Board, Ouija Board" settles for numerous videos of performance footage, it seems like the videos are just an afterthought and not a companion piece.

Still, there are some truly great Morrissey video moments. Grab some veggie chips, pull up YouTube, and enjoy these music videos.

"Suedehead" (1988)

For Morrissey's first music video as a solo artist, he decided to go with something familiar to him (and everyone else) and showcase James Dean and his hometown of Fairmount, Indiana. Directed by Morrissey friend Tim Broad, "Suedehead" had Morrissey enjoying life in Fairmount, doing such Midwestern things as reading *Le Petit Prince* at a stoplight, taking a photo of a Dairy Queen, and wearing a hat. When he is not walking around town freezing his ass off, he rests it on James Dean's Indian motorcycle and on the snow-covered ground as he visits Dean's grave. There was actually a first version of the "Suedehead" video that was not approved by the James Dean estate. Both videos feature a shot of a letter written by Dean, but in the banned version, the shot focuses on the line "I want to die" instead of the "nondying" letter shown in the official video. Also, the cute little boy bringing Morrissey a letter in the beginning of the video (before he visits Fairmount) is Morrissey's nephew Sam.

The "Suedehead" video is featured on the video compilations *Hulmerist*, *¡Oye Esteban!*, and *Very Best of Morrissey*.

"Everyday Is Like Sunday" (1988)

To continue the theme of familiarity, "Everyday Is Like Sunday" has quite a few recurring moments. Taking place in Southend-on-Sea in Essex (which basically is the "seaside town" Morrissey sings about), "Everyday Is Like Sunday" features a young woman milling about, doing everything from watching a Morrissey video on a display window TV (that is quickly changed from Morrissey to *Carry On Abroad*, one of Morrissey's favorite movies) to giving an "etched postcard" about animal rights to an old woman with a fur coat. She is eventually picked up by her mother and taken home, where she proceeds to look out the window through a telescope. Guess who is on the other end of the telescope? Not Orion, but Morrissey, acting embarrassed to be seen through a telescope. Also, his hair in epic proportions. Seriously, like Kid 'n Play huge.

The young woman in the "Everyday Is Like Sunday" video is Lucette Henderson, who is also in the Smiths' "Stop Me If You Think You've Heard This One Before" video and "I Started Something I Couldn't Finish" video. It also features *Coronation Street* actress Cheryl Campbell-Murray and actress and Smiths album cover girl Billie Whitelaw.

The "Everyday Is Like Sunday" video is featured on the video compilations *Hulmerist*, *¡Oye Esteban!*, and *Very Best of Morrissey*. Directed by Tim Broad.

"The Last of the Famous International Playboys" (1989)

Those who clamor for a Smiths reunion should watch this video, because it is the closest they will ever get. Ex-Smiths Andy Rourke, Mike Joyce, and Craig "The Fifth Smith" Gannon perform with Morrissey against a green background cut with footage of a young Judd Nelson-esqe man shadowboxing in his room and running through town. It is not the Coachella reunion of your dreams, but it's not bad.

The video for "The Last of the Famous International Playboys" is featured on the video compilations *Hulmerist*, *¡Oye Esteban!*, and *Very Best of Morrissey*. Directed by Tim Broad.

"Interesting Drug" (1989)

This video starts with a group of schoolboys hanging out in the restroom, wearing high heels, writing Morrissey lyric graffiti, and reading the *New Musical Express*. There is also a mad woman riding a bike around town, protesting various causes. The boys run into her outside of the school, and then they all run into Morrissey (who is handing out animal rights literature), and then they liberate a bunch of lab rabbits. Scenes of Morrissey performing with the Nu-Smiths are cut in throughout.

The "Interesting Drug" video is featured on the video compilations *Hulmerist*, *¡Oye Esteban!*, and *Very Best of Morrissey*. Directed by Tim Broad.

"Ouija Board, Ouija Board" (1989)

"Ouija Board, Ouija Board" is one of my favorite Morrissey videos because it is so wonderfully campy. It starts with Morrissey sitting on his couch holding a Ouija board, looking sad. A medium lures him into the forest to give him a card reading. After the table rumbles, he is thrown onto the ground, and then his creepy zombie friend appears and chases him home. I do not think that she is really his friend, because zombies are pretty carnivorous.

All of this happened without him actually using the Ouija board.

The medium is played by *Carry On . . .* actress Joan Sims, and the zombie girl is played by actress/comedian Kathy Burke, who also appears in the 2002 documentary *The Importance of Being Morrissey*.

The "Ouija Board, Ouija Board" video is only featured on the video compilation *Hulmerist*. Directed by Tim Broad.

Morrissey stirs up trouble trying to get through to an old friend in the "Ouija Board, Ouija Board" video.   *Author's collection*

"November Spawned a Monster" (1990)

Whenever you bring up Morrissey videos, the first thing everyone says is "UGH! That video of him humping a rock!" Yes, that video of him humping a rock.

And that video of him with an apple in his mouth like a luau pig.

And that video of him with a Band-Aid on his nipple.

The video for "November Spawned a Monster" is so ridiculous it's brilliant.

In case you've been living under an unhumped rock, the video is basically Morrissey writhing around with and without his shirt in the desert of Death Valley. Sometimes he's pouting and kicking sand, other times he's sensually licking a bar of chocolate, and most of the time he's spastically dancing among the Joshua trees and sand dunes. And he's also wearing a hearing aid, because why not?

A still from the "November Spawned a Monster" video also spawned the album cover for *Bona Drag* (except his shirt is photoshopped red instead of the black from the video). This video also has the honor of having been "critiqued" by Beavis and Butthead in their 1994 episode "Blackout."

Morrissey tending to his sweet tooth in the "November Spawned a Monster" video.   *Author's collection*

The "November Spawned a Monster" video is featured on the video compilations *Hulmerist, ¡Oye Esteban!,* and *Very Best of Morrissey.* Directed by Tim Broad.

"Sister I'm a Poet" (1990)

Although not a real "music video," this vignette of Morrissey's first solo performance with the Nu-Smiths at Wolverhampton is included on the video compilation *Hulmerist.* It is your typical scene from a Morrissey concert: Morrissey's bare chest and sweaty dudes running up on stage. Directed by Tim Broad.

"Our Frank" (1991)

Did you know that Morrissey made a video for this single?

Me neither, until I wrote this book. I guess I am not the uber-fan I thought I was.

The reason you have never seen this video is that it was only released on the Japanese "Sing Your Life" video single. The video for "Our Frank" was video *non grata* because of the skinhead footage sprinkled throughout the video. Okay, like 80 percent of the video is skinheads. The other 20 percent is Morrissey's eyebrow Band-Aid. With talk of his "racist leanings" growing, the label squashed the release of the video.

Although it is not officially or commercially available, you can view the video for "Our Frank" on YouTube. Directed by James Maybury.

"Sing Your Life" (1991)

Morrissey and his "new" band (Boz Boorer, Gary Day, Spencer Cobrin, and Alain Whyte) make their first official video appearance as a, you guessed it, rockabilly band. Chrissie Hynde of the Pretenders makes a cameo as a dancing girl at the social club where they are performing.

The "Sing Your Life" video is featured on the video compilations *The Malady Lingers On*, *¡Oye Esteban!*, and *Very Best of Morrissey*. Directed by Tim Broad.

"Pregnant for the Last Time" (1991)

In "Pregnant for the Last Time," Morrissey and his band are hanging out in Germany while on the road for the *Kill Uncle* tour. They do stuff like buy Jobriath records and write on tambourines. The live footage is assumed to have been filmed on German dates, such as Berlin or Cologne.

The "Pregnant for the Last Time" video is featured on the video compilations *The Malady Lingers On* and *¡Oye Esteban!* Directed by Tim Broad.

"My Love Life" (1991)

Morrissey and his band cruise along the boulevard in Phoenix, Arizona. His band was pretty brave, considering that Morrissey was an unlicensed driver when this video was made. Lots of Americana was driven past, such as a cool tiki-themed motel, bus stops, and an Earl Schieb Auto Paint & Body.

The "My Love Life" video is featured on the video compilations *The Malady Lingers On*, *¡Oye Esteban!*, and *Very Best Of Morrissey*. Directed by Tim Broad.

"We Hate It When Our Friends Become Successful" (1992)

A fan favorite, the "We Hate It When Our Friends Become Successful" video ushered in the Satin Shirt Era for Morrissey as he and his band members hang out in an abandoned building and empty field. Reminiscent of the Mentos commercials of the time—they frolic around, pose against beams, and enjoy Drumsticks—this video is well known for its sensual ice cream scene. Cathal Smyth, a.k.a. Chas Smash, from the band Madness makes a cameo by the way of photograph—that is him in a hat that is flashed on the screen twice.

The "We Hate It When Our Friends Become Successful" video is featured on the video compilations *The Malady Lingers On* and *¡Oye Esteban!* Directed by Tim Broad.

"You're the One for Me, Fatty" (1992)

Despite the fact that the "fatty" in the title refers once again to Chas Smash of Madness, the video for "You're the One for Me, Fatty" focuses on a fat girl out on a picnic with her dorky boyfriend. I guess some girls really ARE bigger than others. I am just shocked that this video was not added to the "Morrissey is a racist" list because of the black Americana "Mammy" cookie jar the girl eats cookies from. I guess this one slipped passed the *New Musical Express.*

Morrissey and his band also perform in a boring building. And his shiny red satin shirt is fabulous!

The "You're the One for Me, Fatty" video is featured on the video compilations *The Malady Lingers On* and *¡Oye Esteban!* Directed by Tim Broad.

"Certain People I Know" (1992)

The "Certain People I Know" video had a few firsts going on. It was the first official video not directed by Tim Broad. Also a first: Morrissey chest hair. He and the band hang out at a Chicago beach and enjoy the sunshine.

The "Certain People I Know" video is only featured on the video compilation *The Malady Lingers On.* Directed by George Tiffin.

"Tomorrow" (1992)

As I stated in the introduction, this is the video that did it for me. Morrissey and his band stroll through the streets of Nice, France, in black and white with plenty of pouting and ironic gazes. There are technically three versions of this video: the original one mentioned above, which is the most familiar; a shorter version (by twelve seconds) on *The Malady Lingers On;* and a US-only version that has additional bonus footage.

The "Tomorrow" video is featured on the video compilations *The Malady Lingers On, ¡Oye Esteban!,* and *Very Best of Morrissey.* Directed by Zack Snyder.

"Glamorous Glue" (1992)

Morrissey is rocking both the joint and the gold satin shirt in this video for "Glamorous Glue." The Chicago blues bar location is perfect for the thumping blues beat of this song. Moz and the band also befriend a cat and attempt to feed it some cat food. Feeding cats is another recurring theme in Morrissey's videos (see "Alma Matters").

The "Glamorous Glue" video is featured on the video compilations *The Malady Lingers On*, *¡Oye Esteban!*, and *Very Best of Morrissey*. Directed by George Tiffin.

"The More You Ignore Me, the Closer I Get" (1994)

Easily the sexiest video he has ever made, "The More You Ignore Me, the Closer I Get" features a surprisingly threatening Morrissey. In a dimly lit hallway, Morrissey tells us to beware and that he is going to creep into our thoughts. Silly Morrissey—you are already in my thoughts!

Pictures of Morrissey and actor David Baxter line the walls of the hallway as a copy of the "The More You Ignore Me, the Closer I Get" single burns (after all, it was Morrissey's only single to chart on the Billboard Hot 100).

Morrissey shines on in the video for "Glamorous Glue" during the Satin Shirt Era (1991–1992).   *Author's collection*

The cute little girl who is featured and then eventually abducted is Boz Boorer's daughter Billie-Rose.

The "The More You Ignore Me, the Closer I Get" video is featured on the video compilations *¡Oye Esteban!* and *Very Best Of Morrissey*. Directed by Mark Romanek.

"Boxers" (1995)

The "Boxers" video is exactly what it sounds like: boxers boxing.

Featuring boxer Cornelius Carr and Morrissey (who makes a last-second appearance toward the end of the video), it is a decent watch. The album covers for *World of Morrissey* and the Smiths' 1995 "Sweet and Tender Hooligan" compact disc single use stills from this video.

The "Boxers" video is featured on the video compilations *¡Oye Esteban!* and *Very Best of Morrissey*. Directed by James O'Brien.

"Dagenham Dave" (1995)

In this video, Morrissey is the narrator and intertwines with Dagenham Dave while he's out on a date with a lovely woman. Dave's pretty much a schmuck, and his date finally gets sick of his crap and takes off with the Boy Racer (see "The Boy Racer"). During the lyric "I love Karen, I love Sharon on the window screen," Dave is shown sticking Karen's name on the windshield above the passenger side, then ripping it off hastily and putting up Sharon's name instead (his date throughout the video is never identified as either Karen or Sharon) and then finally Moz's. I researched this phenomenon of putting someone's name your windshield and learned that it's a predominately UK thing to do (they're actually called "sun strips"). I'm guessing it's the US equivalent of putting one of those stick figure families on the back window (or even worse—one of those "My Baby Died RIP Forever" stickers).

The "Dagenham Dave" video is only featured on the video compilation *¡Oye Esteban!* It was included with the 2009 remastered edition of the *Southpaw Grammar* album on iTunes. Directed by James O'Brien.

"The Boy Racer" (1995)

"The Boy Racer" video tells the story of the Boy Racer after he picks up Dagenham Dave's date. He must have dumped her because she's nowhere to be seen, and he spends his nights cruising around looking for more chicks. He ends up charming a couple of birds after he makes them drop their fish 'n' chips due to his racing. Morrissey and his band are cut in throughout the video, performing in a strobe-lit room. His face is cut up and bruised, keeping with the "boxing" theme of his 1995 tour.

These last two videos (and *Southpaw Grammar* in general) are the closest thing to a concept album Morrissey has ever done. Granted, it's no *Kilroy Was Here* by Styx, but keeping certain faces and themes together is a nice nod and wink to the hardcore fans.

The "The Boy Racer" video is only featured on the video compilation *¡Oye Esteban!* It was included with the 2009 remastered edition of the *Southpaw Grammar* album on iTunes. Directed by James O'Brien.

"Sunny" (1995)

"Sunny" is the weakest video in the Morrissey catalog. It features three teens hanging out at Victoria Park in East London, and the best part of the video is when one of the teens takes a bite out of a sandwich and spits it out. Probably because it had meat.

The "Sunny" video is featured on the video compilations *¡Oye Esteban!* and *Very Best of Morrissey*. A slightly different version is included on the *My Early Burglary Years* compact disc as an extra. The only difference is that Morrissey performs an introduction of the video with handwritten slides. Directed by James O' Brien.

"Will Never Marry" (1995)

No wonder Morrissey is sick all the time! With people constantly climbing on stage and kissing, hugging, licking, sweating, and bump-n-grinding on him during performances, I am surprised Morrissey is not a germaphobe.

The "Will Never Marry" video features footage from a 1990 live performance of "Disappointed." The video starts off with the fans gathering and waiting in line for his performance. One of the first shots is of a girl showing off her Henry Rollins tattoo. Another is holding up a hand-written sign that states "Because We Must." Because we must climb on stage and tackle Morrissey? Maybe.

The sweat and sideburns are flyin' as guy after guy (and a few gals) rush the stage to invade Morrissey's personal space. Here's the true shocker: "Disappointed" clocks in at 3:05, so that many people crashed the stage in that short amount of time. It was actually more people than that because "Will Never Marry" only runs 2:22.

This footage was added to the end of the *Introducing Morrissey* VHS and the *¡Oye Esteban!* DVD compilation, even though it was never "technically" an official Morrissey music video.

"Alma Matters" (1997)

"Alma Matters" is surprisingly bad-ass (for a Morrissey video). He hangs out in an abandoned building and starts off by eating plain cake donuts and giving some to a cat. First off, who eats plain cake donuts? Second, the cat lives in an abandoned building; it needs a home, not sweets. Once again, we have the skinheads showing up and fighting among each other. One of the skinhead girls starts yelling at Morrissey while he tries to eat some cereal. Finally sick of listening to her tripe, he throws the bowl of cereal in her face! Take that, skinheads!

Unfortunately, "Alma Matters" isn't available on any Morrissey video compilations due to Mercury Records holding the rights to it. But it's available on YouTube (for now), and I highly recommend watching it.

Morrissey and his furry friend take on skinheads in the video for "Alma Matters." *Author's collection*

"Seasick Yet Still Docked" (2000)

Although "Seasick Yet Still Docked" had come out almost a decade earlier, the video was finally finished in 2000 to be included on the *¡Oye Esteban!* video compilation. It's a beautiful video for a beautiful song—Morrissey sings close to the camera while old family photographs flash on the screen in black and white.

The "Seasick Yet Still Docked" video is only featured on the video compilation *¡Oye Esteban!* Directed by Charles Wittenmeier.

"Irish Blood, English Heart" (2004)

In the first video released from his triumphant comeback album, *You Are the Quarry*, it was nice to see Morrissey looking great and on top of his game, but the video is pretty meh. He and the band are playing in the basement of an old building surrounded by hipsters too cool to rock out. I'd totally be rocking out!

The "Irish Blood, English Heart" video is featured on the CD/DVD release and the deluxe release of *You Are the Quarry*. It is also an extra on the *Who Put the M in Manchester?* DVD. Directed by Bucky Fukumoto.

"First of the Gang to Die" (2004)

There are two different versions of the "First of the Gang to Die" video, and they're both extremely lazy. The first version is just Morrissey's performance of the song from the *Who Put the M in Manchester?* live performance DVD, and the second version is of the same performance, but there's behind-the-scenes footage and fan footage cut throughout.

The first version of "First of the Gang to Die" is featured on the DVD single, and the second version is featured on the deluxe edition of *You Are the Quarry*. Both versions appear as extras on the *Who Put the M in Manchester?* DVD. Directed by Bucky Fukumoto.

"I Have Forgiven Jesus" (2004)

Maybe it's because I didn't grow up Catholic, but Morrissey in a priest outfit gets me all kinds of hot. That's why you must watch the video for "I Have Forgiven Jesus." Father Morrissey walks with his band down the street in a broken down park of Los Angeles. He carried the priest theme for a little while: he performed in the priest outfit for his Halloween 2004 concert and had posters of himself dressed as a priest at the merch table in 2007.

The video for "I Have Forgiven Jesus" is featured on the compact disc single and as an extra on the *Who Put the M in Manchester?* DVD. Directed by Bucky Fukumoto.

"There Is a Light That Never Goes Out" (2005)

The video for "There Is a Light That Never Goes Out" is yet another mix of concert footage. It was made specifically to promote the single and the *Who Put the M in Manchester?* DVD.

It appears on the "Redondo Beach"/"There Is a Light That Never Goes Out" compact disc single and as an extra on the *Who Put the M in Manchester?* DVD.

"You Have Killed Me" (2006)

As a lover of anything old and crappy-looking, I find this video is totally up my alley. Made to look like a 1970s Eurovision performance, Morrissey pulls out all the stops (and pays the big bucks) to make such an authentic-looking period piece (real 1970s Eurovision footage was even used). The tape skips and is discolored in certain places, the crowd is very 1970s Italian, and Morrissey himself is rocking the white Fantasy Island suit. Considering

Do you like Eurovision? Morrissey sure does. The video for "You Have Killed Me" was his first homage to the singing competition.   *Author's collection*

Morrissey's love of Sandie Shaw and Lulu (both Eurovision winners) and his own almost-entry into the contest in 2007, this video is entirely appropriate.

The video for "You Have Killed Me" is featured on the limited edition version of *Ringleader of the Tormentors* and on the compact disc single. Directed by Bucky Fukumoto.

"The Youngest Was the Most Loved" (2006)

After being arrested in the "The Boy Racer" video, Morrissey once again finds himself on the wrong side of the law. It must have been for something good, because the paparazzi is crazy as he is led by policemen (who are played by his band members) out to a waiting car.

The video for "The Youngest Was the Most Loved" is included on the compact disc single. Directed by the AV Club.

"In the Future When All's Well" (2006)

Once again, Morrissey finds himself performing back in time at a 1970s Eurovision contest. I'm not trying to cheap out on writing about this video, but seriously—go two paragraphs up and reread "You Have Killed Me." It's the exact same thing.

The video for "In the Future When All's Well" is featured on the limited edition version of *Ringleader of the Tormentors* and on the compact disc single. Directed by Bucky Fukumoto.

"That's How People Grow Up" (2009)

"That's How People Grow Up" is pretty much the same idea as the video for "Will Never Marry," except nineteen years later. A less sensitive, more smug Morrissey performs at the Hollywood Bowl in front of a sold-out crowd. Unlike the "Will Never Marry" video, this one shows clips from throughout the 2007 *Greatest Hits* tour (though it's mostly footage from the Hollywood Bowl gig). Morrissey starts the video in his snappy white Fantasy Island suit, but ends the video as a rumpled mess. Hollywood does that you.

The video for "That's How People Grow Up" is available for purchase on iTunes to help promote 2009's *Greatest Hits* album. It also comes with the purchase of the *Greatest Hits* album itself via iTunes. Directed by Bucky Fukumoto.

"All You Need Is Me" (2009)

For such a simple video, it really is brilliant. "All You Need Is Me" is just Morrissey and the band hanging out in a tropical-looking backyard performing, joking around, and having a good time. There is also footage of each individual band member playing his instrument in a studio and Morrissey and the guys walking around Los Angeles. I think they forgot that nobody walks in LA.

The video for "All You Need Is Me" is featured on the CD/DVD version of *Years of Refusal.* Directed by Patrick O'Dell.

"I'm Throwing My Arms Around Paris" (2009)

Morrissey and the band play in a white room with little dogs (pugs) at their feet. Why not French bulldogs? Or poodles? The song is only called "I'm Throwing My Arms Around Paris." Boz does rock an awesome clarinet solo, though. Directed by Travis Shinn.

31

The Harsh Truth of the Camera Eye

Morrissey on Television

Top of the Pops (1983)

It was the first of many lip-synced performances by the Smiths, but this one was special because it was their first, with "This Charming Man" reaching #30 on the charts. This clip has it all—Morrissey with a raggedy shirt ripped open exposing his chest, waving around a bouquet of flowers, and Johnny being cool and flipping his hair out of his face. The Smiths would end up appearing on *Top of the Pops* a total of eleven times during their short career.

Data Run and SPLAT! (1983, 1984)

A clever marketing ploy or they were just down with the kids, the Smiths appeared on both *Data Run* and *SPLAT!* in 1983 and 1984. Both shows were morning programs on the new and fledgling TV-AM that were aimed at children eight to fourteen. *Data Run* aired from 1983 to 1984 and was replaced in 1984 by *SPLAT!* Both shows featured music videos, cartoons, interviews, and anything else that appealed to England's youth.

The Smiths' segment on *Data Run* gets the award for "Creepiest Appearance Ever." Morrissey and Johnny Marr visit an elementary school and are asked a few questions by the kids (Morrissey is referred to as "Paul Morrissey" during this segment). They also sing a couple of lines of "This Charming Man" with the kids kicking in on the chorus, and there's rehearsal footage with the obligatory Sandie Shaw cameo. If they had just left it at that, it would have been a cute and lightly educational piece. But the producers decided to add a touch of "whimsy" and cut in scenes of creepy-looking puppets reading a magazine and then fighting with each other. Between this and the hideous sweater Morrissey wears during the rehearsal footage, it is a pretty scary and heavily dated segment.

The *SPLAT!* footage is worlds better. "Charlie's Bus" was the name of the music segment on *SPLAT!*, and it featured up-and-coming bands on a double-decker bus full of school kids as they go on an adventure. The Smiths join the kids as they visit the Royal Botanic Gardens and Kew (a.k.a. Kew Gardens), and after an afternoon of learning about botany, Sandie Shaw and a guitar magically appear and she and Johnny perform "Jeane." What most people remember and love about this segment is Morrissey's interaction with a smart little girl:

Morrissey enjoys himself on a double-decker bus (that has not yet crashed) with a group of schoolchildren on the children's show *SPLAT!*
Author's collection

Morrissey (who goes by "Paul Morrissey" in this clip) and Johnny Marr jam out a bit with school kids and creepy puppets on the children's show *Data Run.*   *Author's collection*

> Little Girl: "Where are we going?"
>
> Morrissey: "We're going mad."
>
> Little Girl: "I thought we were going to Kew Gardens?"

Morrissey turns towards the camera and gives the best smirk known to man.

These two clips are Morrissey fan favorites because they show a real human side to Morrissey. Even by this point in his career, he was getting a reputation for being aloof, and by interacting and having fun with kids, it showed that he was not constantly a downer.

The Tube (1984)

Some may call it pompous; others call it being self-assured. I call it keeping it real.

Morrissey's first television interview was in January 1984 for the television show *The Tube*, a few weeks before the release of the Smiths' self-titled album. The interview takes place on the noisy dance floor of the Hacienda Club, and Morrissey does his best to discuss the Smiths and the new album. The highlight of this clip is when the interviewer asks Morrissey if the Smiths plan on making any videos, and he vehemently denies the urge to procreate in this way. Despite the arrogance, Morrissey is so young and fresh—so "first day of rock 'n' roll"—it'll make any hater's heart melt.

Two interesting notes: after the music video comments, the interviewer announces that they are going to show some Smiths footage from the TV show *The Tube* when actually it is footage from the *Data Run* appearance. Also, this night of performers at the Hacienda Club included Madonna, making her second British television appearance.

The Old Grey Whistle Test (1985)

The Smiths find themselves the subject of a rather informational segment about the magic that is the Smiths and how their music comes about. This clip from *The Old Gray Whistle Test* (or just *Whistle Test*, as it was lovingly referred to in the '80s) is one of the best insights into the Smiths that was ever released. Johnny Marr and Morrissey are interviewed, and both come across as likeable and "real"—Johnny even blushes when the interviewer refers to their upcoming *Meat Is Murder* album as "the next *Sgt. Pepper*." Morrissey is at his finest when explaining how he comes up with his lyrics: Johnny puts the music down on a cassette and gives to Morrissey, Morrissey "lives with it" for a couple of days, and then boom—the Smiths' songs are created.

Other outstanding footage included the band in the studio recording various tracks from the *Meat Is Murder* album (such as "Nowhere Fast," "I Want the One I Can't Have," and "The Joke Isn't Funny Anymore"). Each Smith has his own time in front of the camera with his instrument, but when they put Morrissey and Marr together to record their parts for "Nowhere Fast," you can feel through the television screen their magnetic appeal and how the two of them together equal perfection.

This interview also is one of the first times that Morrissey states his annoyance at being referred to as "miserable" and "depressed." When asked if he is as profoundly miserable as people think, Morrissey answers that he is being "pigeon-holed" and never is credited with writing humorously, blaming the accusation of him being depressed on "lazy journalism."

The Oxford Road Show (1985)

A biographical segment on *The Oxford Road Show* features a sideburn-less Morrissey talking about his childhood. He starts off with his first childhood home in Queens Square in Old Trafford, explaining how his grandmother and aunt lived in the same building as his family. The neighborhood was demolished in the late '60s, and Morrissey takes us to the tacky apartments that are there now, where he laments the death of his childhood. He then continues the Morrissey's Childhood tour and takes us to his elementary school. That, too, has been demolished and replaced with a new bright and shiny modern school. Morrissey and I disagree on the building—he says he prefers the old school because it had character, while I prefer the new school because it has style. Morrissey visits with two of his old teachers, and they look through old photos, reminiscing about Morrissey's school days. He then visits his secondary school and complains about how terrible it was and how much he hated going there. The segments continue with Morrissey speaking about how ordinary and boring it was to grow up there in Manchester and how he would write and walk around town to help him deal with it.

This segment is important because it does two things: one of them is showing how truly gloomy and miserable it is in England, and the second thing is that Morrissey is indeed a product of his environment and is able to recognize that, even at a young age. It is also a satisfying look into his personal life—showing the world that he is indeed human and is okay with the fact that the world truly is not all sunshine and rainbows.

Top of the Pops (1988)

It was Morrissey's first appearance on *Top of the Pops* as a solo artist, but it had a slightly Smiths feel, because he was wearing a *Queen Is Dead* T-shirt under his blazer (and let it be known that Morrissey is the only singer ever who looks good wearing his own T-shirts). Without a backing band, Morrissey lip-syncs along to his second single, "Everyday Is Like Sunday," and gyrates to the excitement of the audience. His hair is at an all-time greatness here—full and poofy.

Morrissey would end up performing on *Top of the Pops* a total of eleven times throughout his solo career, starting with "Everyday Is Like Sunday" and ending in 2004 with "First of the Gang to Die." Footage of this performance is included on the 2010 reissue of "Everyday Is Like Sunday" single.

Tonight with Jonathan Ross (1990)

Although he had appeared on *Top of the Pops* before, this was technically his first televised performance as a solo artist, since his appearances on *Top of the Pops* were lip-synced. Morrissey and a pianist perform a lovely and dramatic version of "I've Changed My Plea to Guilty," complete with the eyebrow Band-Aid and Kid 'n Play hair poof. I have to say that the *Kill Uncle* era of Morrissey hair is my favorite.

Hanging with MTV (1992)

If you know any Morrissey haters (and I know you do), I would show them this clip to make them a believer.

Morrissey is at his finest here, promoting 1992's *Your Arsenal* in front of an audience of delightfully awkward teenage fans. The record company pushed *Your Arsenal* big time, and Morrissey did a series of interviews for MTV, his first attempt at really trying to reach his ever-growing American fan base. In this episode of *Hanging with MTV*, the audience members ask him some pretty decent questions, and you can tell Morrissey enjoys interacting with them. He looks great and mugs for the audience and camera. A girl in the audience asks Morrissey if he misses performing with the Smiths and gets embarrassed when the crowd "oooohs" her. Morrissey takes it in good fun and answers that he likes the current band more (and even gets in a jab at the Monkees). His quiff is pleasantly poofy, his sideburns are perfectly pointy, and he is wearing a nice cotton blend shirt instead of the typical 1992 sweaty satin. Morrissey is truly at his best here.

The Tonight Show with Johnny Carson (1991)
The Tonight Show with Jay Leno (1992)

Morrissey's live debut on American television happened to be his first appearance on *The Tonight Show*, and it was legendary. Los Angeles was crazy with Morrissey Fever: he had sold out the Great Western Forum in anticipation of his first return to the Southland since 1986—fourteen thousand tickets were sold in fourteen minutes! Johnny Carson could barely introduce Morrissey without the studio audience (all Morrissey fans, obviously) going crazy with excitement. Finally, Johnny held up the compact disc long box of *Kill Uncle* and pointed to the stage, completely drowned out by the audience.

Morrissey and the band performed "Sing Your Life" and "There's a Place in Hell for Me and My Friends," and while they were good, they were not great. Morrissey sounded weak, and the band just did not have their usual full sound. Granted, it was early in the tour and technically only their third live performance together (they had played concerts in San Diego and Costa Mesa a few days before this). But when you compare it to their next *Tonight Show* performance a year later, the performance was pretty meh.

So it is a year later and Morrissey and the band return to *The Tonight Show* to promote the *Your Arsenal* album and tour. Things have certainly changed (although the compact disc long box remained). Johnny Carson was gone, and Jay Leno was hosting and clearly a fan of Morrissey, getting an autograph from the singer and making a beeline to shake his hand before the other guests. Morrissey sounds rich and full, and his band sounds tight. What a different a year makes!

Saturday Night Live (1992)

Morrissey (and his satin shirt) continued to promote *Your Arsenal* by appearing on *Saturday Night Live* toward the end of 1992. Morrissey and his band were in top shape after being on tour for most of 1992, and it showed—their performance of "Glamorous Glue" and "Suedehead" sounds amazing. I am a *Saturday Night Live* fan, and I remember watching that episode. It was terrible! Even if you hated Morrissey, I am sure you were happy to see him after sitting through the dreck that was the '92–'93 season of *SNL*. I was actually happy to see the satin shirt.

Pop Quiz (1984)

The first thing I thought when I first sat down to watch this was not "Whoa! Morrissey's on a game show?" but "I thought Phil Lynott was dead by then?"

Pop Quiz was a British game show that was basically a shill for record companies to promote their artists. It was also obviously skewed—Morrissey just *happened* to get questions about Nancy Sinatra and Billy Fury? Phil Lynott had guessed Van Morrison previously in the episode, but then got Van Morrison questions later? Either way, it is a fun watch and a flashback to the '80s. Besides Morrissey and Phil Lynott, fellow contestants were Kim Wilde, Alvin Stardust (no relation to Ziggy), Nick Beggs (a non-Limahl member of Kajagoogoo), and Derek Forbes of Simple Minds. Morrissey mugs it up with plenty of smirks and eyebrow raising, and he gets a couple of answers right (even guessing a correct answer of Phil Collins). Unfortunately, Morrissey's team loses, but he comes out a winner in the end. After the host thanks Morrissey for coming and states "who I'm sure will be back again," Morrissey gives THE best "Aw hell no!" look. To my knowledge, that was indeed the only time Morrissey appeared on *Pop Quiz*.

Wrestle with Russell (2009)

It pains me to watch this. Not because of Morrissey, because he is sharp and witty and sexy in it. I cannot sit through this purely because of Russell Brand. He is annoying and British, and I cannot understand anything he says or the questions he asks Morrissey, so everything is over my head. I guess I am just a dumb American.

Wrestle with Russell first appeared on Morrissey's MySpace page and then as a bonus on the deluxe *Years of Refusal* DVD. It eventually was shown on Irish television later in 2009.

The Importance of Being Morrissey (2003)

I have nothing snarky to say about this one. *The Importance of Being Morrissey* is a great documentary. It hits all the right notes: it touches on his family life, his depression, his solo career, his friends, his Latinos, his political views, and the Smiths. There are actually quite a few humorous moments, such as the Mael brothers speaking about corresponding with Morrissey through the fax machine and Morrissey trash-talking Elton John. With *You Are the Quarry* about to be released, *The Importance of Being Morrissey* was the perfect vehicle to get the Comeback Train a-rollin'. Unfortunately, it was never released commercially, but it is available to watch on YouTube, or you can pick up a bootleg copy on eBay (like I did).

Brit Girls Documentary (1997)

Morrissey speaks about some of his favorite British female singers in this multi-part documentary that aired on Channel 4. Cilla Black, Marianne Faithfull, Sandie Shaw, and Twinkle are discussed.

Morrissey and his pooch enjoy the Los Angeles smog while on their daily walk during the filming of *The Importance of Being Morrissey*.   *Author's collection*

The O-Zone (1998)

The O-Zone aired a clip of Morrissey receiving the Lifetime Achievement Award for his "outstanding contribution to British music" at the 1998 Ivor Novello Awards. Although this clip is short, it is a great clip because it shows that Morrissey can actually be nice and give credit where credit is due. Once on stage to accept his award, he thanks Anthony Newley for presenting the award and then thanks "John Maher of Wythenshawe" (Johnny Marr). Those are the only two people he thanks and leaves the stage.

Talk about a class act! Morrissey knows that he would not be Morrissey if it were not for Johnny Marr and rightfully gives him a shout-out. It is nice to see Morrissey being nice.

South (1988)

A spin-off of the popular British soap opera *Brookside*, *South* was able to entice Morrissey to film a cameo appearance. It was not hard to entice him, though—Morrissey was and has been a *Brookside* fan from the get-go. He appeared as himself, waiting in the lobby of Capital Radio to be called for an interview while chatting with actress Justine Kerrigan, who played *South* character Tracy Corkhill. It lasts all of thirty seconds.

Morrissey and Stephen Colbert match wits on *The Colbert Report.*   *Author's collection*

The Colbert Report (2012)

Morrissey makes the usual rounds when he has something to promote—*Top of the Pops*, *The Late Show with David Letterman, Jools Holland*, etc.—but for a nice change of pace, he made an appearance on *The Colbert Report*.

Say what?

Yep, Morrissey agreed to sit down and be skewered by Stephen Colbert. It was definitely some hot Stephen-on-Steven action, and Morrissey took Colbert's jabs like a champ (and managed to get a few of his own in, too). After the interview, Morrissey performed "People Are the Same Everywhere." He also performed "I'm Throwing My Arms Around Paris," but that was a special "Internet-only" bonus video.

Noble Peace Prize Concert (2013)

Morrissey was great.

The band sounded great.

His pants were TERRIBLE.

A weird choice for a performance, Morrissey was the last performer at the Nobel Peace Prize concert. Despite sounding great (especially since he was sick most of 2013), the crowd really did not get into it. He performed "People Are the Same Everywhere" and "Irish Blood, English Heart" with a cover of Lou Reed's "Satellite of Love" squished in between. Morrissey's cover was especially poignant, given that Lou Reed had just passed away that October.

32

Sideburns 'n' All

Morrissey in Popular Culture

A lot of performers have rocked the pompadour (Elvis Presley, Billy Fury, Stray Cats), but no performer has ever rocked the quiff so eloquently (or memorably). Whenever you see a young man with sideburns and a big thick pile of hair in the front, you instantly think one of two things:

Morrissey or ruined pillow cases.

And whenever pop culture needs a sensitive musician or nerdy English singer, Morrissey is the first one they look to. And why not? He's easy to pick on, people misunderstand him, and he is a realistic (and not so obvious) reminder of the '80s. Although he is indeed pretty famous, Morrissey still isn't a household name (especially here in the United States), but popular culture will usually use Morrissey when they are trying to reach its more cultured and enlightened fans.

Mystery Science Theater 3000

In case you have been living under a rock (or on a satellite in the middle of space), *Mystery Science Theater 3000* is a cult classic comedic television show about a man (Joel or Mike, depending on the season) and his robots (Crow T. Robot, Tom Servo, Gypsy, and Cam-Bot) who are stranded in space and are forced to watch B-movies, while making sarcastic quips and zany zingers about the film. Pop culture in general is their target, and no one is spared, not even Morrissey.

In episode 403, "City Limits," the Faux Moux appears in the segment before the film launch. Dr. Clayton Forrester and TV's Frank (the *MST3K* villains) show Joel their latest invention, a Tupperware container to lock in "pop-star freshness, even when their career has gone stale." And their example of freshness is Morrissey! Writer Mike Nelson did a pretty tight Morrissey impression, complete with the pouting, sideburns, and sensitivity.

Faux Moux even wrote and performed a new song titled "Hairdresser in a Coma" (he wrote it during a very sad time in his life: breakfast). It goes

> I cried last night
>
> I died a million deaths
>
> Thinking of your sweet face
>
> And the way you sing
>
> I cried inside
>
> We lied and died
>
> And then I cried again
>
> Not bad for a Morrissey song.

Someone on *Mystery Science Theater 3000* must have been a Morrissey fan because there have been other instances of "gentle ribbing," such as in episode 1002, "*Girl in Gold Boots.*" A man in the movie is playing a slow, sad song on an acoustic guitar, and one of the robots quips: "One of Morrissey's more upbeat songs."

Mike Nelson as Morrissey on an episode of *Mystery Science Theater 3000.*
Author's collection

John Hughes Movies

If you grew up in the '80s (like me), you are totally familiar with all of the John Hughes teen movies: *Sixteen Candles*, *The Breakfast Club*, *Ferris Bueller's Day Off*, and *Pretty in Pink*, to name a few. John Hughes was able to tap into the teenage psyche better than any other writer (except maybe Morrissey). He portrayed them not just as young adults, but also as actual people—people with fears, people with relationship problems, and people with real emotions. John Hughes also had great taste in music, taking charge of the soundtracks for his film and loading them with the best of 1980s modern rock (and in some instances, the soundtrack is better than the movie).

The Smiths fell directly into Hughes's teenage vision. Their "Please, Please, Please, Let Me Get What I Want" was covered by the Dream Academy and used in the museum scene in 1986's *Ferris Bueller's Day Off*. At the time of release, Morrissey insinuated that he was not a fan, but it grew on him over time because he has used the Dream Academy version as intermission music during the later Smiths concerts. But the Smiths' "Please, Please, Please, Let Me Get What I Want" would get its own slot on a John Hughes movie soundtrack, 1986's *Pretty In Pink*.

The Smiths would make yet another appearance on a John Hughes film soundtrack, but with a writing credit only (again!). Good friend of the Smiths Kirsty MacColl recorded her own version of their 1987 song "You Just Haven't Earned It Yet Baby," and it was used on the soundtrack of Hughes's 1988 film *She's Having a Baby*.

Bill Nye the Science Guy

Although it is a little after my time (I will always be a Mr. Wizard girl), Bill Nye the Science Guy brought cool science to the kids of the '90s. Every episode takes a popular song (current and past hits) and remakes it to showcase the topic. In November 1994, it was Morrissey's turn to blind kids with science.

Bill Nye created a scientific cover titled "The Faster You Push Me," a take on "The More You Ignore Me, the Closer I Get." Even his singer was named Momentissey! It stayed pretty faithful to the original while teaching kids about momentum. If you need a refresher on Newtonian mechanics or Morrissey's sideburns, the video clip is available on YouTube for your viewing pleasure.

The Morrissey Broadway Musical

In 2007, the Inter-webs were aflutter with news about a Morrissey musical coming to Broadway at the hands of comedians Thomas Lennon and Robert Ben Garant, both from *The State* and *Reno 911*. Lennon spoke with news outlets and stated: "I have an outline in my head, like a *Mamma Mia*–type musical but with the music of Morrissey called *I've Changed My Plea to Guilty*. It's for a very diehard set of fans."

And then POOF! Nothing.

It was probably 99.9 percent talk, but it would have been amazing if it had happened!

My Life with Morrissey

A surprisingly good and pleasantly cheesy film, 2003's *My Life with Morrissey* tells the tale of a young woman named Jackie who works in a boring office, likes bagels, and worships Morrissey in her spare time (I can relate). Jackie collects Moz memorabilia and quickly moves on to actually stalking him by showing up at his favorite restaurants and hangouts. After actually meeting him (and ingesting his leftovers), Jackie believes they are "dating." After numerous attempts by her co-workers and friends to talk her back to reality fail, Jackie finds herself sliding down a slippery slope into "Moz-teria."

My Life with Morrissey became an underground hit, screening at film festivals throughout 2003. Unfortunately, the real Morrissey could not be part of the film (he does not work for scale), so they got the next best thing—Jose Maldonado, the front man for the Sweet and Tender Hooligans—to fill in (and he does a great job!). Another fun fact: *My Life with Morrissey* was written and directed by Andrew Overtoom, who then became the director of *SpongeBob SquarePants*.

The Wrong Boy

The Wrong Boy is a 2000 novel by Willy Russell that is loved by Morrissey.

What? A somewhat current book that Morrissey likes? And it is not written by some ancient poet who died at age twenty-three from typhoid?

Actually, Willy Russell is an English playwright (and he is still alive) who is responsible for creating the plays *Educating Rita*, *Blood Brothers*, *Shirley Valentine*, and *John, Paul, George, Ringo, . . . and Burt*. *The Wrong Boy* was his debut novel, and its protagonist, Raymond, is a young man who suffers from mental illness, yet is able to function in real life due to his "pen pal" relationship with Morrissey. *The Wrong Boy* is told mostly through long letters that Raymond writes to Morrissey about his life and delusions.

Morrissey did indeed approve of and enjoy reading *The Wrong Boy*: "I thought it was a fantastic accolade. Russell did write to me which was very nice. Even the bits in the book which were a bit critical of me, I don't mind that kind of thing. I was used to that. It was okay."

The Wrong Boy is a perfect example of how deeply Morrissey reaches some people and how his lyrics bring out the intensity (and delusions) of people who need a little help. Sometimes Morrissey is the only thing that can help when you are struggling to survive.

33

I Take the Cue

Cover Songs

"Cosmic Dancer"

A staple of his 1991 tour, Morrissey chose this T. Rex classic because of its ethereal vibe and dreamy lyrics. It was first featured as the B-side to his "Pregnant for the Last Time" single and appears on his *My Early Burglary Years* compilation album, although they're two different versions (the "Pregnant" version was recorded in Utrecht, Holland, and the *Burglary* version was recorded in Costa Mesa, California). The best-known version of this cover is Morrissey's duet with David Bowie live on stage at the Great Western Forum in June 1991.

"Drive-In Saturday"

Okay, I have to be completely honest here.

I do not like this David Bowie song. I do not like the album it came from (*Aladdin Sane*). And I'm not the only one—Morrissey only performed it a total of six times because of the lack of enjoyment by the audience. Not that it was his fault—he totally did a better version of it than Bowie did, but like me, the audience would have rather him do a cover of "Cat People (Putting Out Fire)."

"Drive-In Saturday" was the B-side to 2009's "All You Need Is Me." It was recorded at Omaha's Orpheum Theater.

"East West"

"East West" is the B-side to 1989's "Ouija Board, Ouija Board." Originally it was a Top 40 hit for Herman's Hermits (also from Manchester), and Morrissey fell in love with this song because it told a tale of the lonely life on

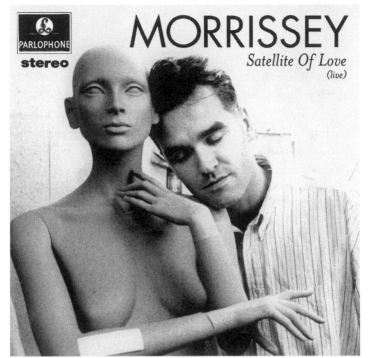

Morrissey's cover of Lou Reed's 1972 song "Satellite of Love."

Author's collection

the road and helped him deal with his homesickness while traveling. Some interesting things to note: Peter Noone, front man for the Hermits, was born in Park Hospital, Davyhulme (as was Morrissey). Graham Gouldman, who wrote "East West," was a member of 10cc (another famous Manchester band AND my mother's favorite band) and had a home recording studio called Strawberry Studios.

And guess where the Smiths recorded their debut single, "Hand in Glove"?

"Human Being"

Once again, here's another song that Morrissey made better than the original. I'm not hating on the New York Dolls at all, but Morrissey's version is tighter and more powerful. Plus it's nice to actually understand the lyrics and listen to the melodies. When Morrissey tries, he can be just as ferocious (if not more so) than New York Dolls front man David Johansen. It only makes sense that Morrissey would cover "Human Being"—after all, he is human and needs to be loved, just like everybody else does.

"Human Being" is the B-side to 2006's "You Have Killed Me."

"Interlude"

For once, a Morrissey cover that was not released as a B-side. "Interlude" was released in August 1994 to little fanfare, even though it features two '80s goth superstars: Morrissey and Siouxsie Sioux. Originally recorded in 1968 by Timi Yuro for the movie *Interlude* and originally NOT a duet, both Morrissey and Siouxsie recorded their versions separately, and then Boz Boorer mixed them together to create the romantic and quixotic love jam. Sadly, Siouxsie and Morrissey had a falling out over the music video for "Interlude," and neither promoted the song when it was released. The B-side to "Interlude" is an extended version and an instrumental version of the song.

"Moon River"

Although it's no "Baby Elephant Walk," "Moon River" is a perfectly suitable Henry Mancini song for Morrissey to cover. It has a strong history of crooner covers: Andy Williams, Frank Sinatra, Bobby Darin, Vic Damone, and a long list of others have tackled this Academy Award–winning song from 1961's *Breakfast at Tiffany's*.

Morrissey made it the B-side to 1994's "Hold On to Your Friends" and included it on his 1995 compilation, *World of Morrissey*. He also performed it live during his UK tour that year, a shortened version instead of the nine-and-a-half-minute beast that appears on the album.

"My Insatiable One"

"My Insatiable One" was originally written and recorded by English indie rock band Suede. Morrissey was in the audience one night while they performed at the Camden Palace and liked what he heard of "My Insatiable One," with its lyrics echoing Morrissey's usual gloom-and-doom outlook about love and life. He decided that he liked it enough to cover it and play it live during his 1992 *Your Arsenal* tour. It is too bad he did not let Suede know about his tribute—Suede's lead singer Brett Anderson found out by picking up a bootleg of one of the Morrissey concerts and heard him crooning his song.

Morrissey would tell the press how impressed he was with Suede and vice-versa with Suede, who stated that they were huge Smiths fans. But the mutual admiration did not last long—after they met in person, Suede singer

Brett Anderson told the press that he "didn't really like Morrissey" and that Morrissey acted like "a useless teenager." After Anderson's shit-talking him to press, Morrissey turned around and said that he "never met Brett Anderson" and that he didn't wish to. Who knows who is right? They both sound like whiny bitches.

Suede continued to have a presence in Morrissey and the Smiths' afterlife. Guitarist Bernard Butler became friends with Johnny Marr after quitting Suede in 1994, and they both worked together on music projects (Johnny even gave him the guitar he used on the Smiths' 1987 *Strangeways, Here We Come* album). And after Alain Whyte suddenly quit the 2004 *You Are the Quarry* tour, Morrissey had his people contact Butler to see if he was interested in taking Whyte's place.

He wasn't.

"No One Can Hold a Candle to You"

I think it is sweet that Morrissey and his best friend from way back, James "Jimmy" Maker, both went on to be front men in bands, although it would be safe to say that Morrissey has had the bigger career. James went on to create the band Raymonde in the 1980s (after a flirtation with the Smiths) and recorded their best-known song, "No One Can Hold a Candle to You," in 1987. Morrissey added it to his set list for the 2004 *You Are the Quarry* tour, and his cover even made it onto the 2005 *Who Put the M in Manchester?* DVD.

Morrissey did pick the original "No One Can Hold a Candle to You" for his 2004 *New Musical Express* compilation, *Songs to Save Your Life*.

"Nothing Rhymed"

Gilbert O' Sullivan was the Morrissey of the 1970's, with his morose and depressing songs. But unlike Morrissey, he managed to take his suicidal intent and turn it into a #1 hit in the United States with his 1972 single "Alone Again (Naturally)." Morrissey paid tribute to the Irish singer-songwriter by performing a cover of his 1970 Top 10 hit "Nothing Rhymed" while performing two nights in Dublin in 2002.

"Redondo Beach"

"Redondo Beach" was the only single released from 2005's *Live at Earls Court*—it was a double A-side with "There Is a Light That Never Goes Out," with "Noise Is the Best Revenge" and "It's Hard to Walk Tall When You're Small" as the B-sides. Originally recorded in 1975 by Patti Smith, it tells the fictional tale of her sister committing suicide and washing up on the shores of Redondo Beach, California (hopefully not near Tony's on the Pier). Fun fact: Morrissey first met Johnny Marr in 1978 at a Patti Smith concert.

"A Song from Under the Floorboards"

"A Song from Under the Floorboards" is the B-side to 2006's "The Youngest Was the Most Loved." It was originally written and recorded by Magazine, a legendary Manchester band fronted by ex-Buzzcock (and friend to Morrissey) Howard Devoto. Devoto has stated that his inspiration for "A Song from Under the Floorboards" was the 1864 novel *Notes from Under the Floorboards* by Fyodor Dostoevsky. Morrissey's version, although not as "punk," is a fitting tribute to his friend and mentor. A better than average Morrissey B-side, Morrissey even performed "A Song from Under the Floorboards" during the 2006 Tour of the Tormentors.

"Skin Storm"

"Skin Storm" is the B-side to 1991's "Pregnant for the Last Time," and unlike the other covers, it was a somewhat current (at that time) song. "Skin Storm" was the 1988 debut single from the band Bradford. Despite the fact that Bradford was inspired by the Smiths and even sported Morrissey-esque haircuts, the song really isn't the usual Morrissey-type ditty. It's pretty lovey-dovey and optimistic, and Morrissey performs it in that style.

"Subway Train"

Morrissey's half-assed cover of the New York Dolls' "Subway Train" first appeared on the 2005 live album *Live from Earls Court,* but it has been in his set list since 2004. He has never performed "Subway Train" in its entirety, but has chosen to perform just the beginning and use it to segue into a different song, usually "Everyday Is Like Sunday" and "Munich Air Disaster 1958." This is done in a similar vein to the Smiths' cover of Elvis Presley's "(Marie's the Name) His Latest Flame" that preceded their song "Rusholme Ruffians."

"Trash"

"Trash" is Morrissey's first attempt at covering a New York Dolls song (the second being "Subway Train" and the third being "Human Being"). Originally recorded in 1973, "Trash" is one of the most beloved songs from their debut self-titled album and asks the eternal question of "How do you call your lover boy?" Morrissey chose to cover "Trash" in 1991 while on the *Kill Uncle* tour once he heard about the death of New York Doll Johnny Thunders. While performing in Dublin (four days after Thunders's death in New Orleans), Morrissey dedicated his version of "Trash" to him. It was not the greatest cover, but to be fair, the original is just so superior, nothing can compare. Morrissey must have liked covering "Trash" because he continued to do so for the rest of that leg of the tour.

Morrissey's cover of "Trash" wasn't professionally recorded or officially released until the 2010 reissue of "Everyday Is Like Sunday," where it makes an appearance as a B-side (the recording was taken from a live performance at Pacific Amphitheatre in Costa Mesa, California, on the *Kill Uncle* tour). It also appears on the 1993 *Live in Dallas* VHS.

"That's Entertainment"

Morrissey's cover of the Jam's 1980 hit "That's Entertainment" is the perfect example of what a cover should be. It sounds enough like the original to keep it familiar, but Morrissey added his own style and touch to make it truly his. It's a little rough, a little English, and a whole lot of dreamy goodness.

"That's Entertainment" is the B-side to 1991's "Sing Your Life."

"You Say You Don't Love Me"

Morrissey performed this Buzzcocks original during the summer of his 2008 tour. Originally released in 1979, "You Say You Don't Love Me" was not a hit for the Buzzcocks but is still remembered for its straightforward lyrics about not falling in love with someone who does not reciprocate. Morrissey did a fine, but unremarkable, cover of this unremarkable song.

Tribute and Cover Albums

A lot of bands count Morrissey and/or the Smiths as an inspiration, but only the serious ones put their money where the mouth is and record or perform their cover of a Morrissey or Smiths song. Interestingly enough, there are more Smiths covers than Morrissey-solo covers. Maybe because it is "cooler" to do a Smiths cover? Morrissey has recorded ten albums as a solo artist—surely there have to be some better songs to cover than "How Soon Is Now?" The following albums are noteworthy tribute compilations.

The Smiths Is Dead (1996)

To celebrate the tenth anniversary of the Smiths' 1986 album *The Queen Is Dead*, French magazine *Les Inrockuptibles* issued a compilation of *The Queen Is Dead* cover songs. The track listing for *The Smiths Is Dead* matches the track listing on the original *The Queen Is Dead*.

The track listing for *The Smiths Is Dead*:

1.   "The Queen Is Dead"—The Boo Radleys
2.   "Frankly, Mr. Shankly"—The High Llamas
3.   "I Know It's Over"—The Trash Can Sinatras
5.   "Never Had No One Ever"—Billy Bragg
6.   "Cemetry Gates"—The Frank & Walters
7.   "Bigmouth Strikes Again"—Placebo
8.   "The Boy with the Thorn in His Side"—Bis
9.   "Vicar in a Tutu"—Therapy?
10. "There Is a Light That Never Goes Out"—The Divine Comedy
11. "Some Girls Are Bigger Than Others"—Supergrass

The World Still Won't Listen (1996)

An album of the Smiths/Morrissey covers by hardcore punk bands, *The World Still Won't Listen* is exactly what you would expect when listening to hardcore bands cover the Smiths, although I do have a soft spot for Anal Cunt and like their cover of "You're Gonna Need Someone on Your Side." I think that A.C. has a soft spot themselves for Morrissey, considering they have a song titled "Johnny Violent Getting His Ass Kicked by Morrissey" (*40 More Reasons to Hate Us*, 1996).

The track listing for *The World Still Won't Listen*:

1.   "Shoplifters of the World Unite"—Dare To Defy
2.   "London"—Down by Law
3.   "You're Gonna Need Someone On Your Side"—A.C. (Anal Cunt)
4.   "What Difference Does It Make?"—Subzero

5. "How Soon Is Now?"—The Meatmen
6. "Heaven Knows I'm Miserable Now"—H2O
7. "Handsome Devil"—Sweet Diesel
8. "Bigmouth Strikes Again"—Slapshot
9. "You Just Haven't Earned It Yet Baby"—Screw 32
10. "The Last of the Famous International Playboys"—Leeway
11. "What She Said"—Youth Brigade
12. "Stop Me If You Think You've Heard This One Before"—Vision
13. "Half a Person"—Edgewise
14. "Panic"—The Business
15. "Sweet and Tender Hooligan"—59 Times the Pain
16. "This Night Has Opened My Eyes"—Home 33
17. "There Is a Light That Never Goes Out"—Walleye
18. "Back to the Old House"—Lament

The String Quartet Tribute to the Smiths (2003 and 2006)

The String Quartet Tribute to the Smiths is exactly what it sounds like: the Section, a string quartet, performs songs by the Smiths and Morrissey. The 2003 release features only songs by the Smiths, whereas the 2006 reissue also has songs by Morrissey solo. The 2003 issue also has an original song, "Not This Time," that was written and performed in the spirit of the Smiths.

The 2003 track listing for *The String Quartet Tribute to the Smiths*:

1. "Last Night I Dreamt That Somebody Loved Me"
2. "Heaven Knows I'm Miserable Now"
3. "That Joke Isn't Funny Anymore"
4. "How Soon Is Now?"
5. "William, It Was Really Nothing"
6. "Back to the Old House"
7. "There Is a Light That Never Goes Out"
8. "This Charming Man"
9. "Please, Please, Please, Let Me Get What I Want"
10. "Some Girls Are Bigger Than Others"
11. "Not This Time"

The track listing for the 2006 reissue:

1. "Suedehead"
2. "Glamorous Glue"

3.   "November Spawned a Monster"
4.   "Everyday Is Like Sunday"
5.   "First of the Gang to Die"
6.   "Heaven Knows I'm Miserable Now"
7.   "How Soon Is Now?"
8.   "This Charming Man"
9.   "Please, Please, Please, Let Me Get What I Want"
10.   "William, It Was Really Nothing"
11.   "There Is a Light That Never Goes Out"

How Soon Is Now? (2004)

How Soon Is Now? is a compilation of Smiths covers by emo bands. It's fitting, because Morrissey really was the original emo kid. Except with better hair and no mascara.

The track listing for *How Soon Is Now?*:

1.   "Girlfriend in a Coma"—Million Dead
2.   "How Soon Is Now?"—Hundred Reasons
3.   "Frankly, Mr. Shankly"—Cursive
4.   "Panic"—Garrison
5.   "Death of a Disco Dancer"—Yourcodenameis:Milo
6.   "Bigmouth Strikes Again"—Read Yellow
7.   "Ask"—Walter Walter
8.   "There Is a Light That Never Goes Out"—My Awesome Compilation
9.   "Last Night I Dreamt That Somebody Loved Me"—Instruction
10.   "Shoplifters of the World Unite"—This Girl
11.   "Handsome Devil"—Lomax
12.   "Cemetry Gates"—The Beautiful Mistake

Stop Me If You Think You've Heard This One Before: A Tribute to the Smiths (2007)

Stop Me If You Think You've Heard This One Before: A Tribute to the Smiths is an odd little compilation. You have big-name '80s bands like Bow Wow Wow and Gene Loves Jezebel, '90s fake lesbian band t.A.T.u., real Smiths/Morrissey cover bands Sweet and Tender Hooligans and This Charming Band, goth legend Eva O, and '80s teen sweetheart Tiffany with her cover of "Panic."

Now if only Debbie Gibson would cover "Suffer Little Children" . . .

The track listing for *Stop Me If You Think You've Heard This One Before: A Tribute to the Smiths*:

1. "How Soon Is Now?"—t.A.T.u.
2. "I Started Something I Couldn't Finish"—Bow Wow Wow
3. "Ask"—Gene Loves Jezebel
4. "Panic (Hang the DJ)"—Tiffany
5. "There Is a Light That Never Goes Out"—Razed in Black
6. "The Boy with the Thorn in His Side"—G. W. Childs
7. "Please, Please, Please, Let Me Get What I Want"—The Autumns
8. "Heaven Knows"—Sweet and Tender Hooligans
9. "Hand in Glove"—This Charming Band
10. "What Difference Does It Make"—Versailles
11. "This Charming Man"—David Glass (of Christian Death)
12. "Bigmouth Strikes Again"—Eva O and DJ Eric Ill
13. "Last Night I Dreamt That Somebody Loved Me"—Orlanddissey & Unwoman
14. "There Is a Light That Never Goes Out" (Spanish)—Sweet and Tender Hooligans

The Smiths Project (2011)

Janice Whaley re-created all four Smiths studio albums and their two compilations by singing and using her voice as an instrument—no actual instruments are actually used on these recordings, just Janice and her voice, a pitch shifter, and crafty editing. She released *The Smiths Project* in 2011 to rave reviews. It was quite an undertaking and beautifully done. For more information or to purchase *The Smiths Project*, please visit http://thesmithsproject.blogspot.com/.

Twinkle Twinkle Little Rock Star: Lullaby Versions of the Smiths and Morrissey (2011)

Rockabye Baby! Lullaby Renditions of the Smiths (2012)

Talk about "The Hand That Rocks the Cradle"! If you loved your baby, you would buy one of these Smiths lullaby albums. Make sure to also buy him or her some little baby Converse and a satin onesie.

Other Notable Cover Songs

Although these songs don't appear on an actual tribute album, many bands have tried their hand at covering the work of Morrissey.

Other Smiths covers:

- "Back to the Old House"—Billy Bragg, Everything but the Girl
- "You Just Haven't Earned It Yet Baby"—Kirsty MacColl
- "How Soon Is Now?"—Love Spit Love, Paradise Lost
- "Ask"—Reel Big Fish
- "The Headmaster Ritual"—Radiohead
- "There Is a Light That Never Goes Out"—The Ocean Blue, Braid, Dum Dum Girls, Noel Gallagher, Neil Finn
- "I Won't Share You"—Pop Etc., Sixpence None the Richer
- "This Night Has Opened Up My Eyes"—At the Drive-In
- "Asleep"—Xiu Xiu
- "Please, Please, Please Let Me Get What I Want"—The Dream Academy, Muse, She & Him, Deftones
- "This Charming Man"—Death Cab for Cutie
- "Last Night I Dreamt That Somebody Loved Me"—Low, Eurythmics
- "Reel Around the Fountain"—Duncan Sheik
- "Girlfriend in a Coma"—Mojo Nixon
- "London"—Anthrax
- "Sweet and Tender Hooligan"—Nouvelle Vogue
- "The Boy with the Thorn in His Side"—J. Mascis
  Other Morrissey covers:
- "Everyday Is Like Sunday"—10,000 Maniacs, The Pretenders, Armageddon Dildos
- "Jack the Ripper"—My Chemical Romance
- "The Last of the Famous International Playboys"—J Church
- "Let Me Kiss You"—Nancy Sinatra
- "The Loop"—Tiger Army
- "Suedehead"—Suggs
- "Why Don't You Find Out for Yourself?"—The Killers
- "It's Going to Happen Someday"—David Bowie

The Disney Connection

It was truly WTF moment when word got out about ex-Disney, ex-teen sensation Miley Cyrus performing a cover of the Smiths' "There Is a Light That

Never Goes Out." But unfortunately it was true—she had indeed whipped it out on stage in May 2014 in Belfast, Ireland, while on tour to promote her *Bangerz* album (I thought my eyes would roll out of my head while typing that "z"). But Miley isn't the first Disney star to take on Moz.

Back in 1994, the All-New Mickey Mouse Club decided to try their hand at adult angst, teen style! Club member Josh Ackerman performed Morrissey's "The More You Ignore Me, the Closer I Get" in a music video, complete with the fake English accent and plenty of pouting. It is pretty terrible—lyrics are changed to make them more "kid friendly," clothing and scenery is extremely dated, and Disney was able to make the song and video even more creepy and stalkery that the original song. I don't blame poor Josh Ackerman, though. When your co-stars are Ryan Gosling and Justin Timberlake, being a Morrissey fan may be your only way to score with a real chick.

Some Bad People on the Right

Animal Rights and Vegetarianism

I f there's one thing that most people associate with Morrissey (besides big hair and whining), it's animal rights and vegetarianism.

Morrissey gave up the meat back in 1970 after viewing a documentary about a slaughterhouse. It wasn't a hard choice for him to convert—his mother is also a vegetarian. Throughout the Smiths (Johnny Marr is also a vegetarian) and his solo career, Morrissey has enforced a strict "no meat and no animal products" rule for his band members and support staff. To help educate the fans, the Smiths recorded and released the *Meal Is Murder* album, with its title track being a haunting tune about the horrors of animal slaughter and consumption. Morrissey still performs "Meat Is Murder" complete with the slaughterhouse footage rolling behind him

I remember the last time I saw Morrissey perform in concert—sure enough, he busted out "Meat Is Murder." Halfway through the slaughterhouse footage, I turned to my boyfriend and asked, "I didn't know people ate baby chicks?"

Yeah, it's that kind of footage.

People for the Ethical Treatment of Animals (PETA)

Morrissey has been a huge supporter of People for the Ethical Treatment of Animals by appearing in their advertisements and by donating money—all of the proceeds of his *Under the Influence* compilation went to PETA, and he promotes PETA by publishing their website and info in the credits of his albums. He has also been seen wearing PETA T-shirts, as well as attending PETA-sponsored events.

In 2005, Morrissey received the Linda McCartney Memorial Award at the PETA Twenty-Fifth Anniversary Gala.

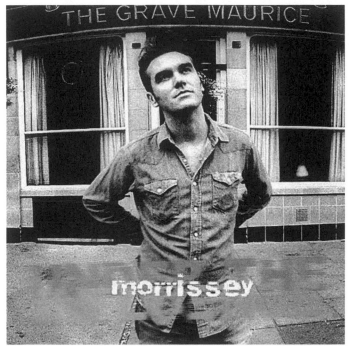

The proceeds from the *Morrissey: Under the Influence* compilation went to the People for the Ethical Treatment of Animals (PETA).

Author's collection

"Interesting Drug" Video

The video for "Interesting Drug" is a whimsical example of animal rights, with a cartoonish woman and a group of boys breaking into a lab and setting rabbits free. Morrissey also makes an appearance in the video, handing out information about animal abuse to the boys. This video is also big on the anti-fur, with one of the boys throwing a fur ad into the toilet, anti-fur buttons adorning their school uniforms, and anti-fur billboards scattered throughout the town.

"The Draize Train"

"The Draize Train" is the B-side to the Smiths' eleventh single, "Panic." John Draize was an American scientist who devised a toxicity test used for testing cosmetics on animals.

Canadian Seal Clubbing

In 2006, Morrissey announced that he would be boycotting the country of Canada because of its annual commercial seal hunt. Every couple of years since then, Morrissey will make an official statement regarding the barbaric ritual of killing seals for fur, meat, and "population control," and reiterating his Canadian boycott. Journalists have challenged his boycott by stating that countries such as Japan, Norway, and Namibia also seal hunt, so why boycott only Canada? In a 2012 interview with the Montreal-based *Cult* website, he answered: "But also because we would expect more intelligence and understanding from Canada than we might from, say, China."

Which leads us to . . .

Chinese People

In a 2010 interview in the *Guardian Weekend* magazine, when animal rights and his vegetarianism came up, he asked the interviewer: "Did you see the thing on the news about their treatment of animals and animal welfare? Absolutely horrific. You can't help but feel that the Chinese are a subspecies."

With the usual "Morrissey is a racist" rhetoric being spewed immediately after the interview was published, Morrissey issued the following statement shortly after, not apologizing for his views on animal cruelty in China: "If anyone has seen the horrific and unwatchable footage of the Chinese cat and dog trade—animals skinned alive—then they could not possibly argue in favour of China as a caring nation. There are no animal protection laws in China and this results in the worst animal abuse and cruelty on the planet. It is indefensible."

Whether you think it was right or wrong, you have to admire a man who sticks by his word. And who loves cats and dogs.

Duck Dynasty

Morrissey was scheduled to appear on Jimmy Kimmel's late-night talk show in 2013, but when it was announced that his co-guests would be the hillbilly family from the popular reality television show *Duck Dynasty*, Morrissey graciously (well, graciously for him) bowed out, stating, "I would love to perform on the ABC late-night show . . . if Kimmel dumped the *Duck Dynasty* gang. If not, I'd have to step away, what with the *Duck Dynasty* clan being people who in effect amount to animal serial killers."

Jimmy Kimmel decided to stay with the *Duck Dynasty* gang, and to capitalize on the drama, he proceeded to take not-funny digs at Morrissey all night, while employing the *Duck Dynasty* hillbillies in a sketch about them making "calls for people who do not kill animals." Yes, it was as unfunny as it sounds.

35

All You Need Is Me

T alk about bigmouth strikes again! Morrissey can certainly take whatever he dishes out, whether it is insults or compliments. Fans and enemies alike never have a shortage of things to say about Moz, but honestly, the insults are never as good as Morrissey's (especially Robert Smith's). Despite being respected and admired, there are a couple of haters in the house.

"I followed Morrissey's career for about the first eight or nine years, but after that point it became apparent that he had a kind of Peter Pan fixation and wasn't interested in growing up. I got to the point where I felt that what he was talking about said nothing to me about my life."

—Lloyd Cole, *Chicago Tribune*, 2006

"When I first heard 'Everyday Is Like Sunday,' I felt very jealous."

—Michael Stipe, REM, *Autobiography* by Morrissey, 2013

"What can I say Morrissey is like, genuinely? I've never been asked to sum him up. Because there was so much emphasis placed on the differences between Morrissey and myself, most people haven't stopped to wonder what it was that made us so close. The thing that brought us really close together is the essence of why he lives his life and why I live my life. And that is that without what we consider to be the art of pop music and pop culture, life doesn't make any sense. And that understanding: He needed it like I needed it."

—Johnny Marr, *Magnet* magazine, 2003

"Take Morrissey. For me, he's been singing the same tune for twenty years. I just don't get it. But he's clearly an interesting character and means a lot to people. He seems to be of a disposition that is very sensitive to criticism and therefore it's appropriately English that he becomes cherished in that kind of Frankie Howard, Tony Hancock

way. Those who are fragile, who need to be cosseted, maybe their shortcomings or their excellence in their field is then woven into the fabric along with Albert Tatlock and Hobnobs."

—Elvis Costello, *London Times*, 2005

"Morrissey just embodies every horrible trait that a human being could possibly possess."

—Henry Rollins, *Rage*, 2006

"One time I was in London and Morrissey came to my hotel to see me. The thing that sticks with me most about that is the hug he gave me because he's just a great hugger."
—Nancy Sinatra, *The Importance of Being Morrissey*, 2002

"The danger of restorative nostalgia lies in its belief that the mutilated 'wholeness' of the body politic can be repaired. But the reflective nostalgic understands deep down that loss is irrecoverable: Time wounds all wholes. To exist in Time is to suffer through

"He's just a great hugger." —Nancy Sinatra.   *Author's collection*

an endless exile, a successive severing from those precious few moments of feeling at home in the world. In pop terms, Morrissey is the supreme poet of reflective nostalgia."

—Simon Reynolds, *Retromania: Pop Culture's Addiction to Its Own Past*, 2011

"Later on, I started listening to the Smiths and Morrissey, which ended up being the most prevalent influences of my life. I mean, Morrissey just consumed me."

—Brandon Flowers, The Killers, JamBase.com, 2007

"I have never liked Morrissey, and I still don't. I think it's hilarious, actually, what things I've heard about him, what he's really like, and his public persona is so different. He's such an actor."

—Robert Smith, The Cure, *Spin Magazine*, 1993

"Had Morrissey claimed freedom of speech in his own defence, I would have supported his stance. Instead, we have the unedifying possibility that a man who once skillfully wielded his dazzling wit to confound his detractors and delight his audience has been reduced to relying on a writ in order to stifle his critics."

—Billy Bragg, *The Guardian*, 2007

36

Morrissey on the Guillotine

Controversies and Enemies

Margaret Thatcher

Margaret Thatcher was elected prime minister of the United Kingdom in 1979 and was the first woman to hold that position. As the leader of the Conservative Party, with her beliefs and politics, she was very disliked by and unpopular with the United Kingdom's working class, so much so that they called her policies "Thatcherism."

Morrissey, of course, hated her and made no secret about it. He always made his feelings known whenever asked (and when anyone would listen).

In a June 1984 interview with *Rolling Stone* magazine, Morrissey had this to say about Margaret Thatcher: "The entire history of Margaret Thatcher is one of violence and oppression and horror. I think that we must not lie back and cry about it. She's only one person and she can be destroyed. I just pray that there is a Sirhan Sirhan somewhere. It's the only remedy for this country right at this moment."

Well, she never was assassinated, but Morrissey's comments brought a lot of press and attention to him and the Smiths. While staying at the Grand Hotel in Brighton for the 1984 Conservative Party Conference, a bomb planted by the IRA went off, killing five people, but not Thatcher (its intended target). Once again, Morrissey had some not-so-nice words about it in a November 1984 interview with *Melody Maker* magazine: "The sorrow of the Brighton bombing is that she escaped unscathed. The sorrow is that she's still alive. But I feel relatively happy about it. I think that for once the IRA were accurate in selecting their target."

Things never got better with the United Kingdom under Margaret Thatcher's control, but you can imagine the number of happy people once she was kicked out of office in 1990 and replaced by John Major.

Morrissey and other people also were not very impressed with John Major, either.

The Royal Family

Morrissey HATES the Royal Family and the idea of a monarchy. Starting with the Smiths' "Nowhere Fast" ("I'd like to drop my trousers to the Queen") and their 1986 album *The Queen Is Dead*, Morrissey still speaks poorly of the Royal Family at any chance he gets.

He is constantly criticizing the Royal Family about their hunting hobby, with the most recent situation being that Prince Charles and Prince William issued a statement about protecting endangered wildlife, but then went on a hunting trip to Spain the next day. He is also critical of Kate Middleton for her consumption of foie gras, but is surprisingly supportive of Prince Charles for banning the serving of foie gras at any event he attends. Maybe Prince Harry gave him a copy of *Meat Is Murder* for Father's Day?

Billy Bragg

Billy Bragg is an English singer-songwriter known for his socio-political electric folk rock. He supported the Smiths on their first North American tour in 1985, even performing his cover of the Smiths'/Sandie Shaw's "Jeane" during his opening set. Bragg became good friends with the members of the Smiths, especially Johnny Marr, and continued to work on various projects with them, such as the Red Wedge concerts of 1986 and one of the biggest albums of his career, 1991's *Don't Try This at Home*. To this day, Billy Bragg lovingly (or sometimes jokingly) tells anyone who will listen about a time when he was a guest at Morrissey's home and had to sleep on rubber sheets.

So why does he hate Morrissey?

Billy Bragg is often critical of Morrissey's views and statements regarding England and other cultures. From Morrissey's blistering comments about England's "jingoism" when it came to the 2010 Olympics (Bragg calls Morrissey a "wet blanket") to his views on how immigration is ruining "his England" (Bragg points out that Morrissey is a product of Irish immigrants), Billy Bragg always has a comment to refute anything Morrissey says to the media (whether it's good or bad). But despite always disagreeing with

Morrissey, Billy Bragg has no problem regurgitating the rubber bedsheets story anytime he has an audience.

You can't hate a man who wants to keep the bed in his guest room clean and piss-free.

Robert Smith

My hairdresser, Brian, and I always get into it: the Cure versus the Smiths/ Morrissey. And we're not the only ones—for the past thirty years there's been a half-assed rivalry between fans of the Cure and fans of the Smiths/ Morrissey. What makes it half-assed is that there's no real rivalry—most fans of the "darker side of new wave" like both bands, and other than when I'm having my highlights redone, it never seems to be a real problem.

The evil Smith. Robert Smith from the Cure has always been at odds with Morrissey, despite Morrissey out-quipping him every time.   *Ebet Roberts/ Redferns/ Getty Images*

So where did all this Smith-on-Smith crime come from?

In a 1984 interview with *The Face*, interviewer Elissa Van Poznack asked Morrissey: "If I put you in a room with Robert Smith, Mark E. Smith, and a loaded Smith & Wesson, who would bite the bullet first?"

Morrissey answered in typical Morrissey fashion: "I'd line them up so that one bullet penetrated both simultaneously . . . Robert Smith is a whingebag. It's rather curious that he began wearing beads at the emergence of the Smiths and has been photographed with flowers. I expect he's quite supportive of what we do, but I've never liked the Cure . . . not even 'The Caterpillar.'"

Like you, I had to go look up "whingebag"—it means "someone who complains or protests." And although it was slightly uncalled for, he was right about one thing—no one liked "The Caterpillar" (except my hairdresser, Brian).

Robert Smith's reply?

"That's fucking nice, cunt!"

The C-word is pretty harsh, so I'm guessing that Robert Smith was pissed at Morrissey's death answer. Their banter would continue with such jewels as:

- "The Cure: A new dimension of the word 'crap.'"—Morrissey
- "If Morrissey says not to eat meat, I'm going to eat meat; that's how much I hate Morrissey." —Robert Smith

And so on. In later interviews, Robert Smith has remarked that the "feud" was ridiculous, and nothing more about it has left Morrissey's mouth. I think both have realized that when you're two steps away from playing an '80s flashback concert at an Indian casino, you have to play nice to play Madison Square Garden.

Siouxsie Sioux

Other than Morrissey himself, no other singer is a finer example of '80s goth than Siouxsie Sioux, front woman and namesake of Siouxsie and the Banshees. I admit it—I love Siouxsie. She is so cool and iconic and an all-around nice person. I only wish I could wear my eye makeup like that!

Morrissey and Johnny Marr were also fans of Siouxsie and the Banshees, but it was not until Morrissey was a solo artist that he started to talk up Siouxsie in the press and play their songs during his concert intermissions. He finally wrote her a letter in 1993 about how much he liked and admired her, and then asked if they could work together. Sounds like a crush to me! Siouxsie agreed, and they decided to record a duets of Timi Yuro's 1968 song "Interlude." They both recorded their parts separately, which were then mixed together by Morrissey guitarist Boz Boorer, and anticipated a release soon after.

But when it came to making a video for "Interlude," Morrissey's crush on Siouxsie ended. They both agreed originally to use footage from the 1956 Diana Dors movie *Yield to the Night*. When the Morrissey was unable to acquire the rights to the footage from *Yield to the Night*, he suggested using footage of a bulldog, which Siouxsie was not keen on, considering the innocent bulldog was usually linked to the British Movement and the National Front. Siouxsie was supposedly cool with using any other dog (or anything else) for the video, but Morrissey insisted on using a bulldog. Because of this, the video for "Interlude" was never made.

Morrissey still speaks highly of Siouxsie and the Banshees to the press, but has not spoken to her since.

New Musical Express (NME)

The *New Musical Express* and Morrissey have a had a love/hate relationship since 1972, when a young Steven Morrissey first wrote into the "Letters" section, praising the new release by Sparks (*Kimono My House*). After failed attempts to join the *New Musical Express* staff as a freelancer, Morrissey soon got his revenge by forming the Smiths with Johnny Marr and becoming fan favorites, despite not appearing on the cover of the *New Musical Express* until February 1984 (their first *New Musical Express* interview was back in May 1983). After that initial cover and interview, the Smiths and Morrissey were a constant *New Musical Express* feature and appeared in the magazine more than any other British act at that time. But once Morrissey established his solo career, the tides began to turn.

After rumblings of racism due to song titles such as "Bengali in Platforms" and "Asian Rut," critics and the *New Musical Express* went full blown with the racism card after the release of "The National Front Disco." To support *Your Arsenal*, Morrissey was scheduled to perform at Madstock, a music festival to celebrate the reunion of Madness. He performed the first night with a set backdrop of two skinhead girls, waived a Union Jack flag around on stage and then lobbed it into the audience, and then busted out "The National Front Disco." Due to the impatient Madness fans pelting Morrissey and his band with a variety of projectiles, he decided to end his set early and cancel his performance the next day. All of this got the *New Musical Express* into a tizzy, and they proceeded to write blistering articles about Morrissey's so-called racism and anything else negative they could drum up. Because of this, Morrissey cut ties with the *New Musical Express*, refusing to have anything to do with them for twelve years.

During these twelve years in exile, the *New Musical Express* would continue to use Morrissey to sell magazines. They resorted to Howard Stern–esque tactics to talk to him: they sent undercover reporters to *Vauxhall and I* album signings to pose as fans asking a few questions and continued to write snipey reviews of any singles he released. Although one of their big "Morrissey is racist" examples is his use of the Union Jack, they hypocritically used pictures of Noel Gallagher and his Union Jack guitar and Spice Girl Geri Halliwell wearing a Union Jack dress.

In 2004, Morrissey and the *New Musical Express* mended fences, and he graciously granted an interview. A free compact disc that Morrissey compiled was included with the issue, and it was a great success for both singer and magazine. Things were fine until 2007 when Morrissey granted the *New Musical Express* another interview. After one in-person interview and a follow-up phone call interview, the interview that was published was a total mess. The *New Musical Express* took two of Morrissey's statements about immigration, "Other countries have held on to their basic identity, yet it seems to me that England was thrown away" and "Because the gates are flooded. And anybody can have access to join in" and made them "The gates of England are flooded. The country's been thrown away"—and this was splashed on the front cover of the *New Musical Express*.

The interview had more out-of-context quotes, "The National Front Disco" rehashing, and even just plain WRONG facts, such as "Bengali in Platforms" being released in 1998 instead of 1988. Instead of disappearing from print for another twelve years, Morrissey took action and sued the *New Musical Express*. After winning a pre-trial hearing and with his case moving forward, the *New Musical Express* published an apology to Morrissey, stating that they were sorry and didn't think he was a racist. Morrissey then decided to drop the case.

Morrissey and Johnny Marr vs. Mike Joyce, a.k.a. "The Court Case"

In 1996, former Smiths drummer Mike Joyce took Morrissey and Johnny Marr to court over his share of nonsongwriting royalties of the Smiths music.

Mike Joyce felt that he and Andy Rourke were entitled to an equal split of profits from the company they formed in 1984, Smithdom Ltd. Under the 1890 Partnership Act (which was created to make sure all partners in a business would be entitled to an equal share of profits and duties), Mike Joyce and Andy Rourke were certainly entitled to receive 25 percent of the band's profits. The only problem was that Morrissey and Johnny Marr believed that Joyce and Rourke should get less because they agreed to receive less, giving Morrissey and Marr each 40 percent and Joyce and Rourke 10 percent. There was never any contract or paperwork signed acknowledging this deal, so the trial was basically a "he said/he said" affair. Joyce and Rourke had the 1890 Partnership Act in their corner and didn't have to prove entitlement, but Morrissey and Marr had to prove that they agreed to a lesser percentage.

The fight for money started way before 1996. After the band had broken up in 1987, Joyce and Rourke started legal proceedings against Morrissey and Marr for their share of Smiths money, while ex-Smiths guitarist Craig "The Fifth Smith" Gannon sued to receive owed payment. But they obviously weren't hating on Morrissey that much, because Joyce, Rourke, and Gannon all continued to perform with him while the litigations were going on—all three performed with Morrissey at the last Smiths/first Morrissey concert in Wolverhampton and also played on "The Last of the Famous International Playboys" and "Interesting Drug." Joyce and Gannon would stop working with Morrissey in 1989.

Andy Rourke settled with Morrissey and took a payment of £83,000, and continued to record with Morrissey until 1990. Craig Gannon and other associates who were due payment from Morrissey (such as producer Stephen Street) received their owed funds and quickly dismissed themselves. Joyce was awarded a settlement of £273,000 in 1995 from Morrissey and Marr after they acknowledged that there was some kind of "partnership" regarding the Smiths, and hoping not to end up in court, but with £273,000 still being only 10 percent of what he believed he was owed, Mike Joyce continued with his lawsuit, finally going before the High Court in 1996.

Although their attorneys worked hard with what they had, there was no real proof of any "10 percent" agreement—just a lot of hearsay, anecdotes, and memories from Morrissey and Marr. Interestingly enough, it came out during the trial that there really might have been a "40 percent/10 percent" agreement—back in the early days of the Smiths, Morrissey had supposedly threatened to leave the group if Joyce and Rourke didn't agree to take a 10 percent share. Johnny supposedly stated that he, too, would leave if Morrissey left, leaving Joyce and Rourke no other option but to take 10 percent. Even if it were true, it didn't matter to the court because there was nothing legal stating that arrangement.

It also didn't help that Morrissey wasn't very nice on the stand, insulting the counsel and acting uncooperative and aloof while on giving testimony. Because of this and the lack of any real contract, the judge sided with Mike Joyce and awarded him £1.25 million. Morrissey and Marr were, of course, not very happy.

A month after the trial ended, Morrissey began to record *Maladjusted* and used it to help relieve his anger with the verdict. The song "Sorrow Will Come in the End" is a scathing piece about his feelings about the trial, so scathing that it was left off the UK release of *Maladjusted* because it could have been considered libel. Morrissey did file an appeal, and it was quickly dismissed in 1998—the bones of Morrissey's appeal were that the judge was guilty of character assassination by referring to Morrissey as devious, truculent, and unreliable. Although Johnny had paid his half of the settlement quickly, Morrissey had not. After his appeals and pleading fell on deaf ears, he sold all of his property in England and moved to the United States.

Bradley Steyn vs. Morrissey

Bradley Steyn supposedly worked on Morrissey's 2014 tour (before he canceled it) as security. According to the lawsuit Steyn brought against Morrissey in July 2014, Morrissey supposedly hired him to "hurt" David Tseng, who runs the Morrissey-Solo.com fan site. Morrissey denies this accusation, stating on the True to You fan site that he never even met Bradley Steyn personally while he worked on the tour.

As I write this, the matter is in the hands of the Los Angeles Police Department.

37

Viva La Morrissey!

Latino on the Streets of London

The French have Jerry Lewis, the Germans have David Hasselhoff, and Morrissey of course is beloved by Latinos. It has always been and continues to be a mystery to some, but I will try my best to decipher this code.

First of the Gang to Listen to Morrissey

Fans of Morrissey not living here in Los Angeles find it hard to believe that there is a huge Latino Morrissey following in Southern California. An audience at a Southern California Moz show will have a majority of fans who are tattooed and sport ginormous greased pompadours. Southern California has many Smiths cover bands, but the most popular and most beloved is the Sweet and Tender Hooligans, led by Jose Maldonado. He explains his opinion about Morrissey's Latino appeal: "Morrissey was raised from Irish roots in England. It's kinda the same experience for a kid growing up with Mexican parents in Los Angeles. As a people, we're working class, Catholic, into boxing and soccer . . . very much like Morrissey is. That experience of not quite belonging somewhere that Morrissey sings about like no one else can—that's a very common feeling among the Latino people here."

In a nutshell, Latinos in America have a deep-seated feeling of disconnect due to being away from their own countries (more so with the first generation) or not finding their place in the United States, and many of Morrissey's lyrics reflect that disconnect and sense of identity crisis. Since his beginnings with the Smiths, Morrissey has always been viewed as an outsider. That view widened with his solo work in which he further positioned himself as an outsider and a loner and, most importantly, a performer with his convictions on the outside looking in.

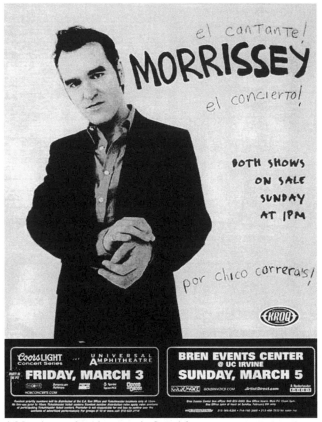

A Morrissey advertisement in Spanish.   *Author's collection*

Just like the United Kingdom, Mexico has a large Catholic population. The population of Mexico is 98 percent Catholic. Okay, so there are a lot of musicians with Catholic backgrounds—why would this make Morrissey any different? I don't believe it is as much of a religious issue as it is a cultural one. Many cultures with populations in poverty embrace religious beliefs in a reach for hope through their despair, and Morrissey's lyrics and themes reflect similar values. The always-nostalgic presence of the past is reflected on the Smiths "Still Ill," as Morrissey laments that "We cannot cling to the old dreams anymore." Native Mexicans have always placed a great emphasis on death and rebirth. Death is not considered final but a natural occurrence and the next step to a new beginning. Morrissey regularly explores the themes of life and the inevitability of death in his music.

Traditional Music

Author Gustavo Arellano points out in his book *Ask a Mexican* that Morrissey's music parallels Mexican ranchera (folk music). Arellano states: "As in ranchera music, Morrissey's lyrics rely on ambiguity, powerful imagery, and metaphors. Thematically, the idealization of a simpler life and a rejection of all things bourgeois come from a populist impulse common to ranchera."

Indeed, Morrissey is not so unlike ranchero crooners Pedro Infante, Juan Gabriel, and Vicente Fernández in his sense of style and passionate, broken-hearted vocals. Arellano also points out similarities between the Smiths' "There Is a Light That Never Goes Out" where Morrissey sings "And if a double-decker bus crashes into us to die by your side is such a heavenly way to die" with "La Cama de Piedra," in which Mexican singer Cuco Sánchez sings "The day that they kill me, may it be with five bullets and be close to you."

Jose Maldonado hosts a weekly radio show in Pasadena dedicated to Morrissey, and El Moz himself has attended a Sweet and Tender Hooligans concert. During a 2004 Morrissey concert at the Wiltern Theatre in Los Angeles, he even introduced the band as the Sweet and Tender Hooligans and himself as Jose Maldonado . . . with the real Jose Maldonado sitting in the audience.

In the 2003 documentary *The Importance of Being Morrissey*, the singer delivers a tongue-in-cheek declaration of his affection for the Mexican people: "I really like Mexican people. I find them so terribly nice and they have fantastic hair and fantastic skin, and usually really good teeth. Great combination."

Southern California Music in the 1980s

As the only remaining Caucasian Morrissey fan, I get a lot of crap from my friends and other music fans I meet. When I tell them I like Morrissey, their response is usually, "But you're not Mexican."

I know that I'm not Mexican, but that doesn't stop me from liking Morrissey. I think people were originally bewildered by the rush and push of Latino Morrissey fans. I have heard numerous Old Timers (well, from the 1980s) say: "But these are the people who would make fun of me and beat me up for liking the Smiths, the Cure, etc."

I have no defense for that. It was probably true. But things change—styles intermingle more, everyone is more sensitive and politically correct, and well . . . maybe the siren's call of the Pompadoured One finally lured them in?

In the '80s, due to KROQ's support of the '80s new wave, alternative, indie, and punk music, the Smiths (and other similar "goth" bands) were huge here in Southern California. KROQ DJ (and King of '80s Music) Richard Blade provided the soundtrack for your life back then—and Southern California Latinos were no exception. Musical genres started to crisscross and Latinos found themselves participating in nontraditional music scenes, such as punk and new wave. The Brat, the Plugz, the Zeros, and the Bags were big-time punk bands in Los Angeles and then that led to death rock and then to goth, and so on. Eventually, it would all lead to Morrissey and the Smiths.

Mexico (and Then Some)

Morrissey's Latino reach goes far and beyond Southern California (and the American Southwest in general). "Moz-teria" has gone south of the border to Mexico, and then south of the border again to Central and South America. He played his first concerts there in 2000 on the *¡Oye Esteban!* tour. In 2002 he joined the Revolución 2000 festival, playing alongside Latino bands Jaguares and Jumbo, and in 2004 he showed his love and appreciation for his new fans by writing two Latino-themed songs, "First of the Gang to Die" from 2004's *You Are the Quarry* and its B-side "Mexico."

38

This I'm Made Of

Miscellaneous Moz

Nicknames

Morrissey is often referred to as "Moz" or "Mozzer" and has mentioned on numerous occasions that he does not like to be called either name—stating in a 1990 interview with *The Face* that the names "make me sound like a racehorse." Either the names grew on him or he decided to just go with it, because he used the name "Moz" on his 1992 T. Rex homage single, "Certain People I Know," and again on the back of the 1995 "The More You Ignore Me, the Closer I Get" single, which features the word "Moz" inked onto assistant Jake Walters's stomach. Supposedly it also says "Mozzer" on Morrissey's passport (insert sarcasm) because that's totally legal.

Boxing

For a short period in the 1990s (1994 and 1995, specifically), Morrissey became obsessed with the sport of boxing. He used boxing imagery throughout this period—from using a picture of boxer Kenny Lane on the cover of his 1995 album, *Southpaw Grammar*, and a picture of boxer Cornelius Carr for the cover of the 1995 *World of Morrissey* compilation, to recording the "Boxers" single, which is about—you guessed it—boxing. Boxer Billy Conn was the obligatory boxer on the cover of "Boxers." A still of Kirk Douglas in the 1949 film *Champion* was used as the backdrop for the *Southpaw Grammar* tour.

And just as quickly as the sport of boxing entered Morrissey's non-aggro life, it left, with the *Southpaw Grammar* tour being the last of anything boxing-related on Morrissey's behalf.

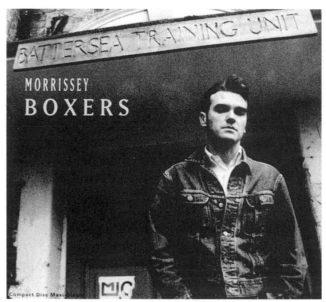

Morrissey extended his boxing obsession to his music with the 1995 "Boxers" single.   *Author's collection*

The *Carry On* Movies

The *Carry On* movies are a series of twenty-nine comedic films that spanned from 1958 to 1978. Having the same cast of actors playing different parts throughout the movies (give or take a couple of one-time actors) provides a nice connection in the series despite the assortment of topics. The *Carry On* movies are known for their sexual innuendos and physical humor, much like that of *The Benny Hill Show.*

Some of the better-known (and better-quality) *Carry On* movies are *Carry On Cleo, Carry On Camping, Carry On Nurse, Carry On Spying*, and the original, *Carry On Sergeant.* When the *Carry On* films first began in 1958, their topics focused more on professions (like nursing, teaching, and police work), but then they started to mock popular movies at the time, like James Bond (*Carry On Spying*) and those boring Hammer vampire movies (*Carry On Screaming!*).

Charles Hawtrey, Hattie Jacques, Joan Sims, and Kenneth Williams are all comedic actors known for playing various roles in an assortment of *Carry On* movies (Kenneth Williams holds the record, having starred in twenty-six different *Carry On* movies), and they're all some of Morrissey's best-loved and most revered actors and actresses. Joan Sims went on to make an appearance in the video for "Ouija Board, Ouija Board," Charles Hawtrey was name-checked in the video for "Interesting Drug" (the schoolboys attended "Hawtrey High"), and a clip from 1972's *Carry On Abroad* is shown on a television in the video for "Everyday Is Like Sunday."

Morrissey and Driving

Morrissey failed his first driving test at the age of eighteen, and I'm surprised we didn't get 586 songs about him not passing it. Despite writing songs where cars and driving are the main themes ("There Is a Light That Never Goes Out," "Driving Your Girlfriend Home," and "The Boy Racer"), Morrissey did not have a driver's license until 1995, although he did own cars that he paid friends and assistants to chauffeur him around in. The first car he purchased was a 1961 Ford Consul, supposedly from an old lady who was selling it because her husband died right after buying it (only Morrissey would buy a haunted car). He also purchased a new Golf GTI in 1988 and would use that to practice his driving.

Morrissey finally passed his driver's test and was rewarded with a license in 1995—and promptly went out and purchased a Porsche 911. Since then, he has also been the owner of a 1977 Aston Martin and a Jaguar. In the 2003 documentary *The Importance of Being Morrissey*, he is seen tooling around Hollywood on a Vespa. How very mod of him!

A clip from *Carry On Abroad* makes a cameo in the "Everyday Is Like Sunday" video.   *Author's collection*

Morrissey's Love Life

When the Smiths first became popular in 1983, they were young and cute, and much was speculated about their personal lives. But right out of the gate, Morrissey spoke about abstinence and staying celibate, with it becoming almost a mantra. With all of the gender trading, androgyny, and S&M-like activities going on in the late '70s and early '80s (I'm looking at you, Soft Cell!), audiences and fans thought Morrissey's celibacy was a nice change of pace and something different. If anything, it accounted for having both men and women excited by Morrissey because they were mystified by him—did he really like women or did he really like men? No one knew because he was not having sex with either.

Eventually the self-sanctioned celibacy began to wear thin for Morrissey, and by 2002, he was making it pretty much common knowledge that he was looking to put out. But what about Jake Walters?

Until Morrissey's 2013 autobiography, *Autobiography*, was released, most people were satisfied with believing that Jake and Morrissey were "just friends." Morrissey and Johnny Marr had an intense and personal relationship that wasn't sexual, so it was possible. Until *Autobiography*, the only personal love life of Morrissey's that anyone was aware of was the mystery person in Italy, and that was only because the songs on 2006's *Ringleader of the Tormentors* were all "lovey-dovey" and "I'm getting laid." With the insinuation of an intimate relationship with Jake Walters back in the mid-'90s coming out in *Autobiography*, no one knows what to think.

And I feel that Morrissey prefers it that way.

Awards

Morrissey has received a few awards, such as the Ivor Novello Award for "Outstanding Contribution to British Music" (the biggest award of his career, so far). He has also received the Icon Award from *Mojo* magazine in 2004, the Best Songwriter Award from *Q* magazine in 1994, and a Silver Clef Inspiration Award. He has been nominated twice for a Brit Award—the first time in 1995 for "Best British Male Solo Artist" and the second time in 2005 for "Best British Male Solo Artist." Morrissey has been nominated only once for a Grammy Award here in the United States—in 1993 for "Best Alternative Album" (he lost to Tom Waits's *Bone Machine*).

He is also the recipient of the Linda McCartney Memorial Award from PETA, awarded to him at their Twenty-Fifth Anniversary Gala in 2005.

Alcohol

One vice that Morrissey does partake in is drinking alcohol. While never a big drinker when he was younger, he would drink wine back in the Smiths days. He took up drinking beer in the 1990s (preferring it in the bottle and not in the glass, which I do agree with him on) and, after his move to Los Angeles in 1997, liked it even more due to the variety of American beers. He does like to drink an Italian beer called Peroni because it is safe for vegans and vegetarians to consume.

Morrissey has switched over to drinking cocktails and has been seen drinking Gray Goose vodka, specifically in vodka tonics. I guess Gray Goose is one animal product he will consume.

Drugs

I think Morrissey would be an awesome stoner. He could take a couple rips off the bong, eat a bag of cookies, and settle in to watch some long, boring movie. "Hey man, we are all human and we need to be loved," he would say while high.

While in the Smiths, Morrissey would often say he didn't use drugs, but he was never outright against anyone who did, since it was fairly common knowledge that the rest of the Smiths would partake. When Andy Rourke's heroin problem got out of control, Morrissey made the executive decision to kick him out of the Smiths. It did not help that Rourke was also busted for buying drugs in a known drug house that was part of a police sting. He eventually got clean and rejoined the Smiths, with Morrissey and the rest of the band welcoming him back.

Morrissey was familiar with legal drugs from a young age, with his use of antidepressants such as Prozac and lithium and barbiturates like Valium, and he continued to take them on and off throughout adulthood. His bouts with medications have inspired some of his best songs, with 2009's "Someone Is Squeezing My Skull" being the most obvious, but drug references are also in 1988's "Late Night, Maudlin Street" ("I took strange pills . . . ") and "Sunny" ("Oh, with your jean belt wrapped around your arm . . . ").

In 1992, Morrissey mentioned that he had tried ecstasy and liked it, although he said he still was not "into" taking drugs. He continues to be drug-free and nonjudgmental of anyone who does.

Coronation Street.   *Author's collection*

Coronation Street

Coronation Street was Morrissey's favorite television program, an obsession that started when he was a young boy in the 1960s and continued as a young man in the 1970s. In typical soap opera fashion, *Coronation Street* was filled with strife, fighting, love, sex, and humor (Morrissey himself was a fan of crabby matriarch Ena Sharples). So in love with *Coronation Street* was he that young Steven Morrissey would write letters to *Coronation Street* producer and writer Leslie Duxbury with storyline suggestions, such as couples divorcing and a jukebox being added to the *Coronation Street* pub. As a child, he would also hang around outside the studio in hopes of getting the autograph of *Coronation Street* actress Margot Bryant.

Like a lot of soap operas (both English and American), *Coronation Street* got kind of silly and stupid (according to Morrissey). He was also upset that the characters on *Coronation Street* never really progressed—there were no vegetarians on the show, and characters became so ridiculous they were irredeemable. Morrissey still speaks about his love for the old *Coronation Street*, but he is no longer a fan.

EastEnders

Yet another soap opera that Morrissey enjoyed watching throughout the '90s (although not as much as the old *Coronation Street*), *EastEnders* takes place in the Walford borough of East London (obviously) and employs the typical soap opera story lines, such as love triangles, kidnapping, and death. While making an appearance on *Top of the Pops* in 1991, Morrissey and his band visited the *EastEnders* set, with pictures of them posing throughout the fake settings appearing in the concert program for the 1991 *Kill Uncle* tour.

Morrissey's love of *EastEnders* influenced his videos for two of his singles off 1995's *Southpaw Grammar*. As Morrissey walks through the house in the "Dagenham Dave" video, there are two framed pictures of *EastEnders* characters Frank Butcher and his wife, Pat, while the video for "The Boy Racer" didn't have characters from *EastEnders*—but two *EastEnders* actresses made an appearance: Nicola Stapleton and Martine McCutcheon were the girls at the end that encounter the "Boy Racer."

Fans

We Morrissey fans are legendary.

We camp out in line twenty-four hours in advance to make sure we get close to the stage. We use our friends for a lift to get on said stage. And then we tackle, kiss, hug, pile drive, and bow down to our lord and savior.

Well, I guess I wouldn't put myself in that equation. I like to arrive in style and claim my seat with cocktail already in hand.

Morrissey has always been a fan of his fans, or as he refers to us, "the audience." Although we were quite intimidating at first with our long letters of strife and tales of woe, Morrissey has gotten used to the passion and urgency of the audience and now welcomes it—he considers it the ultimate form of flattery.

But sometimes that flattery turns into craziness. Fans have been known to call into whatever label he is on at the time and demand to speak to him, threatening to harm themselves unless they can hear his caring baritone on the other end of the line giving sage advice. Or sometimes there is no problem and they're just over-excited—for an example of this, listen to the "hidden track" on the 1991 *At KROQ* EP (fan after fan calls in and leaves enthusiastic messages about Morrissey for DJ Richard Blade). But the KROQ fans were nothing compared to uber-fan James Charles Kiss, who

Morrissey's very own Super Stars trading cards mention his love
of flowers and huge hair.   *Author's collection*

almost held DJs and staff at the Colorado radio station KRXY at gunpoint
to make them play nothing but the Smiths (he wussed out and turned over
his gun to a staff member before things got serious). Another fan found
out where he was living in Los Angeles and decorated Morrissey's car with
Morrissey pictures. He then stripped down naked and started dancing in
the middle of the street.

From good tattoos to bad tattoos, to wearing your hair in a quiff, to
cutting a bitch who cut in the ticket line, Morrissey fans have always been
hardcore for life.

Flowers

"The flowers were a very human gesture. They integrated harmony with
nature, something people seemed so terribly afraid of. It had got to the

point in music where people were really afraid to show how they felt. To show their emotions. I thought that was a shame and very boring. The flowers offered hope," Morrissey told *Melody Maker* magazine in 1983.

Although Morrissey and the Smiths encouraged the bringing, wearing, and throwing of flowers to their concerts (they even had a request in their concert rider for "non-thorn" flowers and a live tree to be provided for them on stage). But around 1985, the Smiths gave up the whole "flowers" theme because of the dangers involved regarding sap, slipping on petals, tripping on stems, and being hit in the face by a projectile bud.

Oscar Wilde's influence on Morrissey showed with his ideas regarding flowers. Wilde preferred to wear a Malmaison carnation that was dyed a bright green, and while Morrissey originally chose the gladiolus as his flower of choice, he is now seen wearing roses (when he does in fact wear flowers on stage).

A blog titled MorrisseysWorld was created in 2011 and was rumored to be the work of Morrissey himself. In 2012, the person behind the blog created the Blue Rose Society, which asked "the audience" to bring red, white, or blue roses to a Morrissey concert. Coincidently (or not), Oscar Wilde started his own Green Carnation Society.

Since then, there have been "Illuminati-ish" claims about the Blue Rose Society and Morrissey's part in it. The members of the Blue Rose Society claim that Morrissey accepts only roses from audience members and then promptly wears them, even when other flowers are offered. They've also pointed out that there was a vase of red roses on the table of the first book signing of 2013's *Autobiography*, and that him wearing white roses around his wrist for the 2013 Nobel Peace Prize ceremony means that he is the wizard behind the curtain of the Blue Rose Society. Anyone can join the Blue Rose Society—just bring a blue rose to a Morrissey concert and try to hand it to him (or at lease throw it up on stage).

Morrissey's Eating Habits

Morrissey is a traditional (if not boring) eater. According to multiple sources (like ex-Smiths bassist Andy Rourke and engineer Danton Supple), Morrissey likes to eat potatoes, toast, and eggs. He seems to favor breakfast-like foods such as yogurt and an assortment of jams, jellies, and biscuits.

He also does not like spicy food or garlic and onions (so basically, good food) and prefers his vegetables steamed, pureed, and bland. Morrissey is also known to munch out on junk food, like chocolate, ice creams, and especially Cheez-It crackers.

Rome

Morrissey moved to Rome in 2005, after leaving his home Los Angeles, his home since 1997. The story that Morrissey told an interviewer was that he was on a layover in Dublin and did not want to endure another long flight to Los Angeles (his original origin). So he asked the airline to get him a shorter flight to somewhere—anywhere—and it ended up being Rome. He holed himself up in a hotel and fell in love with the city.

When in Rome, do what the Romans do. So for Morrissey, that meant making a record. He signed up uber-producer Tony Visconti and brought the boys over and proceeded to record 2006's *Ringleader of the Tormentors*. But because the songs on *Ringleader of the Tormentors* (and Morrissey himself) screamed "I'm in love" and he sounded genuinely happy, fans assumed that he met someone and that was his reason for moving to Rome—especially with the song "Dear God Please Help Me," with lyrics about a clandestine hookup on the streets of Rome and the release of guilt after the encounter. Morrissey has denied that "Dear God Please Help Me" is autobiographical.

In the 2003 documentary *The Importance of Being Morrissey*, Morrissey himself speaks about his lack of flying and how much he does not care for it, letting it affect his touring schedule (in the documentary he is shown visiting Australia for the first time since 1991). To me, the relocation to Rome because of a crappy flight sounds totally plausible. I mean, have you ever flown on Southwest?

Football

As a dumb American, I really have no clue when it comes to football, a.k.a. soccer. But Morrissey likes it (even more than boxing). From a young age, he was a fan of Manchester United, his local football team. Despite the scene being rowdy and full of hooligans, young Morrissey enjoyed himself enough to continue his interest in football. His reasoning for watching it at home is that it gave him a chance to relax and zone out.

Throughout his career, he has also followed teams other than Manchester United, such as the Tranmere Rovers (they had a player named

John Morrissey), West Ham United (because of his friendship with/admiration for the Cockney Rejects, who are big West Ham fans), and Club Deportivo Guadalajara (a.k.a. Chivas) during his exile in Los Angeles in the late 1990s and early 2000s. While touring America and Mexico, he and the band would regularly sport the Chivas uniform on stage.

Morrissey has always added touches of football to various items in his solo career, such as concert backdrops of English football players, album covers (the single for 1995's "Dagenham Dave" features player Terry Venables), and even songs—1992's "We'll Let You Know" celebrates the world of soccer hooliganism, and 1997's terrible single "Roy's Keen" is a play on the name of footballer Roy Keane.

Hearing Aid

Say what?

During his Smiths days, Morrissey was usually seen wearing a hearing aid in his ear, even though he was not deaf. The story behind the nonfunctioning hearing aid would vary from interview to interview—sometimes the story would be that it was a tribute to poor ol' Johnnie Ray (who was hard of hearing in one ear originally and then eventually in both ears), or the story would be that he wore the hearing aid as a tribute to a deaf fan who wrote him a fan letter. Either way, Morrissey continued to rock the hearing aid until 1986.

Eurovision Song Contest

Morrissey has been obsessed with the Eurovision Song Contest since he was a young child, but his Eurovision fever was at an all-time high in 2006—two of the music videos from the 2006 *Ringleader of the Tormentors* album ("You Have Killed Me" and "In the Future When All's Well") were made with a 1970s vintage feel and were intercut with authentic 1970s Eurovision Song Contest footage, and while performing at the London Palladium, he bitched about the performance of the United Kingdom contestant in that year's contest.

After all that, the BBC asked Morrissey if he would consider representing the United Kingdom in the Eurovision Song Contest. Morrissey said that he would, but only if he would automatically "win" the preliminaries by not competing against anyone else (Cliff Richard didn't have to compete against anyone else to represent the United Kingdom back in 1968). The BBC refused Morrissey's request, so Morrissey refused their offer. It is too bad he didn't agree because his entry into the Eurovision Song Contest would have been another link connecting him to Sandie Shaw—she was the United Kingdom entry in 1967, and she won with her song "Puppet on a String."

Factory Records

Everybody knows Factory Records—home of Joy Division, New Order, Happy Mondays, and the Hacienda Nightclub, all of it immortalized in the 2002 movie *24 Hour Party People*. Factory Records was created in Manchester in 1978 by Granada Television reporter Tony Wilson, designer Peter Seville, Alan Erasmus, and Rob Gretton, New Order's manager.

Morrissey and Johnny Marr had separate relationships with Factory insiders—as an angsty teenager, Morrissey would write to Tony Wilson as he worked at Granada TV, praising the gospel that was the New York Dolls or submitting television show ideas. In the cold winter of 1982, Morrissey gave Wilson the Smiths' first demo. Wilson wasn't impressed and passed on signing them. Only after the Smiths signed with Rough Trade did Wilson regret not adding them to the Factory family.

Johnny Marr was good friends with Andrew Berry, DJ and hairdresser at the Factory-run Hacienda nightclub. He also worked with ex–Joy Division/present New Order guitarist and front man Bernard Sumner on the side project Electronic, with their first three singles and self-titled debut album being released by Factory Records.

Morrissey and Tony Wilson would soon become enemies, mostly just shit-talking about each other, with Morrissey calling Tony "fat" and Tony calling Morrissey "an arsehole" (both accusations were true). Morrissey was especially upset over how best friend Linder Sterling was portrayed in the *24 Hour Party People* movie, thereby refusing any use of the Smiths music in the film. Tony Wilson passed away in 2007 at age 57, and Johnny Marr spoke at his funeral, praising Wilson for creating and maintaining the Manchester music scene.

Pseudonyms

Morrissey has a history of using pseudonyms, when it comes to writing, making music, or checking into hotels. He has used the following to dissuade his adoring fans from finding where he lays his head:

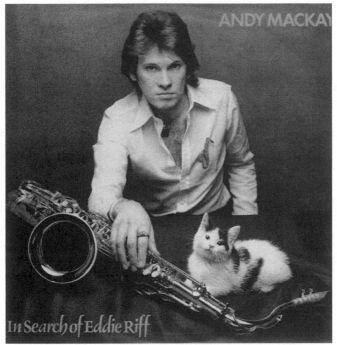

Morrissey's pseudonym Eddie Riff stems from the 1974 Andy
Mackay album, *In Search of Eddie Riff.*   *Author's collection*

- Sheridan Whiteside: A character from the 1942 film *The Man Who Came
  to Dinner,* Whiteside was based on New York critic Alexander Woollcott,
  who was a member of the Algonquin Round Table (fun fact: Alexander
  Woollcott invented the Brandy Alexander cocktail).
- Eddie Riff: Never a real person, just the name of a solo album by
  Roxy Music's saxophone player, Andy Mackay (*In Search of Eddie Riff*).
  Morrissey has used Eddie Riff when checking into hotels and when
  designing album cover art.
- Terence Stomp: A riff on Smiths cover star and actor Terence Stamp.
  Morrissey used the name in the credits of the 1991 album *Kill Uncle.*
- Ann Coates: The name Morrissey used for the recording of the woman's
  voice on 1986's "Bigmouth Strikes Again"—Morrissey filtered his voice
  through a harmonizer to make himself sound more feminine. There
  is an area north of Manchester called Ancoats, and the film editor of
  one of Morrissey's favorite movies, *The Elephant Man*, is named Anne
  V. Coats.

- Burt Reynolds: Unfortunately, Morrissey never rocked the 'stache, but he used Burt Reynolds as a code name for addressing envelopes when asking guitarist Mark Nevin to submit potential songs.

Morrissey and Rockabilly

Morrissey insists that he does not have a "rockabilly band," even though people believe that, due to his 1991 backing band and his two major co-writers having rockabilly roots.

It even happened to me. While having a conversation with an older friend about Morrissey, I asked if he had ever seen Morrissey perform live—"Sure! I saw him back when he had that really good rockabilly band."

So Morrissey is right.

But the real fans know better. Morrissey's songs that qualify as "rockabilly" songs—"Pregnant for the Last Time," "Sing Your Life," and "The Loop"—were written by *Kill Uncle* co-writer Mark Nevin and not Boz Boorer or Alain Whyte. As a matter of fact, Boz Boorer, Spencer Cobrin, Gary Day, and Alain Whyte were hired for the "Sing Your Life" video because Morrissey wanted a "working-class band" in the video. Morrissey has not written or performed another rockabilly song since 1991, so that makes his band just a regular ol' band.

39

I Am Two People

Five Kick-Ass Things Morrissey Has Done

I n the media, Morrissey is usually portrayed as a villain, despite being a hero to many people. Positive actions don't necessarily equal ratings or readership, but the media should give Morrissey credit when credit is due. I'm not exactly the media, but here are five instances where Morrissey was very much the hero.

The Red Wedge Concert

The Red Wedge was a collaboration of concerts spearheaded by Billy Bragg in 1985 to raise awareness and engage youth in politics (and introduce them to the Labor Party). Other bands that performed the Red Wedge concerts were the Style Council, the Communards, Prefab Sprout, Lorna Gee, Junior Giscombe, and Jerry Dammers. Johnny Marr was good friends with Billy Bragg, and he and Andy Rourke agreed to back Billy Bragg during the short tour.

Although Marr and Rourke enjoyed playing with Bragg, the other bands on the Red Wedge bill treated them pretty poorly, creating a hostile and overall crappy concert environment. Marr commented to Morrissey about the situation, and Morrissey decided to show them what's up.

Morrissey and Mike Joyce accompanied Marr and Rourke to the next and final Red Wedge gig. With Morrissey leading the way, the Smiths made their way backstage to the bewilderment of the other bands performing that night. Using the Style Council's equipment and after a quick announcement, the Smiths performed in front of the crowd gathered at the Newcastle City Hall and seriously rocked it, putting all of the other bands on the bill to shame and driving the crowd into a surprised frenzy. They performed four songs: "Shakespeare Sister," "I Want the One I Can't Have," and "The Boy with the Thorn in His Side," closing with "Bigmouth Strikes Again." There is a rumor that Morrissey dropped the mic and the rest of the band set down the equipment and then silently walked backstage with their heads

An advertisement for the 1986 Red Wedge concerts.
Author's collection

held high, showing the rest of the bands that night how it's done. Although I cannot confirm the rumor, I can confirm that they did indeed rock that night, and many people who were in the crowd confirmed it through various interviews and word of mouth.

Although performing well is a normal thing, what makes it a kick-ass thing is Morrissey's loyalty to his friends and his band. No one was going to talk shit to his bandmates and give them a hard time for simply being there to help out a friend. Morrissey often is looked upon negatively for his cockiness, but regarding the Red Wedge concert, it was the right (and kick-ass) thing to do.

New York Dolls Reunion

Like me, you probably were not clamoring for a New York Dolls reunion, especially in 2004. Two of them were dead, and unless you wanted to sit through "Hot Hot Hot" for the millionth time, the other three were not doing much. The reunion fires were kindled when Morrissey was given the honor of curating the 2004 Meltdown festival, giving him the power to select whatever acts he wanted to perform throughout the festival. David Johansen, singer of the Dolls, was already signed up to open for Morrissey's five-day residency, so Morrissey just asked him if he would consider reuniting the Dolls and performing at the Meltdown festival. Johansen, Arthur "Killer" Kane, and Sylvain Sylvain agreed to give it a try.

Giving it a try was the best they could hope for, considering they had not played together since 1975. Arthur Kane also hated Johansen, jealous of his solo success and unfairly blaming him for Kane's musical troubles—his distaste for Johansen was so bad that Kane jumped out of a second-story window when he saw Johansen's performance as the Ghost of Christmas Past in the 1988 movie *Scrooged* (hey, it could have been worse—it could have been *Car 54, Where Are You?*). But all three surviving members were willing to make it work, and they did—for two nights during the Meltdown festival they rocked the house (and made Morrissey cry). Morrissey released the second night's performance as *The Return of the New York Dolls—Live from Royal Festival Hall 2004* on his Attack label. Things were looking up for the remaining Dolls—potential future shows were discussed and all of the previous bad feelings were erased.

Sadly, all of the positive vibes would only last about a month. Arthur "Killer" Kane passed away from leukemia on July 13. Initially thinking he caught the flu while over in England, he came back home to Los Angeles and checked into the hospital, only to never check out. David Johansen and Sylvain Sylvain continued with the newly formed New York Dolls and released an album in 2006 titled *One Day It Will Please Us to Remember Even This* with an assortment of guest stars. All of this was documented for the 2005 film *New York Doll*, although the majority of the film is about Arthur Kane.

What makes this a kick-ass thing is that Morrissey never lost faith in his favorite band and still held hope that one day they would reunite. Morrissey was able to bring peace and happiness to Arthur Kane in his final days and did what was deemed impossible—reuniting the New York Dolls.

Salford Lads Club

Stop me if you think you've heard this one before.

Although none of the Smiths were from Salford, they chose the exterior of the Salford Lads Club in Salford (obviously) for a series of promotional photos for their 1986 *The Queen Is Dead* album. The photo that was chosen for the album gatefold is probably the best-known photo of the Smiths and the most recognizable. Because of this, the Saldford Lads Club has become a tourist hot spot for Smiths and Morrissey fans alike, with all of them posing out front to replicate the now-iconic photo.

In 2007, 103 years after first opening, the Salford Lads and Girls Club received a generous donation from Morrissey in the amount of £20,000 to help with restoration costs. At first he requested that news of his donation be made secret, but the club director asked that the information be made public as to encourage other people to donate. Morrissey agreed to let his donation be known.

Do I have to explain why this is a kick-ass thing to do? Well, maybe I do. Morrissey has a reputation for being somewhat of a miser with his money,

Morrissey and the Smiths pose outside of the Salford Lads Clubs for 1986's *The Queen Is Dead.*   *Stephen Wright/ Getty Images*

so seeing him donate his money to a worthy cause makes it worthy of being a kick-ass thing to do.

Skinheads

Being a dumb American, I have never been too familiar with the English skinheads, but I understand that it is a touchy subject for the English people. Morrissey has often been accused of pandering to the skinhead crowd and outright being a racist. Time and time again, Morrissey has defended himself and his choices to the media. In reality, Morrissey has thumbed his nose at the skinhead movement, from making fun of their dumbness in his 1992 song "The National Front Disco" to showing off their blind ignorance in his video for his 1997 hit "Alma Matters." Morrissey was not afraid to confront the skinhead population while performing at the 1992 Madstock festival (although he did cancel his performance the next day due to being assaulted by items thrown by the audience), and his video for his 1990 single "Our Frank" was banned in the UK and US due to the skinheads featured throughout.

To me, it is pretty kick-ass to not be afraid of a violent and threatening gang of people and just do what you want to do. Morrissey's not afraid to stand up to oppressors and just does not care what people think.

His Smug Mug

Morrissey is fifty-six and doesn't care anymore. He has gone completely gray, he is fat, he has wrinkles, and he is fine with it. It is very kick-ass that he is comfortable with aging, unlike his contemporary Robert Smith, who still insists on wearing the white face paint and eyeliner on top of his stubble. Morrissey still dresses stylishly and dresses his age (except for those pants he wore at the 2013 Nobel Peace Prize concert). He revels in being an elder statesmen of indie rock and can still melt a heart with his clear blue eyes and darling dimples. Morrissey acting his age is a very kick-ass thing to do in a world where image is everything.

40

We Like It When Our Friends Become Successful

Famous Friends

Russell Brand

Never in a million years would anyone associate Morrissey with a crazy-haired wild man, but it happened. English comedian and television personality Russell Brand has been a long-standing Morrissey fan (even going so far as to name his cat Morrissey) and first met him in 2006 during a BBC interview. Morrissey did him the honor of performing on *The Russell Brand Show* (and looking quite gorgeous, might I add). In his television appearances and written words, Brand has continuously spoken about his affection for Morrissey. Morrissey in return has appeared in additional interviews with Brand where they reminisce about football teams, old TV shows, and drinking together at various pubs.

Russell Brand appears in the *Years of Refusal* bonus feature, "Wrestle With Russell," where they banter back and forth about the new album, hair, and fame. Actually, Russell does most of the bantering.

And badgering.

Russell Brand has been a great and surprising friend to Morrissey.

Len Brown

A respected music journalist who has interviewed Morrissey countless times, Len Brown has the honor of being one of the only journalists who has an actual friendship with Morrissey. Len complied all of his interactions and interviews with Morrissey and released the Omnibus book *Meetings with*

Morrissey is interviewed by Russell Brand for the *Years of Refusal* extra "Wrestle with Russell." *Author's collection*

Morrissey, a very good and in-depth book about Morrissey's personal life and outlook. *Meetings with Morrissey* and the videos that accompanied it (available on YouTube) have that friendly, jovial vibe that only real friends can get, with Morrissey being as down to Earth as Morrissey can possibly get.

In a motion of true friendship and respect, Len gifted Morrissey with a copy of a Gregory Isaacs single that was released on Attack Records back in 1974 (before the label was controlled by Morrissey). The single had belonged to Len's brother, Don, who unfortunately committed suicide in 1982. Humbled, Morrissey featured the single alongside himself for a *New Musical Express* photo shoot.

Pete Burns

Morrissey and Pete Burns's friendship was spun right round in the '80s and '90s, starting when they first met in 1985 backstage during a *Top of the Pops* filming and continuing through such events as Dead or Alive reaching #1 with their song "You Spin Me Round (Like a Record)," the Smiths' continuing success and painful split, Morrissey's success as a solo artist, and Burns's transformation into Joan Rivers.

Morrissey has said numerous times that he was drawn to Pete Burns because of his outspoken views and "devil-may-care" attitude. Rumor was that they stopped being friends because Burns purchased a fur coat, but Morrissey stated in 2004 that he never stopped being friends with Burns—it was Burns himself who stopped being friendly. In an instance of schadenfreude, Pete Burns would get into trouble in 2006 while a contestant on the UK version of *Celebrity Big Brother* by claiming that his fur coat was made of gorilla fur (side note: I did not even know you could use gorilla fur until researching this chapter). His coat was confiscated and tested for its "gorilla-ness," and it was discovered that it was made from colobus monkeys instead. Either way, they are both endangered, and Pete Burns was almost prosecuted for having it. Luckily for Pete (but not for the primates), he was able to prove that the coat was made before 1975, before they were officially endangered. Because of this coat fiasco, I highly doubt he and Morrissey are still friends.

Lloyd Cole

Cool black hair, dreamy voice, deep lyrics, and a love of literature and old movies.

Oh, you thought I was talking about Morrissey? Nope—Lloyd Cole.

The resemblance is uncanny, but it did not stop the two of them from being friends. Both like and respect Truman Capote, both had songs covered by Sandie Shaw ("Hand in Glove" and "Please Help the Cause Against Loneliness" for Morrissey, "Are You Ready to Be Heartbroken?" for Cole), and both are English. They met in 1984 backstage at a Lloyd Cole and the Commotions concert and stayed friends well into the '90s, but eventually grew apart, with Cole suggesting that he "grew up" while Morrissey stayed the same ol' Morrissey.

Howard Devoto

Ex-frontman of the Buzzcocks and Magazine, and fellow Manchurian, Howard Devoto was first a mentor to young Steven Morrissey and then a friend. Morrissey was first introduced to Devoto backstage at a Magazine show in 1978 through Linder Sterling, who was Devoto's girlfriend at the time. Their paths would continue to cross throughout the '80s, with the Smiths opening up for Devoto's solo project in 1983 and him opening up for the Smiths in 1986 (with his new project, Adultery). Their friendship would continue until the '90s, appearing together on Radio 1 in 1987 and Morrissey reading Proust on stage during a show by Luxuria, Devoto's post-Adultery project.

James Maker

One of Morrissey's best and oldest friends, James Maker first corresponded with Morrissey after reading his letters praising the New York Dolls (Maker himself a Dolls fan). They agreed to meet, and Maker took the train to Morrissey's home in Manchester. They proceeded to get in a fight with some thugs and listen to records all night. That sounds like the perfect friendship to me!

James (or as Morrissey refers to him, Jimmy) would continue to be Morrissey's closest friend, even supporting the Smiths by performing alongside them for their first two shows, by dancing and playing the maracas. He eventually started his own band, Raymonde, which opened for the Smiths during their final tour. Morrissey would end up covering Raymonde's "No One Can Hold a Candle to You" in 2004 and signed Jimmy to his Attack label, releasing just one single by him, titled "Born This Way." They continue to be friends and inspire each other with their own music, as well as the New York Dolls.

Cathal Smyth

As a member of the legendary ska group Madness, Cathal (also known as Chas Smash) met Morrissey through producer Clive Langer in 1990. Realizing they had certain things in common (like being Irish), Cathal became Morrissey's friend, confidant, and task manager. He hooked Morrissey up with Boz Boorer to join his backing band, and in return, Morrissey wrote "You're the One for Me, Fatty" with Smyth in mind and also included a photo of him in the video for "We Hate It When Our Friends Become Successful." Although not as close as they once were, Cathal has nothing but nice things to say regarding Morrissey. I guess he does not hate it when his friends become successful.

Michael Stipe

Despite the rumors of a "relationship" between the two, Morrissey and REM's Michael Stipe are just homies. They met in 1989, and both realized how similar they were: both loved Patti Smith, both were eccentric front men, and both were highly intellectual. They continued to be and still are friends, with Michael taking Morrissey's side during the Mike Joyce court case and Morrissey aggressively defending their friendship from nosy reporters in 2006. I wonder if Morrissey was the inspiration for REM's "Shiny Happy People"?

41

The Boy with the Thorn in His Side

Morrissey's Best Quips and Quotes

"I always thought my genitals were the result of some crude practical joke."

—*New Musical Express,* 1986

"I am capable of looking on the bright side—I just don't do it very often."

—*Melody Maker,* 1987

"Long hair is an unpardonable offense which should be punishable by death."

—*Star Hits,* 1986

"I think I must be, absolutely, a total sex object. In every sense of the word."

—*New Musical Express,* 1989

"When they bury me in a church and chuck earth on my grave, I'd like the words 'Well, at least he tried' engraved on my tombstone."

—*Melody Maker,* 1987

"The fire in the belly is essential, otherwise you become Michael Bublé—famous and meaningless."

—*Billboard,* 2011

"Sex is a waste of batteries."

—*Melody Maker,* 1986

"Music is like a drug, but there are no rehabilitation centers."

—*Select*, 1991

"The press only write about me in terms of the Smiths story, and the fact that I've had three solo number one albums—or even twenty-five years of eventful solo activity—is never mentioned anywhere. Odd."

—*Pitchfork*, 2011

"Yes I have had a tan, actually. I went to Los Angeles and got one there, but it didn't make it back to Britain. You're not allowed to come through customs with a tan."

—*I-D*, 1987

"Life would be so colourful if only I had a drink problem."

—*Vox*, 1990

No one is as eloquent and insightful with their thoughts (and insults) as Morrissey.

Patti Ouderkirk/ WireImage/ Getty Images

"I see no difference between eating animals and pedophilia. They are both rape, violence, murder. If I'm introduced to anyone who eats beings, I walk away."

—True-to-You.net, 2014

Morrissey Discography

THE SMITHS

Studio Albums

The Smiths
Released: February 20, 1984
Label: Rough Trade
Format: LP, cassette, compact disc
Chart Position: #2 (UK chart), #150 (US chart)

Meat Is Murder
Released: February 11, 1985
Label: Rough Trade
Format: LP, cassette, compact disc
Chart Position: #1 (UK chart), #110 (US chart)

The Queen Is Dead
Released: June 16, 1986
Label: Rough Trade
Format: LP, cassette, compact disc
Chart Position: #2 (UK chart), #70 (US chart)

Strangeways, Here We Come
Released: September 28, 1987
Label: Rough Trade
Format: LP, cassette, compact disc
Chart Position: #2 (UK chart), #55 (US chart)

Live Albums

Rank

Released: October 5, 1988

Label: Rough Trade, Sire
Format: LP, cassette, compact disc
Chart Position: #2 (UK chart), #77 (US chart)

Compilations

Hatful of Hollow

Released: November 12, 1984
Label: Rough Trade
Format: LP, cassette, compact disc
Chart Position: #7 (UK chart)

The World Won't Listen

Released: February 23, 1987
Label: Rough Trade
Format: LP, cassette, compact disc
Chart Position: #2 (UK chart)

Louder Than Bombs

Released: March 30, 1987
Label: Rough Trade, Sire
Format: LP, cassette, compact disc
Chart Position: #38 (UK chart), #62 (US chart)

Best . . . I

Released: August 17, 1992
Label: WEA
Format: LP, cassette, compact disc
Chart Position: #1 (UK chart), #139 (US chart)

... Best II

Released: November 2, 1992
Label: WEA
Format: LP, cassette, compact disc
Chart Position: #29 (UK chart)

Singles

Released: February 20, 1995
Label: WEA
Format: Compact disc
Chart Position: #5 (UK chart)

The Very Best of the Smiths

Released: June 4, 2001
Label: WEA
Format: Compact disc
Chart Position: #30 (UK chart)

The Sound of the Smiths

Released: November 10, 2008
Label: WEA
Format: Compact disc
Chart Position: #21 (UK chart), #98 (US chart)

The Smiths Singles Box

Released: December 8, 2008
Label: WEA
Format: 12 7″ vinyl, 12 compact discs
Chart Position: None

Complete

Released: September 26, 2011
Label: Rhino
Format: 8 compact discs, 8 12″ vinyl, 25 7″ vinyl, 1 DVD
Chart Position: #63 (UK chart)

Extended Plays

GIV 1

Released: 1984
Label: New Musical Express
Format: 7″ vinyl
Chart Position: None

The Peel Sessions

Released: 1988
Label: Strange Fruit
Format: 12″ vinyl, compact disc
Chart Position: None

Singles

"Hand in Glove"

Released: May 13, 1983
Label: Rough Trade
Format: 7″ vinyl single
Chart Position: #124 (UK chart)
B-sides: "Handsome Devil"

"This Charming Man"

Released: October 31, 1983
Label: Rough Trade
Format: 7″ vinyl single, 12″ vinyl single
Chart Position: #25 (UK chart)
B-sides: "Jeane," "Accept Yourself," "Wonderful Woman"

"What Difference Does It Make?"

Released: January 16, 1984
Label: Rough Trade

Format: 7″vinyl single, 12″vinyl single
Chart Position: #12 (UK chart)
B-sides: "Back to the Old House," "These Things Take Time"

"Heaven Knows I'm Miserable Now"

Released: May 21, 1984
Label: Rough Trade
Format: 7″vinyl single, 12″vinyl single, compact disc single
Chart Position: #10 (UK chart)
B-sides: "Suffer Little Children," "Girl Afraid"

"William, It Was Really Nothing"

Released: August 20, 1984
Label: Rough Trade
Format: 7″vinyl single, 12″vinyl single, compact disc single
Chart Position: #17 (UK chart)
B-sides: "How Soon Is Now?," "Please, Please, Please, Let Me Get What I Want"

"How Soon Is Now?"

Released: January 28, 1985
Label: Rough Trade
Format: 7″vinyl single, 12″vinyl single
Chart Position: #24 (UK chart), #36 (US chart)
B-sides: "Well I Wonder," "Oscillate Wildly," "Girl Afraid," "The Queen Is Dead," "Handsome Devil," "I Started Something I Couldn't Finish," "Suffer Little Children," "Back to the Old House," "Hand in Glove"

"Shakespeare's Sister"

Released: March 18, 1985
Label: Rough Trade
Format: 7″vinyl single, 12″vinyl single
Chart Position: #26 (UK chart)
B-sides: "What She Said," "Stretch Out and Wait"

"The Joke Isn't Funny Anymore"

Released: July 1, 1985
Label: Rough Trade
Format: 7″ vinyl single, 12″ vinyl single
Chart Position: #49 (UK chart)
B-sides: "Nowhere Fast," "Stretch Out and Wait," "Shakespeare's Sister," "Meat Is Murder"

"The Boy with the Thorn in His Side"

Released: September 16, 1985
Label: Rough Trade
Format: 7″ vinyl single, 12″ vinyl single
Chart Position: #23 (UK chart), #49 (US chart)
B-sides: "Rubber Ring," "Asleep"

"Bigmouth Strikes Again"

Released: May 19, 1986
Label: Rough Trade
Format: 7″ vinyl single, 12″ vinyl single
Chart Position: #26 (UK chart)
B-sides: "Money Changes Everything," "Unloveable"

"Panic"

Released: July 21, 1986
Label: Rough Trade
Format: 7″ vinyl single, 12″ vinyl single, compact disc single
Chart Position: #11 (UK chart)
B-sides: "Vicar in a Tutu," "The Draize Train"

"Ask"

Released: October 20, 1986
Label: Rough Trade
Format: 7″ vinyl single, 12″ vinyl single
Chart Position: #14 (UK chart)
B-sides: "Cemetry Gates," "Golden Lights"

"Shoplifters of the World Unite"

Released: January 26, 1987
Label: Rough Trade
Format: 7″ vinyl single, 12″ vinyl single
Chart Position: #12 (UK chart)
B-sides: "London," "Half a Person"

"Sheila Take a Bow"

Released: April 13, 1987
Label: Rough Trade
Format: 7″ vinyl single, 12″ vinyl single, compact disc single
Chart Position: #10 (UK chart)
B-sides: "Is It Really So Strange?," "Sweet and Tender Hooligan," "Shoplifters of the World Unite," "Half a Person," "Panic," "London"

"Girlfriend in a Coma"

Released: August 10, 1987
Label: Rough Trade
Format: 7″ vinyl single, 12″ vinyl single
Chart Position: #13 (UK chart)
B-sides: "Work Is a Four-Letter Word," "I Keep Mine Hidden"

"I Started Something I Couldn't Finish"

Released: November 2, 1987
Label: Rough Trade
Format: 7″ vinyl single, 12″ vinyl single
Chart Position: #23 (UK chart)
B-sides: "Pretty Girls Make Graves," "Some Girls Are Bigger Than Others," "What's the World"

"Last Night I Dreamt That Somebody Loved Me"

Released: December 7, 1987
Label: Rough Trade
Format: 7″ vinyl single, 12″ vinyl single
Chart Position: #30 (UK chart)
B-sides: "Rusholme Ruffians," "Nowhere Fast," "William, It Was Really Nothing"

"Stop Me If You Think You've Heard This One Before"

Released: November 1987
Label: Rough Trade
Format: 7″vinyl single, 12″vinyl single, compact disc single
Chart Position: None
B-sides: "Work Is a Four-Letter Word," "Girlfriend in a Coma," "I Keep Mine Hidden," "Pretty Girls Make Graves," "Some Girls Are Bigger Than Others"

"There Is a Light That Never Goes Out"

Released: October 12, 1992
Label: WEA
Format: Compact disc single
Chart Position: #25 (UK chart)
B-sides: "Hand in Glove," "Some Girls Are Bigger Than Others," "Money Changes Everything," "I Don't Owe You Anything," "Jeane," "Handsome Devil," "Half a Person"

"Sweet and Tender Hooligan"

Released: May 23, 1995
Label: Sire
Format: Compact disc single
Chart Position: None
B-sides: "I Keep Mine Hidden," "Work Is a Four-Letter Word," "What's the World?"

MORRISSEY (SOLO)

Studio Albums

Viva Hate

Released: March 14, 1988
Label: HMV, Sire
Format: Compact disc, LP, cassette
Chart Position: #1 (UK chart), #49 (US chart)

Kill Uncle

Released: March 5, 1991
Label: HMV, Sire
Format: Compact disc, LP, cassette
Chart Position: #8 (UK chart), #52 (US chart)

Your Arsenal

Released: July 27, 1992
Label: HMV, Sire
Format: Compact disc, LP, cassette
Chart Position: #4 (UK chart), #21 (US chart)

Vauxhall and I

Released: March 14, 1994
Label: Parlophone, Sire
Format: Compact disc
Chart Position: #1 (UK chart), #18 (US chart)

Southpaw Grammar

Released: August 28, 1995
Label: RCA Victor, Sire
Format: Compact disc, LP
Chart Position: #4 (UK chart), #66 (US chart)

Maladjusted

Released: August 11, 1997
Label: Island, Mercury
Format: Compact disc, LP
Chart Position: #8 (UK chart), #61 (US chart)

You Are the Quarry

Released: May 17, 2004
Label: Sanctuary
Format: Compact disc, LP
Chart Position: #2 (UK chart), #11 (US chart)

Ringleader of the Tormentors

Released: April 3, 2006
Label: Sanctuary
Format: Compact disc, LP, digital download
Chart Position: #1 (UK chart), #27 (US chart)

Years of Refusal

Released: February 16, 2009
Label: Decca, Polydor
Format: Compact disc, LP, digital download
Chart Position: #3 (UK chart), #11 (US chart)

World Peace Is None of Your Business

Released: July 15, 2014
Label: Harvest/Capitol
Format: Compact disc, LP, digital download

Live Albums

Beethoven Was Deaf

Released: May 10, 1993
Label: HMV
Format: Compact disc
Chart Position: #13 (UK chart)

Live at Earls Court

Released: March 29, 2005
Label: Sanctuary
Format: Compact disc
Chart Position: #18 (UK chart), #119 (US chart)

Compilations

Bona Drag

Released: October 25, 1990
Label: HMV, Sire
Format: LP, cassette, compact disc
Chart Position: #9 (UK chart), #59 (US chart)

World of Morrissey

Released: February 6, 1995
Label: Parlophone, Sire
Format: Compact disc
Chart Position: #15 (UK chart), #134 (US chart)

Suedehead: The Best of Morrissey

Released: September 8, 1997
Label: EMI
Format: Compact disc
Chart Position: #25 (UK chart)

My Early Burglary Years

Released: September 1998
Label: Reprise
Format: Compact disc
Chart Position: None

The CD Singles '88–'91

Released: June 19, 2000
Label: EMI
Format: 10 × compact disc single box set
Chart Position: None

The CD Singles '91–'95

Released: September 17, 2000
Label: EMI
Format: 9 × compact disc single box set
Chart Position: None

The Best of Morrissey

Released: November 6, 2001
Label: Rhino
Format: Compact disc
Chart Position: None

Greatest Hits

Released: February 11, 2008
Label: Decca
Format: Compact disc, LP
Chart Position: #5 (UK chart), #178 (US chart)

The HMV/Parlophone Singles '88–'95

Released: October 12, 2009
Label: EMI
Format: Compact disc, digital download
Chart Position: None

Swords

Released: October 26, 2009
Label: Polydor
Format: Compact disc, LP
Chart Position: #55 (UK chart)

Very Best of Morrissey

Released: April 25, 2011
Label: Major Minor
Format: Compact disc, LP
Chart Position: #80 (UK chart)

Extended Plays

At KROQ

Released: September 18, 1991
Label: Sire/Reprise
Format: Compact disc
Chart Position: None

Singles

"Suedehead"

Released: February 15, 1988
Label: HMV
Format: 7″ vinyl single, 12″ vinyl single, compact disc single, cassette single
Chart Position: #5 (UK chart)
B-sides: "I Know Very Well How I Got My Name," "Hairdresser on Fire," "Oh Well, I'll Never Learn"

"Everyday Is Like Sunday"

Released: May 31, 1988
Label: HMV, Sire/Reprise, Major Minor
Format: 7″ vinyl single, 12″ vinyl single, compact disc single, cassette single
Chart Position: #9 (UK chart)
B-sides: "Disappointed," "Sister I'm a Poet," "Will Never Marry," "November the Second," "Trash"

"The Last of the Famous International Playboys"

Released: January 30, 1989
Label: HMV
Format: 7″ vinyl single, 12″ vinyl single, compact disc single, cassette single
Chart Position: #6 (UK chart), #3 (US chart)
B-sides: "Lucky Lisp," "Michael's Bones"

"Interesting Drug"

Released: April 17, 1989
Label: HMV
Format: 7″ vinyl single, 12″ vinyl single, compact disc single, cassette single
Chart Position: #9 (UK chart), #11 (US chart)
B-sides: "Such a Little Thing Makes Such a Big Difference," "Sweet and Tender Hooligan"

"Ouija Board, Ouija Board"

Released: November 13, 1989
Label: HMV
Format: 7″ vinyl single, 12″ vinyl single, compact disc single, cassette single
Chart Position: #18 (UK chart), #2 (US chart)
B-sides: "Yes I Am Blind," "East West"

"November Spawned a Monster"

Released: April 23, 1990
Label: HMV
Format: 7″ vinyl single, 12″ vinyl single, compact disc single, cassette single
Chart Position: #12 (UK chart), #6 (US chart)
B-sides: "He Knows I'd Love to See Him," "Girl Least Likely To"

"Piccadilly Palare"

Released: October 8, 1990
Label: HMV
Format: 7″ vinyl single, 12″ vinyl single, compact disc single, cassette single
Chart Position: #18 (UK chart), #2 (US chart)
B-sides: "At Amber," "Get Off the Stage"

"Our Frank"

Released: February 11, 1991
Label: HMV
Format: 7″ vinyl single, 12″ vinyl single, compact disc single, cassette single
Chart Position: #26 (UK chart), #2 (US chart)
B-sides: "Journalists Who Lie," "Tony the Pony"

"Sing Your Life"

Released: April 1, 1991
Label: HMV
Format: 7″vinyl single, 12″vinyl single, compact disc single, cassette single
Chart Position: #33 (UK chart), #10 (US chart)
B-sides: "That's Entertainment," "The Loop"

"Pregnant for the Last Time"

Released: July 15, 1991
Label: HMV
Format: 7″vinyl single, 12″vinyl single, compact disc single, cassette single
Chart Position: #25 (UK chart)
B-sides: "Skin Storm," "Cosmic Dancer," "Disappointed"

"My Love Life"

Released: September 17, 1991
Label: HMV
Format: 7″vinyl single, 12″vinyl single, compact disc single, cassette single
Chart Position: #29 (UK chart)
B-sides: "I've Changed My Plea to Guilty," "Skin Storm," "There's a Place in Hell for Me and My Friends"

"We Hate It When Our Friends Become Successful"

Released: April 27, 1992
Label: HMV
Format: 7″vinyl single, 12″vinyl single, compact disc single, cassette single
Chart Position: #17 (UK chart), #2 (US chart)
B-sides: "Suedehead," "I've Changed My Plea to Guilty," "Pregnant for the Last Time," "Alsatian Cousin"

"You're the One for Me, Fatty"

Released: July 6, 1992
Label: HMV
Format: 7″vinyl single, 12″vinyl single, compact disc single, cassette single
Chart Position: #19 (UK chart)
B-sides: "Pashernate Love," "There Speaks a True Friend"

"Tomorrow"

Released: September 1992
Label: Sire
Format: 12″ vinyl single, compact disc single
Chart Position: #1 (US chart)
B-sides: "Let the Right One Slip In," "Pashernate Love," "There Speaks a True Friend"

"Certain People I Know"

Released: December 7, 1992
Label: HMV
Format: 7″ vinyl single, 12″ vinyl single, compact disc single, cassette single
Chart Position: #35 (UK chart)
B-sides: "You've Had Her," "Jack the Ripper"

"The More You Ignore Me, the Closer I Get"

Released: February 28, 1994
Label: Parlophone
Format: 7″ vinyl single, 12″ vinyl single, compact disc single, cassette single
Chart Position: #8 (UK chart), #46 (US chart)
B-sides: "Used to Be a Sweet Boy," "I'd Love To"

"Hold On to Your Friends"

Released: May 30, 1994
Label: Parlophone
Format: 7″ vinyl single, 12″ vinyl single, compact disc single, cassette single
Chart Position: #47 (UK chart)
B-sides: "Moon River"

"Interlude"

Released: August 8, 1994
Label: Parlophone
Format: 7″ vinyl single, 12″ vinyl single, compact disc single, cassette single
Chart Position: #25 (UK chart)
B-sides: "Interlude" (instrumental)

"Now My Heart Is Full"

Released: August 23, 1994
Label: Sire
Format: Compact disc single, cassette single
Chart Position: None
B-sides: "Moon River," "Jack the Ripper"

"Boxers"

Released: January 16, 1995
Label: Parlophone
Format: 7″ vinyl single, 12″ vinyl single, compact disc single, cassette single
Chart Position: #23 (UK chart)
B-sides: "Have-a-Go Merchant," "Whatever Happens, I Love You"

"Dagenham Dave"

Released: August 21, 1995
Label: RCA
Format: 7″ vinyl single, compact disc single, cassette single
Chart Position: #26 (UK chart)
B-sides: "Nobody Loves Us," "You Must Please Remember"

"The Boy Racer"

Released: November 27, 1995
Label: RCA
Format: 7″ vinyl single, compact disc single
Chart Position: #36 (UK chart)
B-sides: "London," "Billy Budd," "Spring-Heeled Jim," "Why Don't You Find Out for Yourself"

"Sunny"

Released: December 11, 1995
Label: Parlophone
Format: 7″ vinyl single, compact disc single, cassette single
Chart Position: #42 (UK chart)
B-sides: "Black-Eyed Susan," "A Swallow on My Neck"

"Alma Matters"

Released: July 12, 1997
Label: Island
Format: 7″ vinyl single, 12″ vinyl single, compact disc single, cassette single
Chart Position: #16 (UK chart)
B-sides: "Heir Apparent," "I Can Have Both"

"Roy's Keen"

Released: October 6, 1997
Label: Island
Format: 7″ vinyl single, 12″ vinyl single, compact disc single, cassette single
Chart Position: #42 (UK chart)
B-sides: "Lost," "The Edges Are No Longer Parallel"

"Satan Rejected My Soul"

Released: December 29, 1997
Label: Island
Format: 7″ vinyl single, 12″ vinyl single, compact disc single, cassette single
Chart Position: #39 (UK chart)
B-sides: "Now I Am a Was," "This Is Not Your Country"

"Irish Blood, English Heart"

Released: May 4, 2004 (USA); May 10, 2004 (UK/Europe)
Label: Attack/Sanctuary
Format: 7″ vinyl single, 12″ vinyl single, compact disc single
Chart Position: #3 (UK chart), #36 (US chart)
B-sides: "It's Hard to Walk Tall When You're Small," "Munich Air Disaster 1958," "The Never-Played Symphonies"

"First of the Gang to Die"

Released: July 12, 2004 (UK); July 13, 2004 (US)
Label: Attack/Sanctuary
Format: 7″ vinyl single, 12″ vinyl single, compact disc single, DVD
Chart Position: #6 (UK chart)
B-sides: "My Life Is a Succession of People Saying Goodbye," "Teenage Dad on His Estate," "Mexico"

"Let Me Kiss You"

Released: October 11, 2004
Label: Attack/Sanctuary
Format: 7″ vinyl single, compact disc single
Chart Position: #8 (UK chart)
B-sides: "Don't Make Fun of Daddy's Voice," "Friday Mourning," "I Am Two People"

"I Have Forgiven Jesus"

Released: December 13, 2004
Label: Attack/Sanctuary
Format: 7″ vinyl single, compact disc single
Chart Position: #10 (UK chart)
B-sides: "No One Can Hold a Candle to You," "The Slum Mums," "The Public Image"

"Redondo Beach"/"There Is a Light That Never Goes Out"

Released: March 28, 2005
Label: Attack
Format: 7″ vinyl single, compact disc single, DVD
Chart Position: #11 (UK chart)
B-sides: Double A-side single

"You Have Killed Me"

Released: March 27, 2006 (UK); March 28, 2006 (US)
Label: Sanctuary
Format: 7″ vinyl single, compact disc single, DVD, digital download
Chart Position: #3 (UK chart)
B-sides: "Human Being," "Good Looking Man About Town," "I Knew I Was Next"

"The Youngest Was the Most Loved"

Released: June 5, 2006 (UK); June 27, 2006 (US)
Label: Sanctuary
Format: 7″ vinyl single, compact disc single, maxi single, digital download
Chart Position: #14 (UK chart)
B-sides: "If You Don't Like Me, Don't Look at Me," "A Song from Under the Floorboards," "Ganglord"

"In the Future When All's Well"

Released: August 21, 2006
Label: Sanctuary
Format: 7″vinyl single, compact disc single, maxi single, digital download
Chart Position: #17 (UK chart)
B-sides: "Christian Dior," "I'll Never Be Anybody's Hero Now," "To Me You Are a Work of Art"

"I Just Want to See the Boy Happy"

Released: December 4, 2006
Label: Sanctuary
Format: 7″vinyl single, 7″picture disc, 12″picture disc, compact disc single, digital download
Chart Position: #16 (UK chart)
B-sides: "Sweetie-Pie," "I Want the One I Can't Have," "Speedway," "Late Night, Maudlin Street"

"That's How People Grow Up"

Released: February 4, 2008
Label: Decca
Format: 7″vinyl single, compact disc single, digital download
Chart Position: #14 (UK chart)
B-sides: "The Boy with the Thorn in His Side," "Why Don't You Find Out for Yourself," "The Last of the Famous International Playboys"

"All You Need Is Me"

Released: June 2, 2008
Label: Decca
Format: 7″vinyl single, compact disc single, digital download
Chart Position: #24 (UK chart)
B-sides: "Children in Pieces," "My Dearest Love," "Drive-In Saturday"

"I'm Throwing My Arms Around Paris"

Released: February 9, 2009
Label: Decca
Format: 7″ vinyl single, compact disc single, digital download
Chart Position: #21 (UK chart)
B-sides: "Because of My Poor Education," "Shame Is the Name," "Death of a Disco Dancer"

"Something Is Squeezing My Skull"

Released: April 27, 2009
Label: Decca
Format: 7″ vinyl single, compact disc single, digital download
Chart Position: #46 (UK chart)
B-sides: "This Charming Man," "Best Friend on the Payroll," "I Keep Mine Hidden"

"Glamorous Glue"

Released: April 18, 2011
Label: Sire
Format: 7″ vinyl single
Chart Position: #69 (UK chart), #13 (US chart)
B-sides: "Safe, Warm Lancashire Home," "Treat Me Like a Human Being"

"Satellite of Love"

Released: December 2, 2013
Label: Parlophone
Format: 7″ vinyl single, 12″ vinyl single, digital download
Chart Position: #124 (UK chart)
B-sides: "You're Gonna Need Someone on Your Side," "Mama Lay Softly on the Riverbed," "Vicar in a Tutu," "All You Need Is Me," "You Say You Don't Love Me"

"World Peace Is None of Your Business"

Released: May 13, 2014
Label: Harvest/Capitol
Format: Digital download
Chart Position: #83 (UK chart)

"Istanbul"

Released: May 20, 2014
Label: Harvest/Capitol
Format: Digital download
Chart Position: None

"Earth Is the Loneliest Planet"

Released: June 3, 2014
Label: Harvest/Capitol
Format: Digital download
Chart Position: None

"The Bullfighter Dies"

Released: June 17, 2014
Label: Harvest/Capitol
Format: Digital download
Chart Position: None

Selected Bibliography

While writing this book, I have consulted a great number of books, maga-zines, websites, and other sources. The sources in this list were the most instrumental in my research.

Articles

"24 Hours to Live Questionnaire." *Maxim*, February 2009.

"Q Questionnaire." *Q*, January 1995.

"Q Questionnaire." *Q*, November 2001.

Albert, Billy. "The Smiths: What Might Have Been." *Record Collector*, June 2009.

Ali, Lorraine. "The Man You Love to Hate." *Alternative Press*, February 1993.

Ambrose, Chris. "Morrissey." *Tokion*, March/April 2004.

Armitage, Simon. "Bigmouth Strikes Again." *The Guardian Weekend*, September 2010.

Arnott, Jake. "A Major Part of Me Is Always Dark." *Time Out London*, June 2004.

Aston, Martin. "Witty, Sad, Poignant, Green . . . " *Q*, October 1994.

Bailie, Stuart. "The Beautiful Morrissey Looked at Me." *New Musical Express*, March 1994.

Billen, Andrew. "Sex, Depression, and Gentility." *Times 2*, May 2006.

Bird, Cameron. "Morrissey Rising." *Filter*, Winter 2009.

Black, Johnny. "We Could Be Heroes." *Q Classic*, March 2006.

Boon, Richard. "Morrissey." *The Catalogue*, September 1988.

Bracewell, Michael. "Heaven Knows I'm Not Miserable Now." *The Times*, November 1999.

———. "A Walk on the Wilde Side." *The Observer*, February 1995.

Brown, Len. "Bona Contention." *Vox*, November 1990.

———. "Born to Be Wilde" (part 1 of 2). *New Musical Express*, February 13, 1988.

———. "I'll Astonish You." *Details*, March 1991.

———. "Stop Me If You Think You've Heard This One Before" (part 2 of 2). *New Musical Express*, February 20, 1988.

———. "Viva Morrissey." *Spin*, June 1988.

Browne, David. "The Great White Mope." *Entertainment Weekly*, October 1992.

Burchill, Julie. "Meeting My Morrissey." *The Sunday Times*, March 1993.

Cameron, Keith. "Who's the Daddy?" *Mojo*, June 2004.

Cavanagh, David. "The Good Lieutenants." *Select*, April 1993.

———. "Nothing to Declare but Their Genius." *Q*, January 1994.

Chalmers, Robert. "Morrissey Flowers Again." *Observer*, December 1992.

Clark, Lee. "Paint a Vulgar Picture." *Outlook*, January/February 1992.

Corbett, Ara. "Morrissey Sings His Life." *Creem*, April/May 1991.

Crossing, Gary. "Heaven Knows I'm Happier Now." *The Big Issue*, July 1997.

Cummins, Kevin. "Annoying Nagoya." *New Musical Express*, October 19, 1991.

David, Andy. "Morrissey; Glorious Esteban." *Record Collector*, January 2000.

Deevoy, Adrian. "Men of the Year: Morrissey." *GQ*, October 2005.

———. "Ooh I Say!" *Q*, September 1992.

Dieckmann, Katherine. "Morrissey Suffers the Curse of the Reasonably Unique." *Musician*, June 1991.

DiMartino, Dave. "The Loneliest Monk." *Raygun*, March 1994.

Earl, Andy. "Do You Fuckin Want Some?" *Q*, September 1995.

Eubank, Chris. "The New Roman Emperor, Part 1." *New Musical Express*, February 2006.

———. "The New Roman Emperor, Part 2." *New Musical Express*, March 2006.

Evans, Julian. "The Object of Love." *The Guardian*, February 1994.

Goddard, Simon. "Born to be Wilde." *Record Collector*, June 2003.

———. "Crowning Glory." *Uncut*, January 2006.

———. "Jailhouse Rock." *Uncut*, September 2002.

———. "The Last Rites." *Q*, May 2007.

———. "Stop Me If You Think You've Heard This One Before." *Record Collector*, October 2001.

Goldsworthy, Tim. "Morrissey." *Index*, February/March 2004.

Greenstreet, Rosanna. "The Correspondent Questionnaire." *The Sunday Correspondent*, October 28, 1990.

Hanley, Jack. "This Charming Man." *Boyz*, September 2001.

Harris, John. "The Last Great Pop Eccentric." *The Independent on Sunday*, October 1999.

———. "Trouble at Mill." *Mojo*, April 2001.

Harrison, Andrew. "The Band That Dreams It Never Broke Up." *Word*, June 2004.

———. "Hand in Glove." *Select*, May 1994.

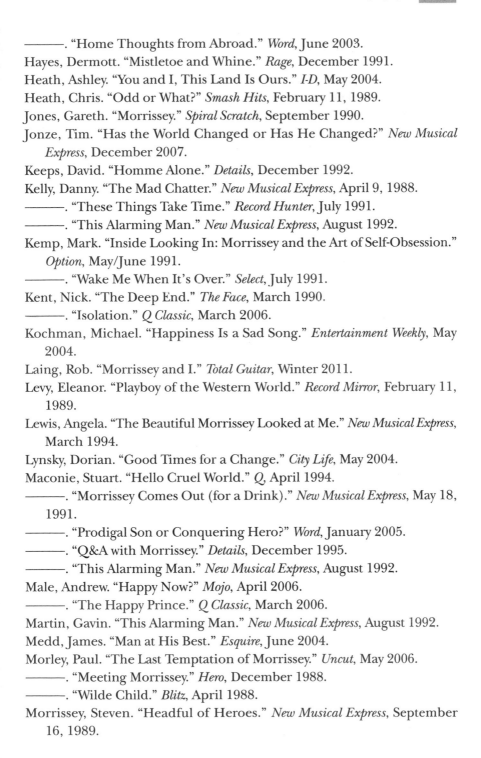

———. "Home Thoughts from Abroad." *Word*, June 2003.

Hayes, Dermott. "Mistletoe and Whine." *Rage*, December 1991.

Heath, Ashley. "You and I, This Land Is Ours." *I-D*, May 2004.

Heath, Chris. "Odd or What?" *Smash Hits*, February 11, 1989.

Jones, Gareth. "Morrissey." *Spiral Scratch*, September 1990.

Jonze, Tim. "Has the World Changed or Has He Changed?" *New Musical Express*, December 2007.

Keeps, David. "Homme Alone." *Details*, December 1992.

Kelly, Danny. "The Mad Chatter." *New Musical Express*, April 9, 1988.

———. "These Things Take Time." *Record Hunter*, July 1991.

———. "This Alarming Man." *New Musical Express*, August 1992.

Kemp, Mark. "Inside Looking In: Morrissey and the Art of Self-Obsession." *Option*, May/June 1991.

———. "Wake Me When It's Over." *Select*, July 1991.

Kent, Nick. "The Deep End." *The Face*, March 1990.

———. "Isolation." *Q Classic*, March 2006.

Kochman, Michael. "Happiness Is a Sad Song." *Entertainment Weekly*, May 2004.

Laing, Rob. "Morrissey and I." *Total Guitar*, Winter 2011.

Levy, Eleanor. "Playboy of the Western World." *Record Mirror*, February 11, 1989.

Lewis, Angela. "The Beautiful Morrissey Looked at Me." *New Musical Express*, March 1994.

Lynsky, Dorian. "Good Times for a Change." *City Life*, May 2004.

Maconie, Stuart. "Hello Cruel World." *Q*, April 1994.

———. "Morrissey Comes Out (for a Drink)." *New Musical Express*, May 18, 1991.

———. "Prodigal Son or Conquering Hero?" *Word*, January 2005.

———. "Q&A with Morrissey." *Details*, December 1995.

———. "This Alarming Man." *New Musical Express*, August 1992.

Male, Andrew. "Happy Now?" *Mojo*, April 2006.

———. "The Happy Prince." *Q Classic*, March 2006.

Martin, Gavin. "This Alarming Man." *New Musical Express*, August 1992.

Medd, James. "Man at His Best." *Esquire*, June 2004.

Morley, Paul. "The Last Temptation of Morrissey." *Uncut*, May 2006.

———. "Meeting Morrissey." *Hero*, December 1988.

———. "Wilde Child." *Blitz*, April 1988.

Morrissey, Steven. "Headful of Heroes." *New Musical Express*, September 16, 1989.

Murphy, Peter. "The Unbearable Lightness of Being Morrissey." *Hot Press*, April 2009.

Naughton, John. "Viva Morrissey." *City Life*, April 1988.

Needham, Alex. "The Guv'nor Returns, Part 1." *New Musical Express*, April 2004.

———. "The Guv'nor Returns, Part 2." *New Musical Express*, April 2004.

Nelson, Jim. "Morrissey Returns." *GQ*, April 2004.

Nine, Jennifer. "The Importance of Being Morrissey." *Melody Maker*, August 1997.

Nixon, Pete. "Morrissey." *Record Collector*, September 1991.

Nolan, Paul. "I've Got Something to Get Off My Chest." *Hot Press*, July 2008.

O'Kane, Dan. "Morrissey: Laughing Through the Tears." *CD Review*, April 1994.

Parsons, Tony. "What Now, Mozzer?" *Vox*, April 1993.

Reynolds, Simon. "Songs of Love and Hate" (part 1 of 2). *Melody Maker*, March 12, 1988.

———. "Songs of Love and Hate" (part 2 of 2). *Melody Maker*, March 19, 1988.

Rogan, Johnny. "All Men Have Secrets." *Vox*, May 1994.

———. "What Difference Does It Make?" *Vox*, June 1992.

Ryecroft, Hugh. "Mozza." *Outlook*, January/February 1992.

Sandall, Robert. "A Gentle Adoration." *Q*, January 1992.

Savage, Jon. "Still Clumsy, Less Shy." *The Observer in London*, March 19, 1989.

Shaw, William. "Homme Alone 2: Lost in Los Angeles." *Details*, April 1994.

Simpson, Dave. "Manchester's Answer to the H-Bomb." *Uncut*, August 1998.

Simpson, Mark. "You're the Bees Knees, but So Am I." *Outlook*, January/February 1992.

Smith, Sean. "Goodbye Oxfam, Hello Gucci." *The Big Issue*, November 1999.

———. "Strange Ways Indeed." *The Big Issue*, June 2003.

Snow, Mat. "The Soft Touch." *Q*, December 1989.

Spitz, Marc. "The Roman Spring of Mr. Morrissey." *Spin*, April 2006.

———. "These Things Take Time." *Spin*, May 2004.

Sullivan, Kate. "Moz the Cat." *LA Weekly*, February 2007.

Thomas, David. "Mad About the Boy." *You*, September 1992.

———. "The Sorrow and the Pity." *Spin*, November 1992.

———. "Therapy?" *Select*, December 1992.

Uhelszki, Joan. "LA Confidential." *Mojo*, April 2001.

Van Poznak, Elissa. "Morrissey Strikes Again: The Mouth That Roared." *Elle*, March 1988.

Walters, Sarah. "Bigmouth Back Again." *City Life*, July 2012.
Wilkinson, Roy. "The Single Life." *Mojo*, November 2002.
Wright, Christian. "Morrissey." *Spin*, April 1990.

Books

Goddard, Simon. *Mozipedia.*New York: Plume, 2010.
———. *Songs That Saved Your Life: The Art of the Smiths 1982–1987*. London: Titan Books, 2013.
Morrissey. *Autobiography*. London: Putnam Adult, 2013.
Rogan, Johnny. *Morrissey and Marr: The Severed Alliance*. London: Omnibus Press, 2012.
Simpson, Mark. *Saint Morrissey*. Seattle: Amazon Digital Services, 2010.
Woods, Paul A. *Morrissey in Conversation: The Essential Interviews*. New Jersey: Plexus, 2011.

Websites

Billboard, http://www.billboard.com/
Fuck Yeah Moz, http://fuckyeahmoz.tumblr.com/
Morrissey Scans, http://www.morrisseyscans.com/
Morrissey Solo, http://www.morrissey-solo.com/
Passions Just Like Mine, http://www.passionsjustlikemine.com/
True to You, http://true-to-you.net/

Index

THE FAQ SERIES

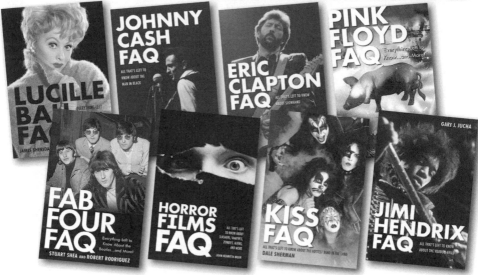

HAL•LEONARD®
PERFORMING ARTS
PUBLISHING GROUP

FAQ.halleonardbooks.com

Prices, contents, and availability
subject to change without notice.